YOU LOOK LIKE
THAT GIRL...

For J
Every day

YOU LOOK LIKE THAT GIRL...

A Child Actor Stops Pretending
and Finally Grows Up

LISA JAKUB

Library of Congress Cataloging-in-Publication Data

Jakub, Lisa, 1978-
  You look like that girl : A child actor stops pretending and finally grows up. / Lisa Jakub -- First edition.
      pages cm
  ISBN 978-0-8253-0746-1 (hardcover : alk. paper)
  1. Jakub, Lisa, 1978- 2. Actors--United States--Biography. I. Title.
  PN2287.J2854A3 2015
  791.4502'8092--dc23
  [B]
                          2014035733

For inquiries about volume orders, please contact:
Beaufort Books
27 West 20th Street, Suite 1102
New York, NY 10011
sales@beaufortbooks.com

Published in the United States by Beaufort Books
www.beaufortbooks.com

Distributed by Midpoint Trade Books
www.midpointtrade.com

Printed in the United States of America

Interior design by Jane Perini
Cover Design by Michael Short

CONTENTS

Composite headshot, showing my versatility as an actor.
As you can see, my hair can go forwards or back.

PHOTO: NICK SEIFLOW

LISA JAKUB

PROLOGUE

1985. Ontario, Canada.

B
eing a seven-year-old actor does not make you popular; it makes you fascinating, much in the way that dissecting a frog is fascinating. It's an interest tinged with a feeling of uneasy tension. It's a look-but-don't-get-too-close kind of curiosity. It was a lot for potential friends in my Grade 3 class to wrap their minds around. There I was, sitting next to them during art period, dipping pipe cleaners in Elmer's glue, when just that morning while they were eating breakfast, I had been singing the praises of Cottonelle toilette paper through their TV. It might have been normal for me, but they found it rather disconcerting.

Mikki was the perfect confidant. She would set her thoughtful, chocolate-milk-colored eyes on me and suddenly the weird, sideways glances and confused whispers would fade into the background. Mikki was four years older than me but our age difference never seemed to pose a problem. She had a dirty grey muzzle and long fur that poked out from between her toes. Her tail was always matted with a collection of dirt, leaves, and the occasional dead ladybug. She was arthritic and deaf. A thyroid condition made her rather obese and she possessed very little control over her bodily functions. While my dog was indeed my best friend, it would be untruthful of me to omit the fact that she had very little human competition.

That Saturday afternoon, they came on bikes. Five of them. One I knew; Karen. She was cute, tall, blonde, and the earliest known representation of everything I found intimidating about women later in life. The other four kids I had seen around. They were Older Boys. They were nine-year-olds, and anyone nearing double digits was, of course, automatically and rightfully awarded a daunting level of prestige.

From the dining room window, I could see them coming. Karen's pink streamers were waving from her handlebars, trumpeting the gang's arrival. It was both thrilling and horrifying to realize that they must have been coming to my house to play; no other kids lived on my block. Clearly, they wanted to ride bikes with me. I had a bike, but riding it had proven challenging. My mother had kindly blamed my compete lack of balance and coordination on an ear surgery I had undergone half my life earlier, but since I still can't ride well, the blame likely lays with a general lack of physical grace.

Since there was little chance of becoming proficient on a bike by the time the posse reached my front door, I required an alternate strategy. I grabbed my skateboard from the hall closet. This had become my way of seeming beyond the bike. I was cooler than the bikers. I rocked a board. My skateboard deck was laminated with tie-dye blue and green swirls and had a glow-in-the-dark sticker on the underbelly that said "SLIME-BALL" in all capital letters. I never really understood the purpose of such a sticker but it came with the board and it made me feel tough. Nobody had a bike with a mean word on it.

The plan was in place. When they asked me to ride bikes, I would take a cool moment to consider their offer and then offhandedly say the line, "I'd rather skate," while flashing my edgy sticker. They would be suitably impressed with my independent, bad-ass choice and we would ride off into the sunset on our respective modes of transportation.

BANG. BANG. BANG. They were here. Karen and The Older Boys had come for me. Trembling a little with nervousness and excitement, I adjusted my board just so, attempting to make it look casual in my arms, the mean sticker facing out.

When I opened the door, there they were, fanned out on my front step. The boys seemed to be mostly inspecting their shoelaces, but they took quick glances up at me. Karen stood in front of them, flashed a smile and flipped her hair in a way that made her suddenly look like she was seventeen. Karen pointed to my face as she addressed her gang.

"See, I told you guys the girl from TV lived here."

The Older Boys took this as their cue to really examine what stood before them. One pushed his glasses up to get the clearest view possible. They squinted in scrutiny, trying to picture it, then nodded in agreement. My face did indeed match the television face. After murmuring to each other, "That's pretty cool," they each handed Karen a dollar before they got on the bikes they could all ride proficiently. And they left. Without ever saying a word to me.

They had dissected their subject. They had inspected me and poked around, displaying my most tender guts. When they got their fill of the weirdness they moved on, leaving me splayed out, pinned to a board, and rejected. I told Mikki that Karen was a SLIMEBALL. She agreed by peeing on the carpet.

Twenty-five years later, Virginia, USA

My adopted hometown is small and sweet and adorably southern. We like grits and sweet tea and sing-songy little phrases laced with just a tinge of sarcasm. There are rolling hills snaked with post-and-board fencing and everyone waves at everyone. I spend a great deal of time now doing yoga, because after a yoga class, I feel wrung out and cleansed like my soul just went through the deluxe carwash.

In the dressing room after class, I was marinating in that state that yogis affectionately call "yoga stoned." That's when everything feels still and beautiful because you have cleared your mind and loosened up your hamstrings. The room was busy but quiet as everyone reveled in their spiritual accomplishments, as evidenced by their sweaty Lululemons. I was peeling off my yoga gear when a girl wrapped in a towel stepped out from the shower. She was running her hands through her freshly-washed hair and I could smell fair-trade organic tea-tree conditioner. Suddenly, she froze, fingers entwined in the wet tangles near her scalp. She furrowed her brow at me.

"Hey, why do I know you?" she asked.

"Oh, well, I go to UVA. Do we have a class together?"

"No. I'm still in high school. But I totally know you."

"I am here at the yoga studio a lot, maybe that's it," I deflected.

"No, that's not it...I'll figure it out," she said slightly ominously. Just as she was starting to turn away she jerked her head back.

"Oh my God, wait. I know you from movies, right? You're one of those actors who decided to move away from Hollywood and escape it all?"

At that point, the dressing room got even quieter and all the exhausted, yet suddenly interested yogis turned to look at us, wondering if she was right. I glanced down at the bra I was about to put on and was reminded how gross it is getting recognized while naked; this wasn't the first time. I gave her the "hold on one second" signal and fought with my tangled bra straps, all while trying to plaster my most sparkly Hollywood smile on my face.

INTRODUCTION

gave up acting but I'm not convinced it's possible to give up being an actor. Celluloid is eternal and if you happen to have been in films that are constantly on the Sunday afternoon cable circuit, it's like you never left at all. I'm stuck to that film life like it's fly paper; regardless of how much I flap and try to get away, another leg just gets stuck in the gooey mess. Although I am no longer an active member of the world's second oldest profession, the condition of being an actor remains. I'm overly emotional, overly sensitive and under confident.

At the age of twenty-two, I decided to leave L.A. in an attempt to save myself from my smoldering misery. I had no right to my misery, it wasn't earned through great loss or physical pain, but there it was anyway, sitting on my chest and quietly suffocating me. Leaving seemed to be my one and only shot at a fulfilling life, a life where I could be myself... whoever the hell that was. When I finally dragged myself out of the Hollywood fog and into the blinding light of the "real world" I realized that I was no longer able to hide behind the veil of needing to be emotionally raw for the purpose of furthering my craft. In the creative realm, my endless psychosis was passed off as sacrifice and dedication. In the "real world," I was just a mess.

A Canadian says sorry

If you are looking forward to a tell-all, full of dirt and scandal, I would like to apologize in advance. This is not a chronicle of the millions of celebrities I have slept with, as I have not slept with millions of celebrities, and I refuse to count early 90's MTV personalities nor the brothers of famous people as "celebrities." This book does not contain tales of wild nights trashing hotel rooms, romps through rehab, or orgies with rock bands. I have no eating disorders. I have never "accidentally" tweeted a naked photo of myself. This book is neither seething nor bitter. I am not crafting an exposé of anyone. All of that hackneyed Hollywood crap is overdone.

I am a pretty normal person. I just lived an unusual life for a while, and what follows are my observations of the people, places and things that one sees while living that existence. I am telling what I believe to be the truth of my life, with a few exaggerations thrown in because it's funnier that way.

It's all about the pretty

Some people really want to be actors. They take classes and discuss the Stella Adler method with their friends. They can feel the longing deep in their marrow and cannot imagine themselves being anything but an actor. I enjoyed acting for a while, but eventually I realized that I was doing my job with the same level of passion as someone who grew up working in the family's pizza parlor.

I was acting because it was there and I had always done it. It was fun being on set, and the camaraderie and community that comes from working on a film was extremely comforting to an only child. Everyone working on a show has a common creative goal and it was wonderful to instantly belong to something like that. However, I wasn't invested in the *craft* of acting. When I wandered out of that world at the end of my eighteen-year career, I didn't miss becoming a character; I missed being part of an on-set family that was creating something artistic together.

My other actor friends loved their trade and I was totally jealous of that. They wished that they had my resume and I wished that I had their passion. It would have been easier if I could at least muster the energy and emotion to despise the film industry, but I didn't hate it either. I simply became apathetic. Ambivalent. I had been branded "actor" at age four. Work turned into more work, and at a certain point, it's easy to forget that there are other life options available. Suddenly, I was living in Los Angeles and was "successful" at a prestigious job in that one-industry town. I knew that I was supposed to feel successful, but I didn't. It was like faking a career orgasm. I got so good at pretending that I even fooled myself for a while.

At some point, all that faking gets exhausting. Beyond the apparent glamour, actors are subjected to long hours, mountains of rejection, and a shocking amount of critical focus on your appearance. That stings. I once got turned down for a job because I wasn't pretty enough. They really said that. There was no sugarcoated option offered, no consideration about what that type of "honesty" might do to a seventeen-year-old.

The producers were interested in hiring me for a film role and gave me a full make-over in which I spent hours getting my hair cut and colored, a face full of professionally applied makeup and a new wardrobe from Fred Siegel's. It all felt very Julia Roberts in *Pretty Woman*. The "beauty team" was flitting around, offering glasses of freshly-squeezed lemonade while they decided what color top might be best for my complexion. They strategically placed blond highlights to frame my face and contoured my cheekbones with peach blush.

When the Hollywood wizards were done with me, I stood in front of the producers like a freshly groomed poodle and awaited their inspection. I smoothed out my perfectly colored hair, posed with one hand on the hip of my pricy designer jeans and batted my plumped and extended eyelashes. I flashed my newly whitened teeth. I tried to act like a pretty girl.

The producers gave my new look an up-down and then convened in the corner. There was a brief, hushed conversation. Quick glances back my direction. Nodding and sighing. They adjusted their glasses and scratched their goatees.

"Thanks a lot, Lisa, we think you are a great actor, but you are still just not pretty enough."

"Well, thanks anyway!" I chirped, probably in too high a tone. I removed my designer jeans, handed back the jewelry and thanked them for their time. I accepted the fact that my skill was not what mattered. My movie had a different ending than *Pretty Woman*. Instead of Richard Gere offering me a diamond necklace in a sassy box, I just felt like an ugly, unemployed whore.

Enough isn't enough

There is no such thing as "successful enough" in L.A. Even for those people who are can't-leave-the-house-famous, the striving is grueling and there is no point where you can take a deep breath and say, *This is all I need. This is enough.* It's never enough: it's always on to the next audition, the next job, the next hit. It's addictive, and it started to get dangerous for me. Not like drug abuse/eating disorder dangerous; it was just soul-crushing dangerous. That's all. Just the crushing of my soul.

Maybe there are actors who are confident enough to handle it. People who are poised and self-assured who can take the constant hammering of celebrity. No one has ever accused me of being poised and self-assured. I was an approval junkie always searching for the next fix, the next fleeting moment where I felt accepted and worthy before being plunged back into unemployment and obscurity.

It felt like the world stopped when a casting director once told me that Steven Spielberg knew my work and thought I was "very talented." She referred to him as "Steve" when she said it. I ran around like a fiend for a week, not able to eat, sleep, or concentrate. Then came the inevitable crash, which left me deflated on the couch, staring at the ceiling and chewing on the ends of my hair. Who the hell cares if "Steve" liked my work? He didn't hire me for the job anyway. I fell deeply into the depression that comes post-Christmas when you realize that after you tore into all those beautifully wrapped gifts, they still didn't make you feel whole.

Maybe an escape into high-functioning alcoholism could have been the thing that kept me in Hollywood. Perhaps if I had just been able to pour my discontent into an addiction, I could have managed it, but the only thing I was addicted to was the momentary rush that came from a new gig, new agent, or new boyfriend. Substances were certainly a well-worn route for many of my colleagues. If I could have funneled all my insecurities and self-loathing into a vodka bottle and chugged it back over the bathroom sink at three in the morning, maybe I could have lasted as an actor longer than I did. But two glasses of wine left me nauseated and taking drugs seemed appallingly stereotypical. Since I wasn't innately equipped and recreational substances were out, the rigors of the film industry seemed beyond my abilities.

But no one wants to hear actors whine about how hard their lives are. There are real problems in the world. People with cancer are going bankrupt over medical bills. Children are being kidnapped and forced to fight grown-up wars in the jungle. Polar bears are drowning. Regardless of how unhappy my job was making me, this was destined to be a poorly attended pity-party.

Pity was never the goal, anyway. I just wanted to clear up this notion that an actor's life was all about limousines and exotic locations. Even if it was entirely those things, it didn't matter: it just wasn't my scene anymore. I didn't want to be an actor, much in the same way that I didn't want to be a paleontologist or a professional ice dancer. It was time to make a change. People all around me were dying to be in my shoes, but I needed to go barefoot.

Along came a boy

It might have appeared that I left Los Angeles for a boy. Being in love with someone who was leaving L.A. to get his master's degree gave me the perfect excuse to tiptoe out of my life. LOVE! Who could argue with love? Especially when I had such a disastrous past in that arena. It made me seem righteous and romantic. I really *was* in love but I was also kind of using him. I could break free from the strong, sparkly grip of Hollywood and point the finger at love.

To this day, online commenters blame my husband for the fact that I left acting. They say he was uncomfortable with my career so he made me quit and leave L.A. That's total bullshit, but it's fine with me. Blame him. That way, I don't have to deal with the real reason I stopped acting: I didn't like it anymore. This opinion is about as popular as saying you loathe rainbows. What kind of person wants to leave an acting career? What kind of deranged monster must they be? My kind of monster. Because I left and I'm glad.

People around me only saw the good job, the house that I purchased when I was fifteen years old and the fact that I was part of the elite percentage of actors who never had to take a drink order. I had what I was supposed to want. I had what people thought they longed for in checkout lines as they looked at glossy magazine covers filled with veneered teeth and silky extensions. There were premiers lined with paparazzi yelling for me to look "over here." There were exclusive parties where I sat in hot tubs with hot producers. There was the kissing of famous people on both cheeks and my photo was printed in the party section of *Variety*. There was autograph-signing at dinner. *Star Magazine* reported on whom I was dating. There was a caricature of me in *Mad Magazine* and *TeenBeat* revealed my favorite foods. Why wasn't all that making me happy? Why was it, in fact, making me feel depressed and hopeless? Why was I hollow and desperately longing for something that I couldn't even identify? What was wrong with me?

With the hazy half-consciousness of someone walking into rehab, I went cold turkey, prepared to suffer the Hollywood withdrawals and search for something more satisfying. My friends were horrified that I was walking away from this group of chosen ones. People kept telling me that I had the golden ticket and I was about to rip it up. They said that Jodie Foster left acting, too, but she came back. You'll be back, you'll see. They sounded like a passive-aggressive spouse, demanding my affection for a life I no longer wanted.

Of course, I was terrified they were right. But I still wanted to see what the world looked like outside of my single-minded industry town. I was curious about life in a place that had different priorities and a culture that had nothing to do with box office gross. A place where no one cared what a Key Grip did. I moved to Virginia.

When I arrived, I kind of just stood there in shock and looked around for a while. I had what I wanted. I was free. But it didn't feel like freedom.

It felt like being untethered.

Unmoored.

Unglued.

I had just left a career and life in California and had no clue what was next. I had a boyfriend in grad school who was too busy with managerial accounting and consumer research classes to help me go on a soul-searching quest to find myself. Laid out before me were long, empty days and zero prospects. I had no friends, no plan, I was trained for nothing and was a high school dropout with a fairly shallow and rapidly dwindling bank account. The money just sort of trickled out in a slow leak. I don't really know what happened to most of it. I had never been one of those seven-figure actors anyway, and never felt the need to impress anyone. I drove a ten-year-old Toyota RAV 4 and lived in thrift store t-shirts. But apparently, money can go surprisingly fast just paying a mortgage, buying frequent plane tickets back to Canada and helping struggling artist friends. So, when I walked away from the only money-making skill I had, I wasn't set for life the way people assumed I was.

No one in their twenties knows who they really are, but it is even more jumbled and confusing when you have spent your entire conscious life being praised for your ability to be someone else. When you are considered special because you can leave your own life behind and completely inhabit another personality, there is very little impetus to examine your own authenticity. Suddenly, I was faced with the frightening proposition of doing a character study of myself.

While the details of my childhood might have been unusual, the general experience was not unique. I had seen kids who seemed to be prodigies at something—sports, music, or dance—and who spent most of their young lives devoted to that. Some kids seem to come into the world with a sense that they have a role to fill, a dream to live out, or a problem to fix. Maybe their parents wanted them to be a doctor or sell insurance just like their dad did. Maybe their coaches were determined to see them in the Olympics. I wondered what happened when they took a different path. Did they feel as lost as I did? Did they feel like they had let everyone down?

I used to enjoy my job, but at some point it all became more important to other people than it was to me. My career plodded along, seemingly of its own volition, propelled only by momentum and a deep, foreboding feeling of obligation. It all happened slowly and without me noticing it, all I knew was that when I looked back, I couldn't even see where my enthusiasm had once been. When I left L.A., I felt like I was disappointing every casting director that believed in me, every producer who had fought for me and every movie-goer who was shocked that I would walk away. I was twenty-two and had failed an entire industry of people who had given me a rarely offered chance.

But let's back up. About eighteen years.

CHAPTER 1

Big Eyes = Career

The first few years of my life in the suburbs of Toronto were fairly standard. I was a picky eater, I had my tonsils removed, I fell down and required seven stitches in my chin. My Little Pony was awesome, and getting my hair brushed was terrible. When I was three years old I learned to read, and I fell in love with the way that letters fit together. Words and sentences became my closest companions.

I would lose myself inside of words, feeling victorious when I chose exactly the right one. Seeing others using words well could bring me to tears. I obsessively read everything available, even reading billboards aloud. Neon signs were particularly attractive, and sometimes announced the attributes of the ladies at such establishments as the Crazy Horse Gentleman's Club. Luckily, "Live! Nude! Girls!" are all fairly simple words to get a three-year-old mind around. So, announce them I did, with only a slight grammatical adjustment resulting in an enthusiastic plea for the nude girls to "live."

I don't remember the incident that determined my path in life, but as the family legend goes, my parents and I were shopping in a farmer's market in Toronto. A man approached them saying he worked for an advertising agency and he thought I would be perfect for a commercial they were casting. Apparently, he could see beyond the peanut butter all over my face and felt there was a thespian simmering below. The only acting I had ever done involved coaxing my cats into doll dresses and pretending I ran an orphanage, so how could I be in a real commercial? My parents, dubious of the random market man, accepted his card in an attempt to get rid of him efficiently and they quickly ushered me away. In all likelihood, there were lengthy discussions between the two of them about the chances of him being a pervert.

My family could be the prototype for nice, normal Canadian people. I'm an only child, and my parents and I thought of ourselves as the Three Musketeers. My mom's curly hair was always unruly, and she had worn a size zero wedding dress when she married my father, a week after her nineteenth birthday. At age fourteen she had seen him across the high school gym and announced that she'd marry him. Mom usually got what she wanted.

Dad is the son of tobacco farmers who moved to Canada from Slovakia in the 1940s. My grandparents clung to the old country. They lived in a tightly-knit Slovak community, with people who all spoke the same language and made the same poppy seed rolls. Even though he was born in Canada, my father didn't speak any English when he started school at age five, but he soon learned his way around the educational system and was attending law school when I was born. Law books cluttered up my parent's tiny apartment and Dad would stay up all night studying for the bar exam, while simultaneously trying to rock me back to sleep. My father enjoyed the sport of curling and a couple Labatt Blues after the game with other kind-hearted, bearded Canadian men.

My parents loved home renovation projects and so we lived in a state of perpetual chaos. We moved constantly, because Mom said that packing up and starting over was easier than cleaning. Our kitchen boasted a half-taken-down-wall, exposing the ancient horsehair and mud plaster construction of our 1880s fixer upper. The cashiers at the donut place around the corner got used to us running in as soon as they flipped the open sign in the morning; their facilities were indispensable when our plumbing system was under repair again. Mom would step over a dusty sledgehammer to feed the dog. The cats would drop their toys into the basement through the hole in the living room floor that we never got around to patching.

I seemed to have come pre-programmed with a high tolerance for chaos, and never minded living in the pandemonium of various construction sites. Wherever we lived, the living room always swayed with Carol King's *Tapestry* record playing on our old Victrola while the three of us sat on the floor and played Hungry Hungry Hippos. We were a regular little family who watched TV, not the ostentatious types who longed to be on it. We could not have been further from showy Hollywood; Mom got embarrassed when they called her name out loud in the doctor's office waiting room.

But when my parents told their friends about the man at the market, they said they *had* to call and find out the details.

"You know, a pervert can't really do anything to you over the phone," they reasoned.

Peer pressure prevailed and my mom called the phone number on the card. As it turned out, the guy was legit and was casting for several commercials. When they asked if I was interested in auditioning, I immediately agreed. I'm not sure if I had any idea what I was agreeing to, but much like a dog, I always got excited about a ride in the car. So, we made the big trip from suburbia into Toronto and went to an audition the production company was holding. There, the casting director realized a few things:

✳ My eyes were disproportionally large for my face and evolutionary instincts dictate that big eyes equal "cuteness" to human brain.
✳ "Cuteness" sells stuff.
✳ I could read. Therefore, I could memorize lines.

The casting director sent me to a talent agent, the agent sent me on more auditions and I ended up with a career. It all just snowballed, much in the way that you might only plan to go out to dinner with friends, but then someone mentions wanting to see a movie and then you find yourself still out at a bar at 2 a.m.

They say that your earliest memory speaks volumes about who you are as a person. My earliest memory is being on set for a Cottonelle toilet paper commercial. I was dressed in a frilly white dress and a man was on top of a ladder dumping out a cardboard box full of cotton balls on my head. The commercial was going to be in slow motion; me with my huge eyes, joyously attempting to catch the fluffy cotton balls that rained down on me. It seemed strange that this grown man's job was to dump cotton balls on my head. My job was also ridiculous, catching aforementioned cotton balls, but I had just turned four. I reasoned that it was more acceptable to have a silly job at age four.

I went on to hawk everything imaginable, from floor cleaner to Kmart to the hippest fashion trends of 1983 in a mall runway show. I was the model for a coloring book that was given away by Kmart; bored kids waiting outside changing rooms could color a black and white version of me while I watered plastic flowers and jumped rope. (They gave me stack of these books to keep and for years after, I would color myself instead of cartoon zoo animals.) I was featured in one of those giant wallpaper books you find at a home design store, playing in a brightly papered bedroom with no ceiling and only three walls. I was on a KFC billboard holding a greasy bucket and grinning like it was my birthday. By the time of that shoot, I had been a vegetarian for a year but apparently the fear of being a sell-out isn't prominent for a preschooler.

I did a commercial for Barbie's McDonald's Restaurant playhouse and assisted her in flipping brown, choke hazard mini-patties. I was a hand model for the Egg Board of Canada. My job was to hold a hard-boiled egg steady within inches of the camera lens, because no one can resist eating an egg if it is very close up. I ate cold, uncooked Chef Boyardee and dry heaved into the provided spit bucket at the end of each take, keeping my eyes closed tight so I didn't have to look at the chewed

PHOTO: KMART

up remains of mini ravioli from my previous takes.

By the time I was seven, Mom and I were quite used to running from auditions to wardrobe fittings to commercial shoots. It wasn't the life that anyone else at my school was leading, but it felt natural to me. I saw them juggling piano lessions, basketball camp and math tutoring, so it seemed reasonable to assume it was kind of the same.

Me, in the middle, acting really excited about pasta in a can.

I attended school when it fit into my schedule, but that became an increasingly uncommon occurrence. Unlike most extra-curricular activities, my job was not only during after-school hours. Even if a commercial audition happened to be at 4 p.m., memorizing the lines, getting dressed, commuting an hour into Toronto and finding the casting office, all in the days before GPS, took much of the afternoon. In my mother's small faux-leather day reminder from 1983, her all caps, excited handwriting reveals, "SCHOOL STARTS!" on September 6th. At some point, that got scratched and replaced with an equally enthusiastic "12:30 COMMERCIAL SHOOT FOR FLORIDA ORANGE GROWER'S ASSOCIATION!"

Oh, Craps

It's easy to assume that all children have a childhood. It's right there in the name. At the time, I assumed that what I was doing *was* childhood. What else could it be when you are eight years old? Mine just seemed to be a childhood in which I worked for a living, read through contracts, and was rarely around other kids. But childhood is supposed to be full of freedom, exploration, and silliness. I had those things to some extent, but there was also an enormous amount of responsibility. It was a different kind of responsibility than the one that dictated that you should put on clean underwear and never poke the dog in the eye. It was a responsibility to an entire production company. There was no room for being a moody little kid who wanted to throw a temper tantrum and not show up for work one day—I would have been sued for breach of contract.

The money issue also complicated the whole childhood categorization. My family never focused on the money but I was aware that there was a financial exchange involved. I suspected money was a big deal because my family didn't have a ton of it. When I was nine, my parents talked to me about investments, and asked if it was okay to use some of my commercial income to help buy our modest house. After we moved in, I asked my mother which part of the house I had paid for. She quickly changed the subject and suggested that I go play in my room. I asked for clarification—was my room the part that I had bought? The look on my mother's face told me that this was not a good line of questioning. We didn't talk about money much after that, which seemed to make everyone more comfortable.

By the way, none of this is in the spirit of *Oh, poor me.* A regular childhood doesn't sound all that great, either. There is bullying in school, peer-pressure, and competition. That all sounds like total shit, too. My particular brand of shit was not any worse than that; it's just that childhood kind of sucks. You have so little influence in your own life; you can't drive or pick out your own clothes and everyone is way taller than you. Did I have a childhood? Not really. Did I want one? Not really.

At a thrift store, my mother fished through a wicker basket of buttons and found me a pin for the collar of my faded jean jacket that read, "Why be normal?" I adopted it as my mantra and adjusted to the strangeness of spending the majority of my time with grown-ups. There were surely some kid things I missed. For example, I can't come up with a single nursery rhyme and I have no clue how to play jacks. Instead, I learned different types of games.

Film sets are a unique combination of hectic rushing and incessant boredom. Hours, or entire days, can be spent waiting and then within a moment's notice, people need to spring into action and make their specific contributions. Learning to entertain oneself is of great value to personal sanity on set. The teamsters, who are in charge of coordinating all the trucks and generators for the entire film production, apparently found that teaching a four-year-old to play craps was very entertaining. Simply hearing a four-year-old say, "Yes, thanks, I'd love to play craps," must have been pretty terrific.

Many of the teamsters were classic truckers. Their guts strained the promotional t-shirt of whatever show they just finished shooting. Their long stringy hair was contained under a baseball cap and their use of the English language was deeply and creatively filthy. They were also fun and truly kind and offered me my first sense of belonging to something, a feeling that I'd spend the rest of my life chasing.

These guys, many of whom were older than my parents, were who I considered to be my community, my peers. The teamsters and I would gather together and play craps for hours. They told me about snake eyes, and how to tell if someone had slipped in loaded dice. They gave me spare change to bet with and taught me how to trash talk. I reveled in being one of the guys.

On one commercial shoot, a nice, idealistic person drew a hopscotch board with pink chalk on the floor of the soundstage where we were shooting. When she proudly presented it to me, a little girl who should have been thrilled, I put on my best commercial smile and thanked her. As soon as she was out of sight, I hurried back to the dark corner of the warehouse, to blow on dice with my crew. I didn't know how to play hopscotch.

"G'night, fellas!" I loved yelling when we wrapped shooting for the day.

"Sleep tight, kiddo," gruff voices would respond from behind trailers and generators.

I'd go home and miss them until I was back for my 6 a.m. call time the next day. From shoot to shoot, the faces changed, but somehow the feeling of belonging stayed the same.

✳ ✳ ✳ ✳ ✳

As a result of constant interaction with people a generation or two older than me, I became increasingly uneasy around other kids. My exchanges with them had largely been unpleasant. Being different in school is the kiss of death, as any fourth grader with a foreign accent or an affinity for avant-garde fashions can tell you. A group of kids at school once cornered me on the playground and asked if I thought I was a good actor. I looked at my feet and shrugged, admitting that I didn't know. They proceeded to hold my arms and whip my bare legs with a willow branch.

"Act like that doesn't hurt," they demanded.

I failed my acting test and cried until snot ran down my chin. They finally let me go and walked away, proud that they had broken me so easily. When I went home, I changed into jeans to hide the welts and didn't tell my parents about it.

I was humiliated by the fact that I hadn't been able to act like the whipping didn't hurt. Admitting to the incident would essentially be admitting to being a bad actor. What if casting directors found out that I hadn't been able to fake it, and I never worked again and just had to stay there in school with those horrible kids?

I fed most of my breakfast to the dog, since I got stabbing stomach aches every school morning. I prayed to get another job so that I could be on set, the one place where I could just enjoy casino games with giant men named Tiny and have my freakiness be accepted.

Inevitably, I'd have to spend a few days or weeks trudging though school, wondering what I could to talk to my supposed peers about. Those kids didn't have jobs. They didn't play craps or travel to location shoots. They weren't up late last night because filming went long and they didn't worry because we were losing the light. They didn't know the exhilarating tension of the sun going down and how booking this location for another day would cost the production thousands of dollars that wasn't in the budget, so you just had to get the shot and didn't have time to go "ten-one hundred." And they definitely didn't know that ten-one hundred was the discreet way of telling everyone within earshot of a walky-talky that you were sitting on the toilet. Kids my own age were worried about choir solos and Girl Scout cookie sales, things I was clueless about.

I tried to relate to the kids who practiced gymnastics or cello for five hours a day. They seemed to be comforted by their unusual skills, like I was, but the balance was never easy for any of us. The opportunities were astounding, and were only equaled by the sheer number of things that we gave up. I knew kids who wanted to be firefighters when they were five, but no one decided to suit them up, hand them an axe and send them out there. However, the rules seemed different for those of us who showed musical talent, sports skills, or an affinity for crying on cue.

I saw some families exhausted by early morning swim meets on behalf of their phenomenon the same way my parents skipped family obligations because I had an audition. At a certain level, the assumption on behalf of kids like us was that *of course* this should be pursued. It quickly becomes "you have an audition/performance/competition!" instead of "do you want to go to this audition/performance/competition?" Because the tendency is to think who *wouldn't* want to participate at that level, if given the chance? For the most part, I found it to be fun, but it was clear that there were other kids on set who felt forced and resented it. Those tended to be the ones who felt stifled, so they took control of the only things they thought they could control, and eventually overdosed in a random hotel room.

All I knew at the time was that at school there was simply no common ground between my "peers" and I. When I hung out with kids my own age, I'd inadvertently say something that made them stare at me, snicker uncomfortably, and walk away, leaving me flushed and rejected. The more I worked, the more snickering and staring occurred. It was a vicious cycle that left me feeling ashamed of myself and my job, yet desperate to get back to it since I felt completely unworthy of being part of the things that normal kids did.

Mom said I was an old soul and that I shouldn't worry about kids my own age. I liked the idea of being an old soul. That made it sound like maybe being socially awkward wasn't entirely my fault.

Sometimes you just need to sit on the floor with John Malkovich

Acting is intrinsic to the human spirit. Humans have an innate desire to be someone else. Sometimes, we just want to be anyone else. It's a relief to get the hell out of our own lives and try on someone else's skin.

This desire is particularly prevalent in young humans: kids pretend to be adults, other kids, animals, or tables. They have no sense of one identity being superior to another because embodying a king or a floor lamp are of equal acting gravitas. No one needs to tell them how to throw an elaborate tea party for a stuffed sea lion and they don't need to be smothered in praise and Screen Actors Guild awards for the dramatic reading they did for the pet parakeet. We've been performing since the dawn of time, it's the way we tell our stories in a feeble attempt at immortality. Adults sometimes wonder if kids "know what they are doing" when they act, but it seems more logical to question the capacity of grownups, who have often misplaced their sense of fantasy and forgotten that it's just all playing dress up.

John Malkovich understands this. I was in *Eleni*, my first feature film, at age six. I had a small, yet important part in the film. (Please note: if you are an actor, it is required that you highlight the pivotal significance of a role if you dare refer to it as "small.") In my hugely important and climactic scene, I was to enter the room, while John, who had been plotting this revenge killing for decades, was pointing a gun at my grandfather, who had tortured and killed his mother. My job was to look at John with big six-year-old eyes until he drops the gun, overcome with guilt. Music swells, credits roll, the movie theater audience steps over discarded popcorn bags and Junior Mints.

The day we filmed the scene, my mom talked to me about the gun and explained that it wasn't real and couldn't hurt me. I had become accustomed to fake food, fake families, and fake living rooms, so this felt no different. I wasn't nervous at all. My biggest concern was about getting the heavy sliding glass door open at the top of the scene. In rehearsals, it had gotten stuck and even though I had thrown all forty pounds of myself into opening it, I had missed my cue. They put someone just out of shot, to help me manage it.

We did a few more rehearsals to finalize the camera angles and lighting. John was showing restraint, holding back the emotion during the rehearsals, and saving his acting energy for the actual take. The shaking and spitting and pulsing forehead veins that come with an attempted revenge murder were reserved for when the camera was actually rolling. John had just done *Death of a Salesman* with Dustin Hoffman, so people were starting to know the power of his performances, but this was still years before *Empire of the Sun* and his true minting as a celebrity. But everyone knew this was a powerhouse of an actor about to take on the most important moment in a serious film. The energy in the room was coiled and ready.

We rolled camera, and the slate was clapped very quietly, as a traditional sign of respect before a tense scene. The director called action and John went all out with the shaking and spitting and pulsing forehead veins. Just before my cue, someone on the crew thought it might be helpful for me to feel "real fear" because he figured no six-year-old could really understand acting. He suggested to me, quietly, off camera, that maybe the gun might really be loaded, that perhaps it wasn't a pretend gun and perhaps I might actually die. Maybe my mother lied.

When it was time for my entrance, the crewmember slid the heavy glass door open for me and I saw the gun. And freaked. I screamed, cried, flapped my arms, pitched a fit, and refused to go on set. I must admit, it was a fantastic actress meltdown; current starlets could have learned from my all-encompassing technique. People gathered around to calm me, offer me Kleenex and fix my streaking make-up. I'm sure more than a few rolled their eyes and recalled the time-tested adage about why you should never work with children or animals.

Somehow through the sobbing, I heard John call me over to set. *This is it,* I thought, *this is when I get fired.* How humiliating to get fired at age six. John had just been in character, screaming and threatening to kill Oliver Cotton, and I was a little scared that some of that rage might be reserved for me, for ruining his shot and making him do that thing with the forehead veins over again. I was preparing to apologize and try to talk my way into keeping my job, as John sat down on the floor and gently patted the ground next to him. I sat. The gun master who was in charge of the on-set weapons joined us on the floor and the two of them proceeded to take the gun apart. They showed me that there were no bullets inside. They explained that I was safe and that I was surrounded by a whole team of people who cared for me and would make sure that I was safe. Nothing bad could happen to me here.

I believed him. Not because he was a stunningly talented actor but because he was a nice man who sat on the floor with me when I cried. He acknowledged my concerns and talked to me like I was a person. A fellow actor. He understood that children are capable, he knew I could act. We tried the scene again and with m my newly instilled confidence, I pulled open the glass door and acted. Those big eyes that were the foundation of my entire career did their job as I looked at the pretend gun and I pretended to be scared. When the director called cut, there were high fives all around—we got the shot.

It was at that moment that it became clear that my peers were no longer those kids wielding the willow tree branch—my peers were teamsters and John Malkovich. This was where I belonged. This was where I felt safe. And there was nothing more satisfying than getting the shot.

At least—that's where I belonged for the next few days. Because then we would wrap the movie, and everyone scattered, off to start pre-production on some new project. My little community was ripped apart. The post-wrap crash was always devastating and I would still be navigating the pain of that loss as I was plunged back into school. Back to being the weirdo and back to feeling desperate to return to set. My addiction to working was firmly implanted and I'd be on a hunt for the next fix. The next chance to get the shot.

Meeting the double-edged sword

At the age of seven, it was time to expand my range. I ventured into the world of voice-over acting. It was new territory for me, as it was a dramatically different kind of performance than the kind to which I had become accustomed. There was no sound stage and no fifty-person crew. No craps games. No trailers or generators or lighting trucks strewn about. No wardrobe calls or hair stylists.

This type of work involved going into a little soundproof box all alone and speaking into a huge microphone. On the other side of a thick pane of glass, the adjacent room was filled with reel-to-reel sound tapes and a big board with a sea of buttons. I would perch up on a stool, my feet intertwining with the chair's legs to keep me stable, while the director would lower the metal music stand down as low as it would go. Then, he would leave, sealing the soundproof egg crate-lined studio so securely that when the door closed my ears would pop. For a moment, it would feel like a coffin; small, padded, deathly quiet and deeply lonely. I would readjust the too-large headphones that would always slip backwards off my head and wait. Finally, the director, my lifeline, appeared in the glass window and I would get a silent point to say the lines that were printed out in front of me. Giant doe eyes could not help with this job; it was a new kind of acting. It might not have had my beloved on-set ambiance, but this particular gig was still incredibly exciting. I was going to be on *The Care Bears*.

Now, just to clarify, I was not a Bear. That would have been too good to handle. I played the role of a little girl who was so afraid of bugs that the Bears flew down from their cozy clouds just to lend a hand. They came to teach me about all the wonderful things that creepy-crawlies could do and showed me that there was nothing to fear. I learned how to enunciate clearly and use my voice instead of my eyes. I learned that voice-overs always need to be "bigger" than film, where you can use your whole body to portray a feeling. It all felt a little over-the-top, but the fact that a cartoon Care Bear hugged a cartoon me was the stuff of dreams.

I continued to do some other types of voice-over work, more cartoons, and commercials. I was hired to re-do another girl's dialogue because the producers hadn't been satisfied with her work and they wanted me to "clean it up." I sat in that same little box of a room and dubbed her lines, matching them to her moving mouth. I have no recollection of what the project was, but I do remember having a line about Brian Boitano. When it was done, it looked pretty cohesive. The producers had accomplished their goal, which was to get rid of the original actress's stilted delivery and make it sound more natural.

While it was nice to have a gig, I felt awful for that little girl. She was about seven years old, just like me, and I wondered how she would feel when her family and friends gathered around the TV to watch her big performance. Would she be confused or embarrassed when she saw herself open her mouth and heard my voice came out? Would her family comfort her? Would they make up a story about why the producers had to re-do her lines? Would her friends ask why she sounded different and would she have to explain why I was brought in? Would she want to act again or would she feel so humiliated that she would just quit?

Until that moment it had all just been playing Barbie dolls and dice games. Now, I had taken something away from someone. I was a traitor. A little bit deeper than that was another thorny feeling: if she was a bad actor and I was brought in to fix her work, what did that make me? I must be good. I swelled a little, feeling like I could be relied on to sweep in and make it all better. It made me wonder if this was how the world worked—were accomplishments so limited that I could only have something because someone else didn't have it? Did success always depend on my ability to grab it out of someone else's hands? Was victory always going to feel so dirty? It was my first adrenaline hit from the entertainment industry and it felt like a double-edged sword. That sword and I would get to know each other quite well.

"A beguiling performance"

It was a common occurrence for working kids to receive little treats after they behaved well for the casting directors, much like performing seals being thrown dead fish. For many young actors, auditions were followed by trips to the mall where candy and stuffed animals were tossed at them as rewards for well-memorized lines and professional chit-chat with producers. Even at the time, the blatant bartering between parent and child seemed creepy. This was different territory than getting a gold star sticker for making your bed. With money at stake, the focus shifts and that tension was obvious.

Bribery was not necessary for me because I really liked auditions. They were fun chances to go new places, learn new things, and get out of school. I loved reading scripts and learning how writers created story arc and character development. I liked memorizing lines, pulling them apart, reordering them and putting them back together. I played with words like some kids played with Legos. Milkshake rewards were superfluous.

Casting session waiting rooms were usually filled with other little girls with their mothers (or the occasional dad) who accompanied them. It looked like the sidelines of a soccer game, except instead of cheering for goals, everyone was rooting for speaking parts. Some parents were pushy, obsessively brushing their prodigy's hair and making them recite their lines just once more, and not so fast this time. It was cringe-worthy. The kids rolled their eyes and tried to push away the hands that were trying to smooth down their bangs or pinch their cheeks to cause a "natural" pink glow. Sometimes the moms themselves were done-up with fresh perms and elaborate eye-shadow, as if they were prepared to jump in front of the casting director themselves, should the need for a mother-type character suddenly arise.

In contrast, my mom attended my auditions in her standard outfit of jeans, a baggy t-shirt that was suitable for home renovation work, and no makeup. She would walk past the empty folding chairs, choosing instead to sit cross-legged on the floor, usually near a ficus plant, where she would flip through an old *Reader's Digest*. At one audition filled with particularly fancy moms, I took notice of my mother's hair. A few days earlier she had been tugging at it in the mirror, saying she needed a cut.

"But I just hate going to that haircut place. There are too many mirrors and it smells weird. Why don't you just do it?" She suggested to me.

We dug through my plastic pencil case, dumping out chewed up erasers and leaking markers and found a pair of scissors with bright orange handles. And I cut her hair in the TV room. Clumps of curls fell to the floor and the cats batted them around. I squinted and looked at her from different angles, making minor adjustments like the hair stylists on set did. When it was done, it didn't look terrible. Dark, curly hair is mercifully forgiving. It didn't look like a nine-year-old had cut it. It looked more like a twelve-year-old had cut it.

It seemed unlikely that any of the pushy, primped moms asked their daughters to cut their hair with a pair of safety scissors. My mom was just different. There was no grasping, no pushing, no clamoring for attention. There was just the profound sense that this was simply what we did, because sitting at an audition for Sears was a totally normal thing to be doing on a Tuesday afternoon.

My mother seemed to live in a backwards world where unusual things, like collecting photos of my entirely alive father to be used in a shoot to represent "the dead dad," put her in this state of confident ease. Anything mundane, like making me a dentist appointment or cooking dinner left her looking uncomfortable and uncertain. She was built for adventure and unusual circumstances, but nothing in her life before me would have indicated that. Mom lived most of her life in the town she was born in, down the street from the hospital where her father took his first and last breaths. There was no precedent for her endless capacity for the extraordinary. But if there were ever a crisis or strange goings-on, my mother was the one you wanted by your side, smoothing things over and enveloping you in her coolness. Her confidence led me to never question our life. I would have been more likely to wonder if clothing was really a public necessity.

One of my first starring roles was in a kids' TV movie where I had to fight ghost pirates. I was nine years old and received sword fighting lessons on the deck of a pirate ship in the icy waters off the coast of Nova

Scotia. We worked mostly nights; filming would begin at 10 p.m. and finish up well after sunrise. I liked feeling like a vampire, falling into bed at the hotel as regular people were just emerging from their rooms, in search of coffee and muffins.

The TV movie was called *Trick or Treasure*, and it received good reviews. I was praised for my performance, which the press called "beguiling," and they threw around words like "genius." They quoted my cast mates who reported that I was a "fantastic professional who never made an error," and they told anecdotes about what I was like on set. They noted specific things that I had said or done and even though it was positive, it all felt like gossip. It was suddenly clear that I was constantly being watched. My behavior was being closely monitored so that it could be recorded for the world to read in the *TV Guide*.

By the way that other people reacted to the press, it seemed like I was supposed to feel something like pride. I didn't. I wanted to hide. It was uncomfortable to have people looking at me or talking about me, even if they were saying nice things. In clichéd Canadian style, I had been raised to be humble. We considered birthday parties to be a little boastful and grandiose. In my family, pride was considered to be the greatest imaginable sin. I think my parents would have been okay with me being a drug dealer, just as long as I didn't brag about how many clients I had. So, how was I supposed to react when my dad's work colleagues had a t-shirt printed up for him with one of my glowing reviews on it?

I was confused about who I was supposed to be. My family always told me to just do my best, but my best seemed to be getting me the kind of attention that conflicted with the reserved values I had been raised with. Later in life, I was on an airplane and was dismayed to realize that the in-flight movie was one of mine, *Beautician and the Beast*. I was in a middle seat in coach on the red-eye flight and didn't look anything like the actress on the screen. She had perfect hair and makeup and was even wearing a tiara in one scene. The real life sweatpants, puffy eyes, and frizzy hair didn't correlate.

I put the blanket over my head and prayed that the people next to me would be more interested in the *Sky Mall* magazine than the movie. I tried to fall asleep in the scratchy wool tent I had made myself, but I ended up listening to people as they watched the movie. I hoped they were laughing at the right parts. I was invested and mortified, in equal measure. It was a dichotomy that became very familiar and impossible to reconcile. But maybe that was just the price of being in films. Wasn't everyone's life complicated and full of tradeoffs?

CHAPTER 2

5th Grade Career Building

What do you call a mid-life crisis that happens at age nine? I don't know if double-digits are traumatic for every child, but I had a total breakdown the week before my tenth birthday. What was happening with my career? I'd been at this for six years now but I didn't really know where it was all going. Would this be my life forever? I couldn't imagine doing anything else, but the whole acting thing felt sort of like it had just randomly fallen in my lap. What if I changed my mind and wanted to be a veterinarian? Was there still time? I laid in bed and peeled back the cuticles on my fingers until little drops of blood appeared, leaving crimson stains on my security blanket.

I had pretty much hit the ceiling of the entertainment industry in Toronto. I had been in commercials for everything imaginable, and at times my ads aired back-to-back: Oil of Olay face cream following right after Ivory Snow laundry detergent. I had been on every TV show that filmed in Toronto. Every casting company in town knew me and directors had labeled me "One Take Jake" because I tended to be well-prepared and didn't often need multiple chances to get the shot. The nickname made me feel dependable. Being famous was never the goal, but it was meaningful that adults found me to be reliable and professional. It seemed there was little more work to be done. Maybe this acting thing had run its course and it was time to learn to be happy being a girl who attended school regularly and took up horseback riding.

Shortly after my double-digits crisis, I was shooting an episode of *Friday the 13th The Series*. I had been re-hired for a guest starring role, they just hoped their audience was not observant enough to notice that I had been someone totally different two seasons prior. The boy playing my brother, Robert Oliveri, had been living in L.A. and doing that thing that L.A. is known for: waiting around to be an actor. He recommended that I come to California to meet his manager, who was looking for "new people" and apparently I fit the bill for being both a "person" and "new." I seemed like someone who could wait around to be an actor, too.

We might have had a family conversation where we discussed the impact and decided that this was the right move, but I don't remember it. Looking back it seems like a huge step: pulling me out of school for three months, traveling to another country, and separating our family for a while. Yet, at the time it felt inevitable somehow. It was as if I had gotten the brown belt in karate, so why would I not move on to the black belt if the chance was being offered?

So, in the spring of 1990, my mother and I headed west. My father was a labor negotiator for school boards, so he stayed home and planned to come out to visit when he could. It was the first time we had ever been to Los Angeles, and it felt epic. Flying into LAX, we descended through the thick orange smog that hung in the air, into a town where apparently every single house had an in-ground swimming pool. This place was crazy.

We checked in to the Holiday Inn in Burbank for our ninety-day stay, which is the suggested time required to become somebody. One of the flimsy dresser drawers became a kitchen pantry and we filled it with saltines and Skippy peanut butter. Framed photos of my dad and the dog sat on the nightstand. Mom had read a pamphlet about creating an earthquake evacuation plan, so we left water bottles and rubber-soled shoes by the door. That was the extent of my preparations for life in California. We got ready to wait, for earthquakes or a Hollywood career or whatever else might come.

Mom purchased a Thomas Guide, a spiral-bound atlas with 200 pages mapping out L.A.'s knotted mess of streets and freeways. She'd sit up late at night, flipping through the endlessly winding back roads and overpasses. Within days, she had turned herself into a California native, navigating our white Thrifty rental car, attempting to avoid the omnipresent traffic jams. Outside the car window, the palm trees swayed, framing the wide streets and the hookers who hung out on Hollywood Boulevard.

Old movies had led me to believe that Hollywood itself was going to be glittery and lovely, reminiscent of Lauren Bacall and Marilyn Monroe. I thought everyone was going to be wandering around in silver gowns with long cigarette holders and calling people "darling." The crack dealers were unexpected. However, the rest of L.A. was pretty predictable, including the large billboards of Angelyne, the classic Hollywood bombshell with blonde hair and abundant talent overflowing from her top.

Within the first week, we met with Mark, the manager, and he decided that I had the possibility of becoming someone worthy of someone else's time. A manager is different than an agent. An agent books auditions and negotiates contracts. I wasn't really sure what a manager did but they did it for free until you booked a job and then they got a percentage of the earnings. Since Mom and I knew nothing about how things worked in L.A. and since this person was willing to manage me, we decided I needed to be managed.

As part of the management package, Mark would provide acting classes, which he was qualified to teach as he had appeared in a reoccurring role on a popular 80s sitcom. We would run through my "sides" (the scenes from the script that had been chosen for the audition) while sitting on a slippery brown leather couch in his living room. Mark would take a pink highlighter and circle the lines in which I was to "deliver the meat and potatoes." We would do crying practice and he would click a stopwatch, as I attempted to shorten the time it took for me to transform from bright-eyed and bushy-tailed to plump, slowly rolling tears.

"What makes you sad?" he asked me.

"Dead puppies."

"Perfect. Think about dead puppies. Go!" He clicked the stopwatch.

As part of my new management track, I was also required to take juggling lessons. This was a perplexing part of my career building, as I was generally hired for a role as a runaway or neglected daughter of an overly-driven, slightly evil Working Mom, neither of which required knowledge of circus tricks. It seemed like perhaps Mark was providing me with the fallback skills for a lucrative career in the birthday clown industry if the acting thing didn't work out.

So, I learned to juggle, along with the other half-dozen young clients of my manager. We had fun and it was nice to be with kids with whom I had a little something in common. We covered a variety of age ranges and had come to L.A. from just about everywhere, but we all had stories of being the freaks in our classes. None of us had trophies from basketball camp but we could all do a killer "bite-and-smile" that we had perfected on many food-related commercial shoots. So, we bonded by trying to get fancy with a bean-bag-behind-the-back move and ended up hitting the kid from the Sunny D billboard in the face. We all worked hard, not knowing exactly why we were working hard at this, but assuming that this was what it meant to be a young actor in L.A.

I finally understood the true purpose of the exercise when I noticed that Mark had brought us to the park that was adjacent to the Warner Bothers television studios. There we were, devoted manager with his flock of talent in all our pre-teen glory, frolicking in the California sun in direct sight line of the TV execs. The Big Wigs would be sitting in their corner offices making multi-million dollar deals and wondering where, oh where, could they find the next It Kid? All they needed to do was cast their eyes to the left, where they could view a veritable buffet of quality child actor choices. Chasing after brightly colored beanbags, I was an eleven-year-old cuteness machine, pumping out warm fuzzy feelings all over the place.

After a hard day's work cavorting in front of the television studio windows, Mom and I would return home to the eighth floor of the Holiday Inn. I wondered if the relationship with my new actor acquaintances would extend beyond juggling lessons. Maybe they would come over to the overly-chlorinated hotel pool and hang out, like regular kids seemed to do after school. But they all had their own homework and audition prep to do.

Everyone had acting lessons, read-throughs, and wardrobe calls that kept us too busy for idle socializing. Besides all that, there was the subtle, underlying reminder that we were each other's competition. I watched in awe and horror as a few of the particularly savvy kids vied for the personal attention of the manager. Laughing a little too hard at his jokes, jockeying a little too hard to sit next to him. They seemed to know intuitively that his favor might translate to a persuasive phone call to an influential casting director.

Back at the hotel, I'd call my dad and get updates on how he and the dog were managing without us. He'd tell me about his day at work, and that my cousin made the cross-country ski team, and that Mikki had eaten another shoe, and I'd well up with longing for the mundane. It was obvious that life in Canada continued without missing a beat while I had taken this big leap to Los Angeles. Then I'd get excited to tell Dad about our visit to Mann's Chinese theater and that my hands were almost the exact same size as Mary Pickford's handprints. I'd explain to my dad that on studio backlots they made the Western saloon doors smaller to make cowboys look bigger and that I had seen the *Back to the Future* clock tower on the Universal Studio tour. He'd ask how the sound stages were set up and if people really used golf carts to get around.

I idolized my father and it baffled me to be the one who was explaining things to him. Dad was the one who knew how to turn a blade of grass into a whistle and skip stones so they jumped nine times across the surface of Lake Ontario. How did I suddenly know things he didn't? I felt split in two and wasn't sure which person I really was. Was I the shy Canadian girl who was embarrassed about birthday parties or was I this new L.A. girl who spent her day juggling in an attempt to catch the attention of film producers?

When we got off the phone I'd throw all my textbooks on the bed in a heap. I was required to do all my schoolwork while away on these trips and mail my homework back to the teachers for grading. The assignments would inevitably be a pile of papers that didn't seem to relate to one another and some scribbled notes about which chapters to read in which textbooks. I didn't have a tutor unless I was on set, so I was on my own to begrudgingly lie on the itchy polyester duvet and try to understand sixth grade introductory algebra. While it was challenging being my own teacher, it was always better than being in school and having to deal with aloof classmates and frustrated teachers face-to-face.

While I was in the middle of a particularly confusing section on dividing polynomials, I could have sworn that a pigeon had walked through the open sliding glass door of our hotel room. Nope. I was wrong. Two pigeons had walked through the sliding glass door. They entered the room, cooing and bobbing with their small, scaly feet leaving indents in the stained beige carpet. This was utterly wonderful. I was very still, not wanting to scare my new companions and was keenly aware of the fact that I could hardly be expected to do math with wildlife in the room.

My mother was equally shocked and amused, as she looked up from the 1,000 piece puzzle of the Eiffel Tower that she had set up in the corner of the room. The birds did some laps, checking under the bed as if they might have dropped a sock on a previous visit. Then, as abruptly as they arrived, they walked out to the small balcony and flew off. I collapsed in a delighted pile of giggles. Los Angeles truly was a magical place.

When they re-appeared the next day, it was clearly time to name them. I was convinced that this would be a long-term friendship and I had to be prepared with an appropriate way to greet them. They were christened Gregory and Audrey. I was obsessed with old movies and the idea of a pigeon with the surname of Peck struck me as hysterical. The other pigeon was a particularly lovely one, graceful and clean (for a pigeon) and so Ms. Hepburn became her namesake.

My new feathered friends visited several times a day. They got more comfortable and stayed for a longer time, sometimes settling in for a while on the shade of the shiny brass floor lamp while I attempted social studies homework. Gregory and Audrey's visits to the Holiday Inn provided a dose of ritual and grounding to the chaos that life had become. I was surrounded by people I had just met. There was no schedule for the day, the sheets weren't mine, and we were making Cup-A-Soup with a submersible heating coil for dinner. Life was temporary and flimsy but my pigeons were real. They were predictable. The big question of my life was all up to the movie gods: whether or not I would become someone. But in the meantime, I was already someone who was worth the time of my pet pigeons. For a few moments, that felt successful enough.

Locating the Breathe Button

Mark quickly got me into meetings with agents, all while throwing out mildly self-congratulatory comments about his extensive "connections" and "network." After reading a scene for an agent (complete with the conjuring of dead puppies and crying on cue) she agreed to sign me and started sending me to auditions. Now, instead of just juggling in front of production studios, I actually got to go inside the building.

The audition for *Night Court* felt like the big leagues. The long hallways of the Warner Brothers studios were adorned with massive, larger-than-life photos of Harry, Christine, and my personal favorite, Bull. They stood there, with arms crossed and toothy grins, knowing exactly how awesome they were as they entered their seventh season of the show. Important-looking people with multi-colored scripts and call-sheets dashed in and out of closed doors, conducting vital sitcom business. The

On set of Night Court
with Benny Grant.

PHOTO COURTESY OF THE AUTHOR

standard moms and kids loitered around the casting office, fidgeting with their résumés and head shots.

My audition went well and the casting director for *Night Court*, Justine Jacoby, wanted to hire me. It was a little more complicated, however, because it was my first job in the US and she had to navigate all the red tape surrounding work visas for Canadian citizens. She wrote a letter to the government stating that no American could do this job and requested an H-1 work visa for me. Since the extent of my role in *Night Court* was to walk into a room dressed as a miniature flight attendant and say something like, "Hey, you're cute," it's quite possible that my talents were overstated. But, for whatever reason, the casting director put herself out for me and once you get one work visa it's much easier to get the next one.

Night Court was a multi-camera show that was filmed in front of a live studio audience. We had plenty of rehearsals which progressed in the same way that Canadian shows had. There was a sound stage and a large crew, all standard issue stuff by this point. The show was a well-oiled machine and the large cameras easily wheeled around the three-walled sets. Hair stylists, makeup artists and wardrobe assistants seemed to appear out of nowhere to make small adjustments and then vanish just as quickly. The series regulars navigated the sets like they were in their own living rooms, leaving the guest stars to wonder if that was a functional door or if we were going to look like idiots by pulling on a doorknob attached to a wall.

After a few days of table readings, blockings, and camera rehearsals, tape night came. The audience was big. Really big. There were a couple hundred people who had waited in the hot Burbank sun for hours to see the hit show. The mass of tourists with their white sneakers and neon visors spilled in, climbing up the metal bleachers, all pumped and ready to see Harry and Christine. As they got settled, the stand-up comic got the crowd geared up for the show and pointed out the light-up "laugh" and "applause" signs that dangled above their heads, should there be any confusion about what their specific emotional contribution should be. The audience giggled at the sight of the familiar sets and tried to peer around the corner to see where the dressing rooms were.

During rehearsals, everything had been pretty straightforward. I walked through the door, said my line, John Larroquette mugged a face, the director said cut and we went to lunch. On tape night, though, the electric energy that buzzed through the studio suggested that this was different and it made me nervous. Nerves were an unfamiliar on-set feeling for me, but then again I was not used to filming in front of bleachers. The crew never made me anxious, they all had jobs to do and weren't really watching me—they were watching the details of the scene. But these people came specifically to stare at the actors. My chest felt tight and my eyes refused to focus. I tugged on my costume, thinking my collar had gotten smaller somehow. Why was it so hot in here? And if it was so hot, why was I shivering?

I tried to convince myself that I had seven years of shoots under my belt, this was just another one. I dug my right thumb into my opposite palm. I had always been an anxious kid, who worried and over-thought everything, so Mom had called this my Breathe Button; whenever I got nervous I could just press that spot and remind myself to breathe. Suddenly, the assistant director was calling me to my first position for my scene. I pulled myself together and on cue, I walked into the shot in my tiny flight attendant uniform, a robin's egg blue suit and black patent leather shoes with matching handbag. At the sight of my outfit, the crowd went into hysterics.

Generally, when a few hundred people laugh at you, it's not a good thing. The panic lodged in my throat, but then I remembered this was a sitcom and laughter was likely a positive reaction. But what about my line? Should I wait until the crowd stops laughing? That lengthy gap would feel unnatural. But if I said it while they were being so loud, it would never be heard. This was totally different than in rehearsals when the bleachers were empty. I decided to give the audience a beat to take in my whole ensemble, including jauntily placed pill box hat, and then said my line as the cackling was dying down.

"Hey, you're cute." I put my hand on my hip, just like during rehearsals.

My line still pretty much got lost in the crowd reaction, but at least it didn't feel too awkward. Clearly, no American actor could have managed it.

You're perfect, now change

With *Night Court* on my résumé, the auditions started to increase. The L.A. freeway system became a familiar blur as we spent hours commuting from one casting office to the other. Mom learned that if you took surface streets, you could, in fact, get from a one o'clock audition at Culver Studios to a 3:30 callback at Disney with just a couple minutes to spare for a quick read-through of my sides. She perfected the intricate dance of traffic calculation and I became an expert at changing in the car while eating In-N-Out French fries without spilling ketchup on my audition clothes.

When we were not stuck in traffic, we were spending long hours in the immigration lawyer's office, collecting my credits from the newspaper TV listings and any industry magazine articles that mentioned me. We were like crazed scrap-bookers, attempting to justify to the government why I should be allowed to work in the US. It felt kind of like begging, but in a very specific way that involved filling out forms in triplicate. Our forms eventually paid off, resulting in regular visas so that I could continue working.

But one obvious truth remained—regardless of how many visas I got, I was not an American. A casting director identified the problem: my Canadian accent made me sound like Bob and Doug McKenzie. I said things like chesterfield instead of couch, runners instead of sneakers and I pronounced the word pasta like "passed-a." The situation was clearly out of control when I asked at a restaurant where the washroom was. After a scary ride in a freight elevator, I ended up in the laundry room, still needing to pee. I just didn't speak the proper language of Los Angeles.

Conveniently, a whole industry had sprung up around the need to get foreigners to say pah-sta. We went to the Samuel French bookstore and bought a cassette tape called something like *Achieving the Standard American Accent*, which came with a little stapled booklet with phonetic examples written out. I listened to the tapes on my bright yellow Walkman on the way to auditions. I imitated the people on the tapes, all of us sounding ridiculous with our exaggerated, deliberate focus and our unnatural lilt. I spouted nonsensical phrases and stretched my jaw and lips, attempting to make them more American.

It didn't work. My clipped Canadian talk still seeped through the attempted whitewashing and casting directors continued to complain about it. Mom hired an accent coach who had been recommended by my manager. She and I met twice a week and sat in a small, windowless office, making strange sounds together and trying to get my tongue to hit the roof of my mouth in the correct place. I said my lines and she covered my audition scenes with notes, indicating the proper, generic American pronunciation of words like *project* and *house*. Her eyebrows would raise on the syllable I was supposed to emphasize and she would hold her breath when we got to anything with a *u* sound. She put red squiggly marks over each syllable, creating hieroglyphics that rendered the actual dialogue almost illegible. Her perfect accent oozed slowly and deliberately from her lips as she read my lines as an example, over and over again. It was all so flawless, so vanilla and inoffensive next to my now obvious annihilation of the word *about*. We would repeat the dialogue onto a tape recorder so that I could listen to the flowing verses at home as I drifted off to sleep.

Slowly, the Canadian-ness melted away and I sounded like all the other nonspecific American kids on the radio commercials. That little piece of me was sufficiently hidden and glossed over. I had been smoothed out and prettied up, made more acceptable for the American screen. My new accent felt like hair dye or bronzer. It was a lie, but it was the sort of lie a person is expected to tell.

After a while, I forgot that it wasn't always a part of me. The new cadence stuck, since I was surrounded by other actors from Minnesota or Boston who had hired the same accent coach and whose voices had been cloned to bland perfection just like mine. But when I went back to Canada, everyone said I sounded weird and didn't know that when I asked for a soda I really meant a pop. But that was a sacrifice that needed to be made if I wanted to work in Los Angeles. Hollywood had officially branded me.

CHAPTER 3

The Show Must Go On. Really.

hortly after *Night Court*, I booked another gig. The shoot for *Rambling Rose* felt slow and genteel, embodying the spirit of the South during the 1930s, just like it was supposed to. My role was straightforward and not very demanding. There was a lot of sitting at a dinner table and saying cute things. There was nothing that indicated that this movie would change everything and give me the biggest challenge of my life.

We shot in Wilmington, North Carolina and so began my love affair with filming on location. Getting to go somewhere new for months at a time and immersing myself in an unfamiliar place was intoxicating. It was fun to live out of a suitcase and make my home wherever I landed. It seemed unnecessary to have consistent companions or the comforts of my own bed; the delightful chaos of being on location made up for all that normal kid stuff. This first taste of what would be my life for the next decade proved to be a particularly lovely introduction. The production company had rented a small condo on the beach for my mom and me, with lots of windows and a carpet that always felt slightly damp from the sea air. The apartment was densely populated with cockroaches but I could run across the street and dig my toes into the sand in under a minute.

We filmed at Carolco Studio in Wilmington. North Carolina gave significant tax incentives to production companies that filmed there and since we also had exterior shots that needed to show the sleepy south of the 1930s, it was a perfect location. On the sound stage next door, another production was taking advantage of the tax perks; they were shooting the *Teenage Mutant Ninja Turtles* movie. Our very different films tended to break for lunch around the same time, so we often ate together. The Turtles would remove their heads and sit with us in our original 1930s scratchy wool costumes, while we choked down our soggy sandwiches and wilted salads from the commissary and complained about the slow shooting schedule. Those Turtles were nice guys who increased my knowledge of ninja moves.

I had no clue who Robert Duvall was before working with him. *Lonesome Dove* and *Apocalypse Now* were not on my eleven-year-old movie-watching list. He was very kind, with a laid-back, approachable manner and he asked the cast and crew to call him Bobby. His laugh was deep and heartfelt, and he maintained his character's Southern drawl even when we weren't filming.

In between scenes, the other children on the film and I would be sent to "school." This entailed corralling us into a florescent light drenched office with a few chairs, desks with sticky drawers and walls with peeling paint. It was oppressive on the best of days and it was a stark contrast to go from being a working professional on set, to being a bored 7th grade student with zero interest in memorizing the details of Canada's parliamentary system. My schoolmates were six-year-old Evan, who played the youngest brother and our two stand-ins, Gelene and Jeffrey, who matched us in size, age and general appearance.

One day, Bobby's assistant Brad knocked on the door of the schoolroom and popped his head in and addressed the tutor.

"Hey Ruth, Bobby would like to see Lisa."

My teacher seemed surprised by the intrusion and she protested. She explained that she only had three hours a day, squeezed into fifteen-minute segments between shots, to attempt to get us a decent education. These were the legal rules of children working, she explained and she had to answer to the union. Brad smiled and nodded, acknowledging her plight. Then he simply repeated, "Bobby would like to see Lisa." There was no negotiation, no explanation, no apology.

I shrugged at my tutor, barely concealing the smug look slapped across my face and obediently got up from my desk and followed Brad. It wasn't that I cared so much about being summoned by one of Hollywood's most revered film stars, I was just doing an internal happy dance at the fact that I got out of school. In the back of my mind I wondered what he wanted. Did he want to run lines? Sometimes actors did that during lighting set ups. But for which scene? Did I know all of them? Was I in trouble for something? Was this what happens when you get fired?

Brad wasn't answering any questions as he walked me back to the set where we found Bobby. He was sitting in a rocking chair on the fake front porch of the Depression-era house that was built, to scale, on the soundstage. The place could have been torn out of a plantation in the Deep South, but instead of looking out over kudzu-laced weeping willows, the house gazed over the dirty warehouse floor snaked with heavy industrial cables and the ransacked craft services snack table. Bobby was dressed in his costume—he had his straw hat in his hand and was playing with the brim while he waited for me. He smiled when we arrived and gestured for me to sit in the rocking chair next to him.

"Do you need anything else, Bobby?" Brad asked him as he turned to leave.

"Thanks, we're fine."

I didn't sit but instead I hovered and nervously picked at the porch railing, telling Bobby that my tutor was mad and attempted to re-explain the legalities of being a child actor and the three-hours-per-day schooling requirement. Plus, there were my teachers back home who were never happy that I was working, so all my work really needed to be done perfectly. What I left unsaid was that I wasn't sure which adult I was supposed to obey. There were teachers demanding that school was the priority and then there was Bobby not taking no for an answer. No matter what I did, someone was going to be disappointed and I would always be failing somehow.

He listened to me patiently and then nodded and said, "Tell your teacher that you are going to learn much more here with me than in those textbooks. Sit down, Baby Doll." He pointed again to the rocking chair next to him. I sat.

Bobby called for me often after that. He would let me get an hour of school in before sending Brad knocking at the schoolroom door. My tutor gave up trying to fight it. She would respond to the inevitable interference with a deep sigh and would say, "You can go," just to hang on to the illusion that she still held some control over the schoolroom. Every time I arrived at the porch, Bobby had a new topic that he wanted to discuss. I don't know why he chose me for these porch chats but I loved how freely and openly we spoke. All I knew was that he made me feel special.

Bobby legitimately wanted to know about my past eleven years of existence. He asked questions and really listened in a way that pre-teens are not accustomed to. He shared details about his life. He taught me how to tango. We talked about acting. He had a deep passion for the craft and I suspected I was assumed to have the same. He wanted to tell me how to keep a good head on my shoulders and teach me how to not get burned out by the film industry. He told me to keep people around me who would always tell me the truth and that I should never believe my reviews, good or bad, because both were likely to be exaggerated.

"And if you forget everything else, just remember this one thing," he said. "It's only a movie."

It sounded like good advice, but it made me laugh anyway. I looked around at the hundreds of people who were reverently clocking eighteen-hour days and pouring their souls into this movie. I thought about our seven-million-dollar budget. Every moment on set always felt like it was Saving-the-World important, with people rushing around in an attempt to get everything perfect. And yet, here was a Hollywood legend saying it wasn't that big of a deal. I didn't get it. So, I laughed.

Filming progressed and the show was filled with fun kid-perks. We filmed near sluggish Southern streams and during my lunch break I would try to count all the painted turtles that dotted the muddy banks. My one day off every week was spent on the beach, eating hush puppies, chasing ghost crabs and playing Frisbee with Bobby's dog, Gus. We had just a couple weeks of filming left when everything changed.

I was in the dingy school room, seated at my desk and attempting to avoid some bogus busywork that had been passed on to me by teachers back home who were upset that I was not seated in their classroom. They made it clear that they didn't care for the daunting task of providing several months of work in advance. Some teachers simply refused to grade the assignments I had done on location and covered my report cards with *Not Applicable*. They sent work that had very little relevance to actual subjects, just so that they wouldn't have to deal with me anymore. Each bogus page they gave me was a little academic mutiny in the form of a photocopied worksheet.

That day of work had already been long. We had several scenes still to film and I was exhausted. I looked at those worksheets and didn't know how I was going to survive them. It was the end of October, and my mind easily wandered to Halloween. Trick-or-treating was, of course, thrilling, but I had spent so much time dressing up like a kid from the 1930s that the idea of wearing my own clothes seemed novel and attractive. I wondered if anyone would give me candy if I knocked on their door dressed in jeans and Chucks and told them that I was pretending to be a regular non-working child. I wanted to talk to the other kids, maybe find out their Halloween plans, so I pushed my chair back to stand up and the wheels of the chair got caught on the carpet. I flew backwards like I was in a bad slapstick comedy, with arms and legs flying through the air.

Crack. I heard it. It could have been the chair, but it wasn't. It was my spine. The back of my head smashed in to the wall, my body snapped forward and there was a sharp burn when my knees collided with my nose. The other kids laughed, I must have looked ridiculous disappearing so suddenly behind my desk. I tried to laugh, too but realized I couldn't breathe. I couldn't quite tell what hurt. Maybe it was just my pride, maybe my face burning was from embarrassment rather than impact. I gasped as the wind came back into my lungs. I put my hand up to my nose, but there was no blood. It was fine.

My tutor bolted over and tried to untangle the mess of chair, desk and me. I was dizzy and mortified from my graceless display. When I noticed that everyone was staring at me, I smiled from embarrassment and said, "Ta da!" to my amused but uncertain classmates. One of the kids ran to get my mother from my dressing room down the hall. The producers of the film quickly followed and my tutor requested we call an ambulance. They made me stay lying down, despite my insistence that I was fine. I just needed to walk it off and get a glass of water.

To my further humiliation, they did call an ambulance. But something else quickly took over the embarrassment. Had I known at the time what it was to be drunk, I would have recognized it as intoxication; I became completely drunk with shock. The pain vanished and I became aware of bizarre minor details. Life turned into a tilt-shift photograph, everything was fuzzy except for the almost excruciatingly sharp focus in the middle of my field of vision.

When the ambulance arrived, I learned that the EMT's name was also Lisa, and through my fog this seemed absolutely hysterical. Two Lisas! One strapping the other to a board! I was Velcroed in with thick blue restraints and my head was sandwiched between padded blocks. The Velcro straps pulled at my waist-length hair but by that point my body had gone numb. All I could feel was a light tug, pulling my head to the side. As Lisa put me in the ambulance I remember begging them to not use the siren. They could use the lights, if they absolutely had to; otherwise they just needed to drive normally and calmly to the hospital. There didn't need to be some siren, exclaiming to the world, "Excuse me, coming through, a dumb-ass klutzy kid just fell out of a chair! Coming through!"

I was still in my film costume when we arrived at the hospital. I was wearing authentic 1930s clothing with a large pink bow in my hair. I was quite concerned about what the hospital staff must think of me. I kept trying to explain that I was an actor, not for any presumed prestige, but to explain that I was not this prissy in my regular clothing choices. A sea of faces were smiling and nodding above me as they cut the costume off my body.

That day, the crew had planned a birthday party for my brother in the film. I had seen the cake and the producers were giving the birthday boy a puppy; there was no way I was going to miss that. I asked my mom to call the studio and tell them that I would be back soon and if they would just wait a few minutes, I would get off this stupid board and be back to watch the presentation of the puppy, with a large slice of cake in hand. She rubbed my arm and agreed to make the call. She didn't mention that I had passed out for quite a while, the party had ended many hours prior and I wasn't leaving that hospital any time soon. The doctors were looking at my x-rays. My back was broken and as I slipped in and out of consciousness, I heard the word paralyzed.

The early assessments of my injuries were inconsistent and confusing. They knew that I had damaged three vertebrae and had severe whiplash in my lower back but they could not tell the extent of the spinal injury. They said that it was the kind of damage they see when an adult falls off a roof. Although at first they thought that I might be paralyzed, the prognosis was revised and they said that I would be able to walk but it was unlikely that I would ever be back to my previous abilities.

Tests and drugs were doled out and my days in the hospital blurred together. I'd wake up to various scenes that felt like they were part of a play I was watching. Mom talking to nurses. Mom on the phone with Dad. Nurses poking at me. Mom asleep in a chair. At one point I came out of a drug-induced haze to find a large gorilla standing over my bed.

He had dead, glossy black eyes, and reeked of gorilla sweat. There was a loud, persistent siren-like squealing as the monster attempted to hand me a bouquet of red balloons. When the nurses ran in to comfort me, I finally realized that the horrible sound was me screaming. The film crew ill-advisedly sent a guy in a gorilla costume to cheer me up. It was sweet and well-intentioned, however, let me just say that codeine and gorillas don't mix, people. I still have nightmares about it.

In addition to the gorilla, various co-workers came to see me at the hospital. They brought flowers and books and healing crystals to line up along my spine, but Bobby never came. Brad brought good wishes and a card on Bobby's behalf.

"He just...can't. He can't see you like this."

It was only then that I realized that this might be a big deal. This was not another one of my clumsy spills that I could laugh off. I could almost handle being laughed at, but being pitied scared me. I took more painkillers and went back to sleep.

After a week in the hospital, I was fitted for a back brace and released with the doctor's okay to get back to work. Bobby welcomed me back with a gentle hug, but everything had changed and I was no longer up for our porch sessions. I was pale, fragile, scared, and just trying to get the shoot finished.

They are not kidding when they say that the show must go on.

I was confined to bed rest except for five-minute spans, three times a day, which was the time that the doctor approved me to sit in a chair. Mom went into functional crisis mode, carefully watching the clock to make sure we didn't go over my time limits. Always good in extraordinary situations, she stayed calm and became laser-like in her focus. This film became something to be conquered and she was going to make sure we finished the show and got out of there.

Since I couldn't lift my arms over my head and I was now constantly wearing a metal back brace, the wardrobe department had to cut open my costumes and then hand-sew me back into them every day. The brace was shaped like a cross. It was attached to my front with thick adjustable straps and had large pads that sat along my collarbone, my pelvis, and curved around both sides of my body. The metal was constantly cold, the screws and bolts that held it together were jagged and snagged on everything. Mom covered the brace in shiny dolphin stickers to make it less scary, but it still resembled something you would find either on a construction site or in a medieval torture museum.

My stand-in, Gelene, would take my place for rehearsals. She looked a lot like me, with her long brown hair and slight build, so she was used as my body double for any scenes where I had to be moving. They dressed Gelene up in my costumes and filmed her from behind so you wouldn't see her face. She made a perfectly good able-bodied me; she would run through the frame and no one was the wiser. When the shot required my face to be seen, I was carried to set and seated in a chair with my arms propped up on the table, where I would try to make my drugged eyes not look too stoned. Most of my lines were cut or shortened since I sounded like a meth addict. Normally, having lines cut is devastating for an actor, but I was just counting down the days until I could get back to Canada.

While scenes were being lit and set up, I would be carried to a twin mattress that had been placed on the floor in my dressing room. My mother would often leave me alone to get some rest and I would linger in my twilight stupor, waiting to be called back to work. She would pull the shades so I could sleep but I mostly stared at the pattern on the couch, trying to make out shapes and faces to keep myself occupied.

I took shallow breaths, the only kind that the tight back brace would allow, and wondered what this injury really meant. The doctors said it was really uncertain what kind of recovery I would have and what my physical abilities would be. Was this the end of my career? I wondered if I would even know how to be a kid who went to school full-time.

I knew how to work. There were the on-set politics to navigate and the lines to learn and the motions to replicate at exactly the same time for the continuity of every take. There was hair and makeup to sit still for, even if the hairdresser pulled a little too hard and the makeup felt heavy and greasy. There was the lighting to be aware of so that you didn't stand in a shadow or cast your shadow on another actor. School was foreign territory, with its own unspoken rules that I didn't understand. I worried about my ability to survive it.

But there was no guarantee that my body would be acceptable for film anymore. It felt unfathomable that this was the end of everything that I had known but I'd always felt like it was going to end somehow. Wasn't acting temporary for most kids? I'd drift off to my drugged sleep feeling more confused than ever.

What usually woke me was the assistant director, saying that it was time to go to set. But one afternoon, I had a different visitor: the new puppy that my co-star had been given. He was a sweet little guy who tended to wander the halls of the office building that the dressing rooms were in.

"Hey, Buddy. C'mere," I called from my mattress.

He wandered in to the room in that wiggly-butt puppy way and sniffed around. He looked in my mother's giant carpetbag that held my script and snacks, he sniffed around my stack of untouched schoolwork and attempted to crawl under the side table to reach a lost potato chip. Then he came back to me.

"Whatcha doing, puppy?" I cooed at him.

What the puppy was doing, to my dismay, was peeing on me. There I was, broken-backed, unable to move, and being peed on. I'd never felt more vulnerable in my life. When I started yelling, my mom came running, followed by a couple other production assistants who all tried gallantly to stifle their giggles. The wardrobe people were even more unhappy than I was, as they carefully hand-scrubbed dog urine from my vintage, fifty-year-old wool skirt.

✳✳✳✳✳

When the film was finished, my mother and I returned to Canada where I laid on the couch for many long months. School was out of the question, as I couldn't sit in a chair for more than a few minutes at a time. So, a loop of old movies kept me entertained and distracted from the pain. I watched *To Kill a Mockingbird* and cheered when Bobby as Boo Radley stepped out of the shadows to save the day. It was somehow comforting to see my friend. I watched Scout and Boo sit on the porch together, just like Bobby and I had. It brought tears to my eyes when Mary Badham smiled up at Bobby, recognizing his gentle soul. *Hey, Boo.*

I was incredibly lucky to experience a growth spurt that allowed my spine the space to heal. I slowly came back to myself. After hours of daily physical therapy, only a few minor issues lingered. My right foot would drag when I got tired and some nerve damage in my lower back would act up occasionally. But I gained my weight back, gained my strength back and I was soon back to life. Back to life meant back to work: I didn't have to conceive of a regular life after all. I had a princess to meet.

The People's Princess

While I was wearing a back brace and watching game shows, the editors of *Rambling Rose* were cutting and splicing and creating art. The film would be my introduction to the world of premieres. I had already been in the movie with John Malkovich, but actors of bit parts (even the significant, doe-eyed bit parts) don't get invited to the fancy premieres.

Later in life, it would become clear that attending premieres would feel like getting flayed. Some people must enjoy them, maybe the same kind of people who get excited about getting an invitation to parties at roller rinks or backyard barbeques or anniversary celebrations. Because premieres are much like those regular parties, except add another 700 people, paparazzi, forced ass-kissing motivated by a deep-seated fear that you will never work again, and small, low-carb food served on toothpicks, as required by scrawny Hollywood actresses to keep them that

*Publicity shot for "Rambling Rose." With Laura Dern, Lukas Haas,
Robert Duvall, Diane Ladd, and Evan Lockwood.*
PHOTO COURTESY OF CAROLCO PICTURES.

way. However, my first premier set the standard pretty high. It was a royal premiere in London, which meant the guest list included Princess Diana.

When you are being introduced to royalty there is serious protocol because Brits are not known for screwing around when it comes to tradition. There were many rules to adhere to; when I met the princess, I could not speak until spoken to and when I did dare to open my mouth, I needed to say, "Your Royal Highness." This level of formality felt completely awkward; my instinct would have been to give the princess a hug, offer her a piece of gum, and show her a picture of my dog.

I traveled with my entourage, which for me, consisted of my mother, father, and grandmother. For my Canadian grandmother, attending a royal premiere was akin to having brunch with Jesus. There was no way she was going to miss that. As soon as we arrived in London, I met with a woman whose actual job it was teaching me how to curtsey properly.

My curtsey teacher came to our hotel room, and it scared me a little to let her in. She looked like a cartoon someone had drawn of what a British curtsey teacher should look like. Her entire being was lithe and severe and her hair was pulled back so tightly that it made you wince just to look at it. After a brief history lesson about the curtsey, we practiced the move itself. I was something of a disappointment to her, as my curtsey looked more like I was suddenly tripping over something. She smiled a tight British smile and patiently requested I try again. She seemed convinced that I was about to massacre the ritual in front of her princess, which would inevitably cause the crumbling of the British Empire and everything it stood for. When she had done her best, she patted my shoulder a little too hard and said she was sure it would be fine—but please would I mind terribly spending another hour or so practicing in front of the bathroom mirror?

The whole thing was incredibly intimidating. I worried about what to say to Princess Diana. British weather seemed to be a terrible topic of conversation. Would I have enough time for a real heart-to-heart exchange? Should I tell her she looked beautiful or was that like telling

Mount Everest it looked big?

Right before the main event, the actors, director, and producers of the film gathered together to watch an instructional video on how to properly meet and greet the princess. We crammed around the television in the producer's hotel room. I brought a notebook. The air was thick with nerves and everyone else seemed to be hoping that the video would answer some questions for them, as well. We all sat around looking tense, the ladies smoothing hems and straightening pantyhose, the men buttoning and unbuttoning tuxedo jackets.

I poised my pen and paper as the video started; Rowan Atkinson came on screen as Mr. Bean. It was a spoof in which he was spit polishing his shoes and making a fool out of himself as he waited for his royal introduction. The video ended with him head-butting the Queen of England. I laughed, but it was the kind of laugh where I was simultaneously looking around, hopeful that the real video was about to start because the issue remained that I didn't have a clue about what I was doing. Seriously? This was the "educational video"? The little skit was supposed to help everyone relax, but all it did was encourage me to scribble in my notebook, *No head butting.*

There was no time for questions as my family and I were ushered into a limo that took us to the theater. As we drove, it was the first time I realized we really were in London. There had been so much to think about with the premiere that there hadn't been the chance to take it all in. We passed the silly red phone booths, the double-decker buses, and women with black umbrellas, who could have been stand-ins for Mary Poppins. I loved how different it all felt. Going to North Carolina for work had felt exotic, but international travel was on a whole other level.

When we arrived in front of the marquee, my heart froze. The street outside the theater was teeming with hundreds of people. It might have been thousands. When I panic, I hyperventilate, which often leads to blackouts. That had the potential to result in an unintentional royal head butt, so clearly it needed to stop.

"That's...that's a lot of people."

Mom waved her hands dismissively at the crowd outside the tinted limo window.

"They're waiting for the bus. Look, there's the stop right there."

She was right. There was a stop right outside the theater.

"It's London. Everyone takes advantage of public transportation here. It's very smart. Environmentally responsible, too."

I was about to inquire as to why people would be waiting for the bus by crouching on top of the bus shelter with a long-lens camera, but my dad and Grandma beamed at me from the other side of the limo.

"They're just waiting for the bus," they agreed. There was a lot of nodding.

It seemed best to believe them and it calmed me down a bit as Mom pressed her thumb into my Breathe Button spot in the middle of my palm.

My family took their seats in the theater and left me to join the other people from the film in the reception line. I waited for the princess's arrival, between Lucas Haas, who played my older brother in the film, and Jane Robinson, the costume director. I was wearing itchy tights and a horrendous black, flowery Laura Ashley dress with a wide, floppy lace collar that seemed quite sophisticated to my pre-teen sensibilities. The tights had been a last-minute purchase from a Marks & Spencer in London. I had forgotten to bring tights and my grandmother gasped at the thought of me meeting a princess with uncovered legs. My itchy British tights crushed my waist and made me even more uncomfortable. The princess took a long time to arrive but she was a princess, so no one said anything. I fidgeted and my still-healing back was starting to ache from standing so long.

The dark, rainy London night suddenly turned to daylight with all the flashbulbs and the air filled with the excited yelling of paparazzi. Moments later, Princess Diana stepped into the lobby of the theater and looked just as spectacular as you would expect. As she made her way down the line, being introduced to the representatives of the film, I tried to practice the curtsey in my mind. I slipped my foot behind my ankle a few times to make sure I could still move it.

She chatted a bit with each person she met. It very much resembled a wedding reception line, except Princess Diana was both bride and groom and was more stunning than both put together. When she was presented to the person just before me, I started to freak out again. Do I look at her now? Or is that eavesdropping? Do I stare straight ahead? Do I look at my shoes and feign surprise when she gets to me? "Oh! Hello there!" As if there was some other reason I had flown to another continent and was wearing itchy tights?

Before I was able to work out an answer, suddenly, Princess Diana was standing in front of me, reaching out her hand. I took it and curtsied, losing my balance a little and wobbling to the side. She smiled kindly and supported me with her other hand. Strike one. I was specifically told to not steady myself on the princess, as if she were some sort of bejeweled kickstand. But I was a clumsy twelve-year-old who tripped a lot in normal situations and was still nursing a broken back from falling out of a chair; this fumble was inevitable.

The official presentation was made by some sort of royal aid with a booming voice, "Lisa Jakub, an actress in the film."

"Hello Lisa, it's very nice to meet you." Her words were effortless and felt like sunshine.

"It's an honor to meet you, Your Royal Highness."

Okay, I got through that part. That was the line I had planned. Now we were free-styling. It seems an easy thing, to have a conversation and respond like a human being to another human being, but when there are several cameras in your face and you're holding the hand of a princess, it's not so simple.

"You look so pretty!" she remarked. I blushed and looked at my feet, then remembered that you are supposed to keep eye contact. I looked back up and stared blankly. Saying, "Thank you," seemed like I was accepting the premise that I was pretty, which is hard to do under regular

Trying not to fall down. With Renny Harlin, Martha Coolidge,
Jane Robinson, and Diana, Princess of Wales.

PHOTO: TIM CLARKE

circumstances, let alone while standing next to Princess Diana. Saying, "You look pretty, too," seemed trite, as if I hadn't thought she looked pretty until she thought I did. I fished around in my brain for something else to say. Nope. Nothing.

"I hear you did a lovely job in the film." She kindly made up for my lack of words.

"Thank you, Your Royal Highness."

"I have a son that is just about your age; his name is William. I'm sure he would love to meet you."

Was Princess Diana is trying to set me up with her son? Now, this would be a hell of a first date for me.

"Oh. Yes. Okay. That sounds fun."

"Well, it's settled then, we will have to do that sometime." She beamed more sunshine at me.

Again, I was stymied. How was *that* going to work? I almost said, "Should I just stop by the palace one day, or...?" I went with, "Thank you, your Royal Highness," because I had already said that successfully and was fairly confident that my mouth could make those same sounds again.

She gave me a final, sweet smile and moved on down the line to greet the rest of the people from the film. I just stood there looking forward. We had all flown to Europe for those twenty seconds and now they were done. Had I done a good job? It was a surprisingly intimate public moment that no one could grade me on. I was surrounded by crowds of people and cameras but I suddenly felt very alone. People to my left and right were worried about their own performances, my mom hadn't been there, nor my curtsey teacher or anyone else that I could count on for an honest critique of my behavior. If I had another take I could have done it better, been more charming and articulate. I could have done that curtsey better and would have said something funny so that I could have heard her laugh. But, for better or worse, life didn't just write "Take 2" on the slate, offering another chance to be perfect in that moment. There was no choice but to be content with what had happened, even if

I felt the pressure to have made it worthwhile. So, I exhaled and tried to wiggle my toes within my stiff, shiny black shoes and wondered how we were going to work out this whole William thing.

After surviving the receiving line, we all made our way into the theater and watched the film. I was a few seats down from Diana and kept stealing glances to see if she liked it. She laughed and cried in the appropriate places and seemed to enjoy herself. She was indescribably beautiful, lit by the flickering screen. It's hard to understand the full impact of meeting someone like that at age twelve, but I at least understood that I was in the presence of someone who radiated goodness. It had nothing to do with her status. It had to do with the fact that she was kind and she gave me a loving smile when she had to support my curtsey. She had seen my nervousness and had tried to comfort me, mother me. Her title was meaningless. She was simply a kind person.

And I've decided to forgive William for going a different way with his choice of wife. Even though Kate might not have been his mother's first choice.

✳ ✳ ✳ ✳ ✳

Six years later, I was in a limo coming home from the airport when I heard about Princess Diana's death. I had just finished a shoot and they always send limos for that sort of thing because it's supposed to be impressive and they want to make you feel like you are more important that you really are. I'm always uncomfortable and usually carsick in limos but this was a different kind of awful. The horrible news came on the radio and the driver turned it up for us. My parents and I were all in the backseat and I started shaking. It took a while for the tears to come; my tear ducts were shocked shut.

I stared out the window of the limo and thought of her staring out the window of her limo. She was gentle and had held my hand longer than necessary. She loved her boys. Now, the paparazzi, who had been stoked and encouraged by what I did for a living, were gaining strength like a well-fed dragon. They had chased her. Hunted her. And now she was dead. This job of mine had put me in this unique position to meet this spectacular person, but, I wondered, at what price? My body had been turned inside out and my lungs were too small. I heard my mother whisper to my dad, "Put your arm around her." He did.

Unfurnished lives

Rambling Rose wasn't a box office blockbuster, but the critics enjoyed it. The film earned Oscar nominations for Diane Ladd and Laura Dern, the first time a mother and daughter had been nominated together for the same film. However, the film industry journey is rarely a straight line for an actor. There are huge ups and downs and nothing is a guaranteed stepping stone to the next career conquest. So, shortly after going to a premiere with a princess, Mom and I were back living in an unfurnished apartment, sitting in casting waiting rooms filled with pre-teen brunettes, silently mouthing their lines and practicing their nonchalant hair flips.

My agent and manager concluded that I needed to spend more time in Los Angeles in an attempt to take advantage of the film's modest success. Living in hotels for months on end was getting expensive, even the barebones hotels with the threadbare carpeting where we tended to reside. We didn't know anyone in L.A. who we could stay with. Most of the other people we knew were living out of suitcases, too—kid actors and their moms who lived elsewhere and came to L.A. to chase down a job.

Like any good transients, we turned to the odd world of short-term rentals. My mother and I rented an unfurnished two-bedroom apartment on a month-to-month basis in North Hollywood. It was classic California valley architecture; our place was on the second floor and overlooked an open-air cement courtyard that was decorated with small palm trees in terra cotta pots. We bought a cardboard banker's box for me to use as a school desk. We picnicked on the floor and slept on lumpy, leaky plastic air mattresses that were intended to be used in a pool.

Such a fleeting and precarious life felt thrilling, like we were just dandelion seeds waiting for a strong breeze to scatter us absolutely anywhere. One good audition would mean a new job and we would fold up our lives and our cardboard furniture and simply vanish as if we had never lived in apartment 2F. The sparse, minimalist look of the place also offered a significant change from our small, cluttered house in Canada where there was often a dog/turtle/piece of construction equipment in the way. I could practice cartwheels unencumbered by something as invasive as a couch. Mom pointed out that one of the leading causes of injury in an earthquake was from bookcases or other pieces of furniture falling over, so we were likely in the safest place in all of Los Angeles, seismologically speaking. Her ability to make our peculiar life seem normal, and even sensible, was extraordinary. I reveled in the thought that maybe "different" didn't have to mean "wrong."

Auditions were picking up, but I'd still only have two or three a week, so there was a lot of time to fill. I could memorize about a page of dialogue a minute, so audition preparation was hardly time-consuming. Three months moved slowly. We didn't really have friends, and you can only walk around at the mall for so long, even in California. I would sit around the bare apartment and read *A Wrinkle in Time* over and over again. Mom and I would play cards and browse the video store for old movies. We bought an annual pass to Universal Studios and went three times a week to go on the E.T. ride and watch the lady in a Lucille Ball costume pose for photos with tourists.

And I would write. I always wrote. I wrote fantasies, war epics, and pop-up books. I journaled constantly. Everything that happened to me had to be chronicled in a spiral bound notebook or else it didn't really count. An event could only be processed and become real when it had words and phrases and commas associated with it. Otherwise, who could ever say it really happened? I tried to make sense of my life, and attempted to work out my complicated feelings about auditions and the idea of possibly becoming famous. I wondered what it would be like to play soccer or violin. I wondered how it felt to take home a permission form for a field trip and not immediately wonder if I'd be out of town filming something when it was time to go to the museum.

However, I also felt badly for the kids who didn't know how to walk into camera frame and stop exactly at a T mark on the floor without looking down. It was impossible to imagine a life that didn't include table reads and wardrobe calls; it was like trying to imagine what the world would look like without the color blue.

About three weeks into our stay in California, distracted by Uno tournaments and daily trips to browse the sale racks at Macy's and eat greasy Chinese in the food court, I realized that my schoolbooks had yet to be opened. My mom believed that I should be responsible enough to set my own schedule. There was no such thing as "school hours." I was in charge of keeping track of that myself. The books were still stacked in the corner of my closet, complete with instructions from my teachers back home. I panicked. What if I was detrimentally far behind when I got home? I imagined sitting in class and being completely lost as they discussed viscosity levels or inferential logic. I imagined failing a grade and more deeply entrenching myself in weirdo status. Paralyzed in my fear, all I could do was stare at the books, piled up in the corner and threatening to bury me in an academic wasteland.

When I finally found the courage to crack the spine of my French textbook, it turned out that I could actually do a whole week's worth of work in about two hours. I caught up pretty quickly and wondered why all that time spent in school was necessary if it could all be done so efficiently. Learning by myself was easy. I could just get to the important parts and not be distracted by that whole idea of socialization. When I went back to Canada and sat in the classroom, it all felt like boring filler, like glorified group babysitting. I looked forward to getting back to my own version of independent study in L.A., at my homemade desk rigged up with an air mattress and a sagging cardboard box.

For our next stay in California, we landed at the Oakwood Apartments, a well-known temporary housing complex where production houses and theater companies often put their actors up. Oakwood did have one perk over our place in North Hollywood; the apartments were furnished. I use the word *furnished* with some trepidation because in the early 1990s they were furnished the way an Eastern European hotel by the airport might have been furnished in the late 1970s. There were dusty fabric flowers in vases filled with some sort of plastic resin that was supposed to look like water, and which was almost certainly carcinogenic. There were brown polyester bedspreads with frayed edges and cigarette burns. The watercolor prints of landscapes were bolted to the walls, as if anyone would actually be tempted to steal them. But the whole set up was better than our cardboard tables and I could just scotch tape a *Back to the Future* poster over the still-life print of peaches in its shiny gold frame.

We did several stints at the Oakwood over the years. Mom and I tried out a variety of floor plans. We rented the 400-square-foot studio apartment and shared the Murphy bed. I always hated making my bed, so just folding it back into the wall seemed an ingenious way to tidy up. Bedtime became much more exciting as I tried to ride the bed on its descent from its cave. It was a great disappointment when I was working more frequently and we got a two bedroom, which had an eat-in kitchen, a little balcony, and two separate beds that kept all four of their legs on the ground. It didn't occur to me then that it was unusual that my jobs dictated the type of living arrangement that we had. Since that was the case with all the other actors in the complex, it just seemed like that was the way life in L.A. worked. Everyone's apartment size was an indication of how good the last few months of auditions had been for them.

It was mind-blowing to me, even then, that there were people who lived at the Oakwood full time. By nature, corporate housing is a temporary situation but there were a hardy few who had been there for upwards of twenty years. It was very expensive to live there for any ex-tended period of time and I wondered why anyone would do it. The architecture was wildly unattractive and the mind-numbing sameness of the twenty-six low, square buildings, lettered A-Z was the aesthetic equivalent of living in a McDonald's.

It soon became clear that the true allure of the Oakwood was Hol-lywood itself. By living within the paper-thin walls of corporate hous-ing, you were immersed in the acting community. There was something comforting about being with people who were struggling, just like you. You could pick up your mail and chat with a neighbor who understood what it meant to have a good audition or a bad one. They understood what it felt like when you nailed the scene, when the dialogue flowed seamlessly and the tears fell on cue or the joke got a laugh. Then, the pro-ducers would give you that smile and nod to each other and say, "you'll be hearing from us very soon." Those good auditions were such a high that you'd float back to the car and not even care about spending two hours in traffic to get home.

But, the neighbors also understood how it felt when you finished your scene and the producers sat stony-faced behind the long table. You knew you had flubbed the line and not tapped the emotion and had done that unnatural gesture with your hand. The producers sat quietly, their silence piercing the air and clearly expressing that they will not call you back. Definitely not for this job and maybe not for any other job, either. You had walked out with your head down as you passed the better actors just waiting for their turn. Everyone understood how that drive home felt even longer than two hours.

Oakwood residents knew what was filming, who was in town, which show just lost their backing, and which manager was open to new cli-ents. It was the center of the universe for the not-quite-theres. One of our neighbors had been a professional extra for twenty years. He had made a career out of being the guy in the background. When he worked, he worked for fourteen hours a day, was treated like cattle, never had any lines, was paid poorly, and rarely got any real screen time. That was his chosen profession because he liked to be close to that intoxicating on-set energy. Being part of a film community was so venerated, that it was worth the sacrifice.

Down the hall from us lived a woman named Sandra who had spent decades working as a stand-in. She was almost beautiful. All of her individual features should have added up to a movie star, but everything was just a quarter-inch off. Just a little bit too big or too small or too much to the left side. Her posture was not quite graceful, her voice just a little too high and grating. So, it was her job to stand in the shot while the lighting crew set up, so that the actress could take a break. That's a real job. A set, while being a communal project that everyone is working on together, is also incredibly hierarchical. Who is lording over the top? Actors. Directors. Producers. They get all the glory and the praise, they pose in front of the step-and-repeat at premieres and get draped in loaner jewelry from Van Cleef and Arpels.

But a film couldn't get made without Sandra standing in for her actress. She's never been on a single frame of film, yet, she is important. Those people are integral to the process but like many others who devote their lives to filmmaking, they get little credit. That's why she lives at the Oakwood and she'd never have it any other way.

Here was an entire community of people where I could finally belong. It was a place where everyone spoke on-set lingo, and no one looked twice at the people who paced by the pool, talking to themselves and gesturing wildly while rehearsing their lines. Hollywood's superficiality, the politics that demanded to be played, the deep insecurity and brokenness that seemed to fester with each new rejection—it was all worth it to be part of the process. In a million subtle ways, my new neighbors showed me that this life was worth giving up everything for. I breathed in their admiration for the film industry and absorbed it so deeply that it almost felt like it originated from myself. It didn't feel like it was merely devotion by proxy. I was hooked.

CHAPTER 4

My Love Is Blind

was twelve years old when I discovered my propensity for falling instantly, madly in love. It's the kind of love where I dive headfirst into someone else. It's that kind of lose-my-soul-and-don't-ever-care-to-find-it kind of love. The intensity is borderline violent. I prefer to think, even now, that my first love was equally crazy in love with me, but it's likely that he was unaware of the whole thing.

I was going to be appearing in a mini-series called *Vendetta II* in which I was playing a blind girl. I was not blind throughout the whole film but rather, my character went blind after a mobster threw her off the side of a mountain in an attempt to kill her mother, a nun, who was played by the supermodel Carol Alt. So, for half of the mini-series, I was blind until a trip through the Italian countryside restored my sight, as beautiful views are prone to do.

For the first time in my eight-year career I was playing a role that I actually had to work on. Until this point, I was always hired to be the kid who was somehow upset about something. Playing the role of a moody pre-teen was a comfortable niche for someone who was overly sensitive and could weep at the mere suggestion of a dead puppy. I was good at acting upset.

This new job required research. I had to learn how to do that fixed stare and how to use a cane. It was a staggeringly melodramatic mini-series but I was still striving for realism.

My grandmother's friend Margaret was a teacher at the School for the Blind, helping blind students adjust to sightlessness and manage daily tasks. I arranged to meet with her and one of the students, to ask some questions and learn about life as a blind person. That's when I met Scott.

The day of my training, my mother and I arrived at Margaret's house and my heart dropped. Scott was beautiful. When he heard us at the door, he stood up, cane at his side. He looked confident and vulnerable at the same time, traits that would dominate my search for the ideal man for the next decade. He smiled in my general direction and I wondered if the blind have a version of love at first sight.

"I'm Scott," he said.

"Lisa." I staggered, suddenly short of breath.

"I hear you act in movies. That's cool. How old are you?"

He was clearly a couple years older than me, and the fact that my age didn't even end with –teen made me feel like I might as well be wearing diapers. I glanced at my mother and wondered if she recalled my exact age. If I stretched it a year or two, would she really notice? Probably. Besides, I didn't want my whole future with Scott to be built on a lie.

"Twelve," I admitted.

"I'm fourteen." I hoped he would follow up with, "But I have always had a thing for twelve-year-old girls." He did not make any such confession.

"Oh," I wittily replied.

Margaret interrupted our intimate moment to ask if we should get started. My mother grabbed her purse, saying she would be back later to pick me up. I waved goodbye without even looking in her direction.

Margaret blindfolded me in an act of cruel and unusual punishment. Keeping me from looking at Scott was like taking someone to the Grand Canyon and not letting them look down. We got to work and I learned how to navigate a room blind and how to pour drinks without spilling. I poured a few glasses of sticky soda all over my hands before I learned the proper technique. Scott sympathized with my struggles and tried to help me but we just made a bigger mess. His laugh made me delightedly dizzy, and somehow made me feel like laughing at my mistakes was okay.

As we went through the day, I found him easy to be with, open and sweet. He was always kind and helpful as I messed up the tasks he dealt with on a daily basis. He had been blind since birth, and tolerated my inelegant questions with ease. I was accustomed to boys at school who treated me like I was an aberration because I was on television, or the boys I met on movies who only cared to brag about how much money they had made on their last film. Scott was different.

I was given the task of making lunch while blindfolded. Margaret left us alone and Scott sat at the kitchen table while I knocked things over in the cupboard as I tried to remember the ordering system to find the peanut butter. I wondered if I would still make him peanut butter and jelly after we were married. I assembled the sandwich wrong, so the jelly was on the outside, which I only realized after I put my hand in strawberry goo. There was still a little remnant of peanut butter on the top but Scott was forgiving and I hoped he found my flaws charming. I poured him a Coke and tried to not let the foam break over the lip of the glass.

"You got the jam to peanut butter ratio perfect! And you got the glass of Coke so full!"

"I spilled a bit over the side," I deflected. "It's super fizzy."

It's super fizzy? I was not bringing my A-game. We didn't have much time together; I needed to be doing something more memorable than discussing the exuberant carbonation of his beverage.

With the bandana still over my eyes I told him the most interesting things about my twelve-year-old life thus far. I talked about my pets and tried to impart the fact that I was a loving individual who would be good to our children. I told him I was looking forward to spending several months in Italy and that I was trying to learn Italian, which was partially true in that I was throwing "Ciao" into my daily lexicon. I said I was excited about seeing Italian art because that made me appear mature.

I didn't mention the fact that my mother had promised an educational field trip to Florence to see the statue of David, which I was looking forward to because I had never seen a penis before. After I mentioned the art, I felt the need to say something a little more normal, so I didn't seem like some stuck-up child actor who is not relatable.

"And I really like pizza!"

Damn. I had been doing so well and now I said something stupid about pizza. I wished I could see him and search his face for a reaction. Finally the silence was broken.

"Oh man, I bet the pizza over there is so good!"

I was saved. My man also liked pizza. All was well in my world.

"So, what do you look like?" Scott asked, his mouth half full of peanut butter.

I didn't know how to answer the question.

"Do you want more to drink?" I stalled to buy more time to come to terms with my appearance, because clearly that is something that a girl can work through on the way to the fridge.

"I'm good, thanks. Seriously, what do you look like?"

"I have brown hair."

He laughed. "Doesn't help me. I don't know what brown is. Never seen it."

"Oh, right. I'm short."

He sighed at me. "What else?"

"I don't know. It's a hard question."

"Are you pretty?"

There it was. The question that I would struggle with for the first thirty years of my life. It was unanswerable and yet, the only person in the world that I cared about at that moment wanted me to answer it.

"No."

"Liar. You sound pretty."

"Sounds can be deceiving," I said.

"Not really. Can I touch your face?"

"Okay," I answered too quickly.

I reached out for his hands as he reached out for mine. After a moment of awkward grasping, I guided his hands to the sides of my face.

"So, here's my face," I said, completely unnecessarily.

He used the softest touch to feel my cheeks. He silently slipped the bandana off my eyes. I could finally see him, looking even more lovely than I had remembered, his head tilted to the ground with a look of concentration on his face. He outlined my eyebrows and grazed along my lids. I tried to mirror his intense look as I felt this was a serious moment but I couldn't help my lips from forming a dopey grin.

"You're smiling," he said when he outlined my mouth.

"It tickles." I didn't mention that the feel of him was the most wonderful thing I had ever known.

"As I suspected," he declared. "Pretty."

My heart leapt out of my chest and bounced along the floor.

"Here, let's get your blindfold back on. Margaret wanted you to wear it all day." I had a hard time getting the blindfold back on over my slightly swollen head.

I tried to go back to eating my sandwich, but it's hard to chew and grin at the same time. Suddenly, lunch was over as Margaret interrupted our date and put us back to work. She placed Scott on one side of the room, acting as bait, and I was twirled around and had to find him by tracking the sound of his voice. There was a stereo playing loudly and I was supposed to block out the ambient noise.

"Hey, Lisa, I'm over here," Scott shouted at me.

I could hear that he was down low and figured that he was sitting on the floor. When I got to where I thought he was, I knelt down and reached out, intending to touch a perfectly proportioned shoulder. Instead, I grabbed something soft and warm and thoroughly unfamiliar. Over the stereo, I might have heard Margaret gasp and I whipped off the blindfold. Squinting through the bright sunlight pouring into the room, I saw Scott sitting in a chair in front of me, my hand squarely in his crotch. I was frozen, slowly registering what I held in my hand. With a look of surprise in his face, he squirmed slightly to get away from my grasp. Margaret stared, appalled by the sight of the actress on her knees, hand in her student's lap. I finally retracted, as if I had been bitten. Hot, humiliated tears filled my eyes. I was molesting the blind kid.

"Well," My victim spoke. "You found me."

My unshielded eyes watched him break into a smirk. I smiled, too, and my tears poured out onto the carpet.

"Let's move on to more cane work," Margaret suggested in an unnecessarily loud and high-pitched voice. Less penis-grabbing involved in cane work, I suppose.

Far too soon, the day with Scott was over. I thanked him for spending time with me, but what I meant was, "I love you."

"I had a blast. I can't wait to see your show when it comes out," he said.

"You mean hear it?"

"Hey, no making fun of the blind guy." He swatted at my shoulder and I melted.

"I'll make sure you know when it's on."

"Do me a favor?"

"Anything." I meant it.

"You know how you were telling me about that scene in the movie when you get really mad and throw stuff around? When you film that part, you should throw something through a window."

"Why?"

"I'll hear the smash and know you are doing it for me."

"I will. Promise," I managed to say through the lump in my throat.

We hugged good-bye and I inhaled the warm, musty scent of teenaged boy. I wanted to stay there forever, in Margaret's living room, being held by this sweet, thoughtful, kind boy. He didn't let go and I wondered how long it would be before someone peeled me off him. Eventually, Mom ushered me out the door and I stumbled to the car in my love haze.

Soon after, I left for the shoot and spent the following four months working on the mini-series. I thought about Scott often and tried to make him proud of my authentic portrayal of blindness. I used the cane the right way and instructed the other actors, explaining that I needed to hold their arm just above the elbow if they were walking with me in the scene. I fought with the producers about how the role should be played and changed details to make them more realistic. It appeared that I was a devoted method actor; I was really just a kid with my first crush.

While I was on location in Italy, my grandma heard from Margaret that Scott had received a scholarship to a prestigious blind school and moved across the country to live in the dorms. It was over, whatever it had been. I'd never see him again. I was heartbroken imagining him out there somewhere, feeling some other girl's face and eating a better-balanced PB&J.

Filming continued, despite the fact I was navigating my first broken heart. I threw myself into my work and enjoyed the distraction of being on location in a foreign land. Mom and I made friends with the waiters at the restaurant across the street who liked to practice their English. I attempted to get my schoolwork done, even though it felt ridiculous to try to study French in Italy. I found plenty of enjoyment from the education provided by wandering through Roman ruins and sampling every gelato shop in town.

The day we filmed the scene of my emotional breakdown, I remembered my promise to acknowledge Scott in the show. During rehearsals, I saw that there was no window to smash, so I asked the director if I could throw a lamp.

"It's something my character would do," I said with all the passion a twelve-year-old actor could muster.

After checking with prop masters and sound people, the director reluctantly allowed it.

"Let's try to get this in one take, people! She's gonna be breaking shit."

I broke that lamp with enormous intention, gratitude and love. I broke it for a boy who took things in stride, who lived his life with joyful gratitude and zero pity. A boy who didn't surrender to the challenges of life and who taught me it was okay to laugh at my mistakes. A boy who smelled really good and waited for me to let go first. A boy who thought I was pretty, even though he never saw my face.

It's still some of my best work.

✳ ✳ ✳ ✳ ✳

One of the wonderful things about a film shoot is its intensity and ability to consume every moment of your waking life. Filming hours are demanding and it's easy to become totally immersed and forget about one's love interest back home. (This would be a skill I would perfect, to quite a fault, later in my career.) I worked hard, studied my script, and enjoyed living in Rome. It was always one of my favorite parts of film life, the opportunity to live somewhere new while on location for several months. I learned to shut off my other life, the one in which I went to school with kids whose careers involved lemonade and dog walking.

I acclimatized to a life where home was a hotel that stood behind a Bernini fountain, where a merman with rippling abs rode a clamshell and blew a conch. The weekends meant taking the train to Venice and strolling the canals while eating loaves of olive bread from greasy brown paper bags. My off-set social interactions largely revolved around the crazy homeless man who lived in the piazza in front of the hotel. He wore a long, ragged black trench coat and would do pirouettes and spring his long, lanky body into the air. As he landed, he would bonk Vespa drivers on the head with a fairy wand while they sped through the traffic circle. All the while, my eccentric friend would sing the word "sara" repeatedly, long into the night. Perhaps it was the name of the long-lost-love that drove him to madness, or, maybe it was *sará*, the Italian word for "it will be." Maybe he was a Buddhist poet.

When working internationally, key crewmembers are usually imported from L.A. or New York and the rest of the crew is hired locally. It's of utmost importance that the drivers be locals when working in a foreign place. That way, you don't have a bunch of freaked out Americans trying to figure out the rules of a Roman traffic circle. My driver was Roberto, a Roman man in his early forties with dark, intense eyes and a firm handshake that made everyone feel that everything was under control. His car was pristine and smelled of polishing wax, and the dangling tree air freshener always got tangled with the rosary that hung from the rear view mirror.

One of our locations was high up in the mountains above Rome in a secluded monastery. The series might have been melodramatic, but the scenery was stunningly beautiful. The fog would roll in across the mountain and you could hear the clanking bells of the sheep long before they broke through the mist. Their herder, seemingly nonplussed by the presence of a production company, expertly guided the flock through our trucks, trailers, and light stands. It looked like a scene that belonged back in the 1800s, but there they all were, solidly in 1992, hooves tripping over Panasonic cables as the sheep bleated their way past.

The drive up the mountain was treacherous. It required hairpin turns that were so narrow that only one car could fit at a time. We were usually traveling before dawn, so that I had time to get into hair, makeup, and wardrobe before the cameras started rolling at sunrise. Roberto would give two friendly beeps of the horn as we began each turn, a noise that sounded like a peppy, "Coming through!" but really meant, "If you can hear this, please pray because we are about to collide and shall all be plummeted over the side momentarily!" So, we curved and beeped and prayed for an hour each way. Roberto was obsessed with the Enya album *Watermark* and would play it constantly on the car stereo. To this day, the peaceful, soothing notes of "Sail Away" make me violently nauseated.

Once, while navigating the streets of Rome, Roberto avoided some traffic by hopping our little black Fiat onto the sidewalk and driving along next to the umbrellas of the outdoor cafés. A couple of people leapt out of the way like we were in an action film, except for the fact that no one was chasing us. Roberto seemed thoroughly nonchalant about the maneuver. It was both thrilling and terrifying. When we drove on the sidewalk past a group of police officers, I was convinced we were all going to jail for Roberto's recklessness. But the *Polizia* just smiled and waved their cigarettes in the air.

"Roberto? Why did they just wave at you?"

"Because we a-passed by."

"No, I mean, why did you not get in trouble for driving on the sidewalk?"

"Ah, Leeza," he tisked at me. "You do not know? I am special."

"You are special?"

"Yes. Special. Special police. Important police. Carabinieri. I am very important man."

The guy who was driving a twelve-year-old to set each day was part of the military branch of the Italian police force. It seemed like everyone wanted to be in the movie business.

✳ ✳ ✳ ✳ ✳

Late that night, there was a protest in the street outside of our hotel. Crazy Sara Man was excited, waving his fairy wand in the air and catapulting his pirouettes even higher. His Sara song got louder as hundreds of angry protesters swarmed into the street.

We saw the protest from the hotel window and Mom started to put on her shoes.

"Let's go see what's going on." She threw me my flip-flops. "Hurry up."

Never one to miss an adventure, my mom held my hand tight as we made our way into the crowd. People were yelling things I couldn't understand and holding torches. It reminded me of the townspeople in

Beauty and the Beast. We didn't know what the protest was about, but if history has taught us anything, it's that you want to be on the side with the people carrying the torches. The infamous Italian passion was palpable as people shouted slogans and pumped their fists in the air. The police circled the crowd on horseback, holding the reigns tightly as the horses strained and flared their nostrils at the trailing torch smoke. I wondered if any of them were friends of Roberto's. We marched with the mob for a while, until Mom decided we were getting too far from the hotel. We turned back, giving one last fist in the air salute to the warriors of whatever cause we were supporting.

I laid in bed that night, electrified by our adventure and still hearing the chants ringing in my head. When I closed my eyes the torches were still swinging and I could feel the stinging smoke. Calculating the time zone math, I noted that back in Canada, my classmates would just be arriving home from school about now. Maybe they were eating Fruit Roll-Ups and watching *Full House*. There wasn't a judgment attached to that realization; it was not better or worse that I had been avoiding the hooves of the mounted *Polizia* while protesting an unknown cause in the streets of Rome; I merely noted the striking difference. It was an unusual way for a pre-teen Canadian girl to spend a Tuesday night.

But by that point, I needed to sleep. I had a 5 a.m. call time in the morning. In just a few hours I'd be tip toeing around in the dark to find the catering truck. I'd order the Italian version of a breakfast burrito, my standard on-set meal, and eat it while getting my hair done. The hair and makeup trailer was always lively and the hub of all the on-set information and gossip. It was a comforting and exciting way to start each day, getting the scoop on everything. I'd have to ask the Italian makeup artists if they knew what I'd been protesting.

CHAPTER 5

Life Imitates Art

Whenen you are growing up and learning to navigate your heart, you tend to get crushes on the people who have immediate access to. A traditional school setting offers a nice, deep pool of crush-worthy candidates upon which one can hone one's liking skills. It's an opportunity to learn if the heart is drawn to the nerds or funny guys or slackers. Do you like the aggressive types or the shy guys who need to be drawn out of their shell? Pretty boys or bad boys? How important is personal hygiene?

Because I wasn't in school much, my options were drastically limited. I crushed on the boys I met at work. This often meant other actors on my show, or possibly on shows that were filming at the same studio. I once filmed next to the location for the *Mickey Mouse Club* and giggled around one of the perfectly wholesome boys with his Ken-doll hair, piercing blue eyes, and sweet dance moves. In hindsight, he was clearly gay; however, that did not stop me from swooning when he lip-synched his Boyz II Men cover.

Several years later I would have a crush on one of the stunt men on TV movie. The stunt coordinator on the project had said that he was going to be bringing in his son to help out, playing a cop that would chase me down an alley and arrest me. His son turned out to be C. Thomas

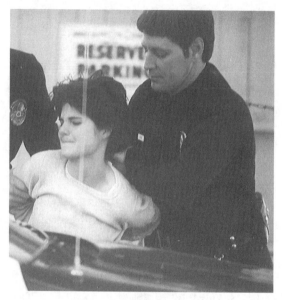

With C. Thomas Howell.

Howel, who had played Ponyboy in *The Outsiders*. I had watched that movie at least thirty times and every time Ponyboy recited Frost's poem, "Nothing Gold Can Stay," my stomach flipped in a circle.

The director asked me if I wanted to rehearse, and I most certainly did. Tommy (as I was told to call him, which felt totally intimate and sweet) chased me down, half-dragged, half-carried me back through an alley, slammed me face-down on the hood of a police car, put handcuffs on me and threw me in the backseat. Tommy was very kind and made sure I was comfortable with everything he was doing. The rehearsals went well, except for the part when the director yelled:

"Hey Lisa, can you look a little less pleased that the cop is frisking you?"

I'm pretty sure that when you watch *On the Edge of Innocence*, you can see me blushing as Tommy, in his fantasy-worthy police uniform, flings me into the backseat of a cruiser.

✳ ✳ ✳ ✳ ✳

My very first kiss was committed to celluloid and carried out with a boy who found me to be quite annoying, in front of sixty crew-members and my mother. This was something I'd get used to, as I did pretty much everything on film before I did it in real life. Some things, I did in movies and then decided that experience was enough and didn't bother to do it for real:

✳ I did a movie about going to summer camp. It had everything you were supposed to get out of summer camp; there was love, drama, politics and canoe handling skills. I checked that one off the list and never went to a real camp.

✳ I had sex on screen before I did it in real life, playing an 1850s pros-titute in the Wild West. That experience was not much like the real deal but I got the gist of it; it demonstrated the bounciness of the whole thing.

✳ I got married on a show before I really got married. When I was sev-enteen, I got married in a quaint, 18th century Irish village ceremony for a TV movie.

It might seem like real life would be ruined after the movie experi-ence, but it's not like that at all. Having a test run at everything signifi-cant made the real deal a little less nerve-wracking. My real wedding felt a little less stressful, because I'd had that other one, although sadly, my real wedding wasn't attended by goats and Irish extras in hoopskirts.

When we shot *Matinee*, I was thirteen, and my kissing partner, Si-mon Fenton, was sixteen. We just never really clicked, and he thought I was a stupid little kid, which was quite true, but we still had to kiss. Originally, the scene was written to include some breast fondling as well. That was a horrifying proposition to read in a script, when my only real physical interaction with boys had been a completely accidental moles-tation of a blind guy. I gathered my nerves and requested a meeting with Joe Dante, the director. We sat on a curb outside of the soundstage and I told him that I was uncomfortable with the groping, as it was gratu-

On the set of Matinee with Simon Fenton.
PHOTO COURTESY OF THE AUTHOR.

itous and unnecessary. Would he consider changing the scene? I felt very brave and grown up to be talking about something so gross with a man who was technically my boss and about the same age as my father. Joe listened to me kindly, then laughed, punched my arm, and said, "Well, of course I was going to change that. There is nothing to grab, anyway."

The scene was reduced to only a kiss, which was in absolutely no way, "only a kiss." It was my first ever kiss; it was monumental on multiple levels. What if I did it wrong? What if I was destined to be labeled a terrible kisser because it would be forever documented for any potential suitors to study and determine my worthiness as a possible kissing partner?

In the days leading up to the kiss, my co-star and I tried desperately to avoid each other in the small trailer that we used for our schooling, but avoidance proved to be difficult in a space that was only eight feet wide. Teenaged angst permeated the trailer, where we sat as far apart as possible and pretended it was unintentional that we kicked each other's chairs on the way to the bathroom.

We were filming on a sound stage on the Universal Studios backlot in Orlando, so when we weren't needed on set and our three hours of daily school was done, my co-star and I could ditch each other and escape into the theme park. This must be one of the most fun ways to avoid a boy. Having a theme park as your office includes perks like a front-of-the-line pass, which means that you can skip the hour-long wait and get in a quick ride on King Kong or Indiana Jones after lunch. I got to know the Rocket Pop vendors by name and learned where the performers in character costumes stored their giant heads.

What's problematic about working on a backlot is when the trams of tourists ride by, and the guide with the headset points you out as being one of the stars of a new movie filming on the lot as you're walking to the bathroom. Then, you find yourself wanting to hide behind a churro cart, but feeling like you are contractually obligated to pose and smile while they whip out their disposable cameras. After all, you are a Universal Artist and you need to earn that front-of-the-line pass. So, I'd just stand there, uncomfortable with the attention and imagining that I was one of the performers who wore the big suits and giant heads to pose with tourists. They were just taking photos of the costume actor on the outside. They couldn't see the real, tiny me who was hiding underneath, sweating and dying to go home.

The day of the kiss finally arrived. My co-star, equally horrified by the task before us, dealt with it like sixteen-year-old boys are apt to do: he made it even more terrible. He refused the Binaca breath spray that was standard issue for any actor doing a kissing scene. He joked and jabbed and I felt like shit. The scene turned out fine. It looked clumsy and stressful; exactly what it was. I don't know how many takes we did, although I would guess it was 593. It was more likely five.

I comforted myself by deciding that the kiss didn't count. It couldn't count. This couldn't be the big first kiss that I would remember forever. I'd heard other girls talk about their first kiss, which had been sweet and never *ever* involved a lighting crew. Those girls had actually *liked* the person they were kissing, or at the very least they were friends carrying out a dare. It couldn't count as a real kiss if the two people were not really speaking to each other at the time, could it? I'd hugged lots of people on film, maybe it was just an extension of that. A lip hug.

I would later sign a release to have the kissing scene played in the film *Beethoven's Second*. When they show movies in movies, the actors involved need to agree to the release of their images. The contract didn't say what the clip would be used for and in retrospect perhaps it would have been a good idea to ask for more details. As it turns out, Beethoven the dog and his girlfriend go see *Matinee* at the drive in, and apparently my wounding kiss created some romantic moments for the canine couple. Even though the event did nothing for my co-star or me, I guess it's nice that we could turn on some dogs.

Smells like teen spirit

It was after *Matinee* that the fan letters started coming from prisons. They came through my agent, and she would mail the stacks of envelopes to my house in Canada. They were perfectly polite, written on lined paper with frilly edges where the page had been torn out of a spiral notebook. The handwriting was slow and careful as the convicts listed the television shows and movies that they had enjoyed watching me in. After the request for a signed 8x10 photograph, at the very bottom of the page in smaller, slightly reluctant lettering, they identified the name of their prison and their prisoner number. They kindly included return envelopes, self-addressed to places like San Quentin and Folsom. It was exciting to get mail from a notorious prison.

My parents implemented a strict no-writing-back-to-fan-letters policy, one of the few rules about anything in my childhood. I obeyed, even though I always felt badly about the prisoners spending their allowance on stamps and taking up their (perhaps not so precious) time to write to me. A few young colleagues of mine were having problems with obsessed fans and stalkers. The reigning wisdom was that while it was nice that people took the time to express their affection, becoming pen pals with fans opened up the possibility for something scarier. John Hinckley Jr. had shot Reagan in an attempt to get Jodie Foster's attention and none of us wanted to set ourselves up to be the next fixation.

Fan letters arrived from non-felons, too. People shared select pieces of information about their lives, hoping to trade some sort of faux intimacy for a signed photo. Not knowing what to do with the letters, I left them all to pile up in the corner, where they would eventually slide under the china cabinet and co-mingle with dust bunnies and lost cat toys. I quickly stopped reading fan letters all together, because it was uncomfortable to have people know you if you don't know them. It's like seeing someone at a party who asks about your parents by name, but you have no clue who they are. I secretly wished these fans could be my real-life friends and would occasionally poke through the envelopes to check the return address for their geographical proximity. The number of meaningful relationships I was able to maintain was dwindling fast and these fans already had some sort of affinity for me, even if their motivation had nothing to do with who I really was.

My mother and agent kept an eye on the increasing stacks of letters, scanning them for anything threatening or dangerous. There were a few creepy ones, I think, but I was never privy to the details of them. My mother's normally lax leash on me seemed to get a little tighter after a fat envelope of mail would arrive. Was this what fame felt like? Was it supposed to feel awkward and dangerous?

✳ ✳ ✳ ✳ ✳

Regardless of my trepidation about the realities of fame, I went back to L.A. and went back to my job looking for work. Each year from January to April, television shows would cast for their new seasons and L.A. was even more densely populated with chiseled cheekbones and blinding veneers. Pilot season is like migration season for birds. Would-be-actors flock to Hollywood, feeding and mating and milling around. They cluster together at hip new clubs, acting studios and gyms offering the latest fitness trend. They all preen their prettiest feathers, flap their wings to get attention and peck out the eyes of potential competition. I'd be there, too, snagging whatever audition crumbs the production companies threw out to me.

The rest of the year would be spent bouncing around working on shows and occasionally going home to Canada in an attempt to be a regular kid. This transition was always a little bumpy. When I was home, I was stressing about my science project examining the effect of Diet Coke on carnations and trying to navigate where to sit at lunch. It was different from L.A., where I was going to parties in which Dolly Parton was telling me that my performance made her cry and that, "tears were splashing off my big ole boobs." She was a delightful, tiny little thing and it was hard to know what to say. *I'm sorry? Thank you?* Do you look at her boobs or not? It seems like a really rude thing to do at a party, but when it's Dolly Parton, and when she's gesturing to them, who knows what the rules are?

Instead of entering through a red carpet with photographers, going to a party in Canada involved tripping over a pile of Reebok High Tops that were mixed with dirty, melted snow in the front hallway of a suburban three-bedroom house. A newly-made friend of mine had a party in his parent's unfinished basement and I added my high tops to the slushy pile. As I walked through the sheets stapled to the exposed beams to delineate rooms, I saw Fritos in giant plastic bowls and cases of warm Sprite stacked on the cement floor.

There were couples making out, sprawled over the worn armrests of the couch, the boys testing to see how far they could get with under-the-girl's-flannel-shirt action. Smashing Pumpkins' *Siamese Dream* blared in the background, drowning out the sounds of overeager hands being slapped away. I longed to be one of those girls who was having her shirt buttons tested, but it didn't seem like I was ever going to be wanted like that. There would always be movies in the way, positioned strategically between me and anyone I tried to have a relationship with. They thought of me as "The Girl from the Movies" first, anything else was secondary.

I was already learning to be wary of people's intentions. Everything seemed to be going well with this one girl I was starting to be friends with, until I commented that a shirt in a shop window was cute. She immediately ran in, bought it for me and then asked if I would wear it on TV. I tried to decline the shirt and explain that I had no control over what I wore on set, but she stomped off and we never spoke again. If it was that awkward just trying to have friends, a boyfriend seemed out of the question. It was obvious that I would always have to settle for boys who were paid to kiss me while a crew stood around and watched.

Just beyond the masses of enraged hormones, a group of guys huddled around an old TV, the kind that looks like furniture, in the corner. There was a news show on, reporting that Kurt Cobain had been found dead in his home, with a shotgun and a suicide note nearby. Several of the guys were crying. I had never seen boys cry before. It was totally disconcerting. Suddenly, they looked ten years younger, and like they had accidently been separated from their parents at a theme park. They were lost. Devastated and broken. Their puffy pink eyes filled the place where the standard teenage boy irreverence and snark should have been.

One of the guys went over to the tape player, silenced the Smashing Pumpkins, and putting in the *Nevermind* cassette. We all listened to "Come As You Are" with a quiet reverence, except for the making-out people, who were too thrilled with the possibilities of the dark basement to take a moment of grief-filled respect.

As I watched the guys wipe their noses on their sleeves, mumbling, "Fuck, man," into their chests, I realized that entertainment could really mean something to people. It could be art. Regular people, like these Canadian 9th graders, felt connected to Cobain. They felt his pain and they mourned the loss of him like they would a dear friend. Performers held a lot of responsibility to the world that watched us. We asked to be invited in to people's lives and hearts and when we entered, it came with emotional responsibility. It didn't need to be logical. It was a gut thing.

That accountability sat heavily on my shoulders. Of course, I was clearly not famous like Kurt Cobain and I had no desire to kill myself. But it was the first time that the flip side of this relationship was so clear to me. I saw the people who were on the other end of the fan mail I got, the people who said that they felt a connection and had been impacted by my work. I didn't know if I was an artist, I was no more confident in my acting chops than I had been when the first graders whipped me with willow branches. But it was clear that whatever I was, I was involved with art and art could mean something. It could be epic and genuine, essentially human and primal. It could also be painful and heart-wrenching and occasionally fatal. It was serious and needed to be taken seriously.

CHAPTER 6

I Am Not Applicable

My history teacher was not impressed that I was missing my test because I had to go for tea at the White House with Barbara Bush. Being Canadian, the whole thing was less remarkable than it would have been if I actually knew the words to the Pledge of Allegiance, but it was neat anyway. I did a TV movie with Jessica Tandy called *The Story Lady* and it was about reading being a good thing. It was shocking to think that this was news to anyone, but apparently Barbara Bush enjoyed it and wanted people to watch a movie about books. She was involved in a symposium called, "Developing the Lifetime Reading Habit: Libraries, Youth and Elders," so Mom and I got to go to the White House.

The director, producer, writer, and some other actors from the film were also invited and we stood around a very flowery room at the White House and drank tea with the First Lady. She seemed nice and was wearing a suit with white sneakers that had the word "READ" on them in puffy gold paint. I wondered if she had done that herself or if there was an official White House bedazzler. We drank tea from tiny floral china cups and I learned how to eat finger sandwiches without dropping the saucer. There were photo ops and Mrs. Bush gave a little speech about the movie and then my mother and I just stood around awkwardly for a while, trying not to touch anything. Neither Mom nor I ever felt comfortable in fancy situations. We were the kind of family that went camping for vacations and considered dinner at Sizzler to be only for extra extra special occasions. So, we passed our uneasiness back and forth, while we stood below a larger-than-life-size painting of Jackie O in a gilded frame that probably cost more than our house.

After tea with First Lady we went back home to Canada and life continued along its strange but enjoyable binary. I never felt totally comfortable being a regular kid, but being an actor kid didn't quite fit, either. I was starting to notice that actors talked about their work with this reverence that I didn't have. I would always respond with, "Yeah, set is fun." I was clearly missing something.

At least bouncing around from one to the other gave notable relief from the specific discomfort of each. I could avoid the horror that was the school bus because I had to leave for a shoot. I could also turn down an audition for the film with the dreadful dialogue because I had to go back to Canada for my driving test. There was no shortage of handy excuses to weasel my way out of things.

I would be a student for a couple weeks here and there, but when my report cards came, the number of days absent was usually about seventy. The comments from teachers were things like, "Lisa seems like a nice girl, however, we *really* hope to see more of her next year." In that underlining would be a whole world of subtext and judgment about the path it seemed that I had chosen in life.

Besides teacher guilt, there were the legalities involved that demanded I at least try this school thing. And then there was my father. Dad was a labor negotiator for school boards, the son of Slovakian immigrants who became a lawyer, and a big believer in pulling up bootstraps. He truly believed in education, and for various reasons thought it might be a good idea if his daughter attended high school. So, while I had more than my fair share of doubts, I tried to be a student.

It generally went poorly. I did all my homework with tutors while away on films and got decent grades when the teachers could be convinced to dole them out. Apparently educators think school is about more than that; they believe it's beneficial for you to actually be seated in their classroom. The fact that I was cultivating my career while learning about photosynthesis didn't impress anyone.

Walking into a classroom you have not seen in several months is very daunting. I had stomach aches that would keep me up all night and leave me clutching my belly as I walked through the low-ceilinged hallways. It was the pressure of the first day of school jitters all over again, except it was the beginning of December and everyone else already knew how to find the computer lab, and so was much worse. My unfamiliarity with the school combined with my dreadful sense of direction meant that it was quite likely that I would show up for homeroom in the janitor's closet.

Since I was there so infrequently, I didn't really have friends to call for updates before going back to school. There would be no excited waves or warm hugs to mark my return, just unabashed stares from my classmates with whispers of, "She's back," as I tried to sit in the far corner of the room and remember the teacher's name. Once, I returned to an empty classroom because I didn't know there was a field trip that day. I waited alone in the room until everyone came back, entertaining myself by leaning out the window to clean the chalkboard erasers. It would have been way too embarrassing to go to the principal's office to tell them that I was attempting to attend a class that had gone off without me.

When I was in school, I tended to either be far ahead of where the class was, or completely confused because the work the teachers assigned me on location had little relevance to what was going on in the classroom. I vacillated between feeling totally bored and totally stupid, both options bringing me to tears. Every time a teacher referred to, "the readings from last week," I'd cringe and remember that my reading for the previous week had been memorizing ten pages of dialogue and flipping through some film industry magazine. Those were unlikely to be the readings she meant.

During a review of the French perfect participle, I'd daydream about being back on set. There, the work day starts early. There is a beautiful slow silence as everyone moves around the trucks, stepping over heavy cables trying to get to the catering truck for coffee in the pre-dawn darkness, mentally gearing up for a day that would likely slide into tomorrow. The first stop, with warm breakfast burrito in hand, is the hair and makeup trailer, traditionally staffed with sassy women and gay men who have the closest pulse on the day. They know who was out late last night with whom and who requires extra makeup on the bags that they brought home from the bar. They know that the first assistant director is in a bad mood because the studio execs are supposed to stop by later and that always slows down the schedule.

After makeup it's time to put on the wardrobe that is waiting in the small, cramped trailer that smells like those aquamarine toilet chemicals. Maybe my wardrobe involves uncomfortable costumes, with corsets and tall lace-up boots, but maybe it's jeans and a shirt that is worth "losing" at the end of the shoot so that it ends up in my own personal closet. The day might be rushed with a heart-pounding run to set because the lighting is ready and we need to go NOW. Or it might be painfully boring with shots that should take twenty minutes stretching out for five hours. The scenes might be emotional and gut wrenching with long, complicated speeches, or they might be easy and mindless, making it possible to wonder during the shot if the adorable camera assistant is smiling at me.

But then they call lunch. The catering truck has a decent vegetarian selection, but the pasta is kind of mushy, and that one time there was a dead fly in the pesto. We all eat together at big long tables, and people save seats for other actors, who are wearing oversized men's button up shirts backwards, like little kids in a finger-painting class, to protect the wardrobe from the hot sauce. It's always worthwhile to rush through eating and squeeze in a little nap before getting back to work. (As I get older, I enjoy spending part of my lunch break sprawled out on the couch in my trailer with some company. It's a good time to fool around with costars or camera guys, should you be into that sort of thing.) Then the assistant director knocks on the door, interrupting napping or nookie or whatever, and it's time for the hair and makeup folks to cover up the sleep lines or hickeys and tousled hair before heading back to work.

Maybe the afternoon speeds past, with the adrenaline of fast-paced scenes or perhaps there is time to sit in a corner of the warehouse and write in a journal or learn to knit from a library book. The craft services table tends towards more quantity over quality, but it's always there, and peanut butter pretzels help ward off the boredom while the other scenes are shot. There are candy bars and seventeen types of crackers and some sort of dip with a random long blond hair in it. And then there is more waiting and then running to set to be told that they are not quite ready. And that goes on. For hours. Until the realization hits that this corset has been digging into your ribs for twelve-and-a-half hours and it must be time to wrap for the day. So, it all gets peeled off and a million bobby pins are removed from hair pieces and there's a whole ten hours until it's time to come back tomorrow.

Even though the cast and crew and script and location would change, the feeling was consistent. Whether we were in Dublin or Denver, the makeup sponges always smelled the same. But none of that comfort and familiarity could be found at school.

So I'd trudge through the halls until, like a lightning strike, my agent would call. Life in Canada would be upended within moments and I'd be put out of my misery. I booked a job and life would become a flurry of activity. Flights were arranged and hotels were booked and there were teary farewells with various pets. My father's face would be filled with a painful combination of pride, sadness and impending loneliness as he watched his wife pack for months of traveling with his only child. We were moths that flitted in and out of his life with little prior notice. He was happy for me, certainly, but the realities of my career were much more apparent on his end than on mine. He was always the one left behind. Dad would hug me and say congratulations and then just hold on a little longer, knowing the hugs were going to be few and far between.

My father never said anything negative about my career. Besides his don't-rock-the-boat Canadian-ness, Dad was proud. It was something that I had fun doing and he never objected, even if the logistics of my career broke his heart a little. Mom had no need for routine, she was an excitement junkie and a vagabond who was equally thrilled to go to Prague or Saskatchewan. So, my per diem money all went to the gigantic phone bills that resulted from my nightly conversations with Dad from whatever far-flung location we were in. Our lives would continue without each other, along this parallel path that would occasionally cross when I had time off and when he could take a vacation from work. The dull consistency of family life was a luxury we'd never have.

I never considered the impact that my career could have on my parents' marriage. Like most kids see it, my parents appeared to be one cohesive entity. They had started dating when my mother was fourteen years old, so it was impossible to see them as two separate people. They were one, large parental unit that was big enough to stretch from home to whatever location shoot I was on. Some other kid actors had hired chaperones as parental stand-ins, usually someone barely older then they, who enforced no rules and commanded no authority. I was always happy to have my mom with me; she never cared about rules anyway and she was my best friend. I missed my dad terribly when we went away, but it never occurred to me that watching him wave good-bye to us from the front porch as we left for another three month jaunt could have been even more painful for him than it was for me.

Murderous mansion

The next time we returned to L.A., we had a new place to call home. I had recently worked with a producer who was relocating to New York for a few months, so she and her screenwriter husband needed a house sitter. My mother and I were happy to oblige; their mansion in Beverly Hills was a nice step-up from even the two-bedroom apartment at the Oakwood corporate housing. There was a minor hitch about the place, but the producer was sure we wouldn't mind: it was the house that the Menendez brothers had killed their parents in just a few years earlier.

The house was about 9,000 square feet and had twenty-three exquisitely decorated rooms. If those felt too confining, there were manicured grounds, a pool, tennis court, and great trees to climb. The place was so enormous that the producer had decided to keep the live-in maid employed while we were there, just to help us take care of the place. Maria had her own wing of the house, near the kitchen.

The tennis court had one of those automatic ball shooters so that one can work on one's backhand before the ladies come over for tiny sandwiches that the maid brings out on a sparkling silver tray. I spent hours outside trying to master that machine while stinging, gray ash from the L.A. fires floated down angelically around me. Los Angeles frequently burns in a phenomenon nonchalantly called "fire season" and the Santa Ana winds carry the ash even into the exclusive 90210 zip code. I'd play tennis until the burning in my lungs got to be too much, and then retreat to the air-conditioned mansion to cool off by lying face down on the marble entryway floor.

Besides burning ash, there was another obstacle to spending time outside. Graveline Tours frequently cruised the house, telling tourists the chilling tale of the brothers who shot their parents in cold blood. The decked-out hearse stopped in front of the house as the windows rolled down and sightseers stuck their long lens cameras out. The tour guide detailed the slayings through a speaker.

"On August 20, 1989, Lyle and Eric, who were twenty-one and eighteen at the time, *allegedly* shot their parents to death in this very house. Jose was shot point-blank in the back of the head. Kitty, who attempted to run for her life, was shot several times before she died. The brothers then came out to this very lawn out front here, crying and wailing that someone had killed their parents..."

I heard the monologue so many times I could have given the tour. The house was a particular hot spot because the trial for the brothers was going on while we lived there. People apparently felt that it might help their cause to stand in front of the house and yell at us, "Lyle and Eric are innocent! It was self-defense for years of abuse in that house of horror!" They came at all times of the day and night, pleading for the lives of these boys they didn't know. They rattled the gate and begged for their mercy. They held up handmade signs and sobbed. I wasn't sure how to explain to them that I had no control over the legal details. I just slept in Lyle's bedroom, that was all.

Surprisingly, the house was not that creepy. It didn't feel like a place of torture and murder. You expect that from dark places with low ceilings, not from a house with a brightly wallpapered sunroom and a restaurant quality kitchen. How could terrible things happen in a place with a screening room that was fully stocked with movies that were still in theaters?

The maid seemed unbothered by it all so I tried to take my cues from her. Maria was a tiny, quiet woman, not much bigger than me, who seemed to simply appear in the middle of a room without ever approaching. At first, the idea of having "help" that was always around was wildly unnerving. Home to me was always the place I could walk around in my underwear or pick my nose in privacy, but this was like having company all the time. The kind of company who wore a crisply pressed uniform and raked the plush carpeting with a little tool after I walked through the living room.

Maria was endlessly intriguing. After a while, I started operating under the assumption that the house came with a built-in buddy for me. Still a little short on companions, I followed her around as she did her work, attempting to befriend her. Not sure if something got lost in translation or if she just had no interest in the kid who stalked her and bellyflopped on the down-filled designer pillows. Regardless, Maria didn't show much interest in me beyond saying, "Excuse me, Missus," as she re-fluffed everything that had been in my path.

When Maria went home for her day off every week, I would stand outside the door to her quarters and try to guess what was inside. What do you keep in your work bedroom? What do you need for your half-life? Maybe it was a sad place, covered in photos of the children that she had to leave behind, so that she could dust the original Botero statues in the foyer. Or maybe it was her secret hideaway, removed from the constraints of family responsibilities, where she could decorate to her own taste and keep all the things she didn't want to share. I never got the guts to go in and see how Maria lived. I would just touch the door to her room, outlining the grooves in the heavy wood and wonder how she managed it. Maybe everyone felt split in two by their work, feeling, like I did, that in either place we were always leaving an important part of ourselves behind. I never was able to explain that I had hoped Maria could teach me how to live with it.

The master bedroom had large, connecting his-and-hers bathrooms. One was drenched in pink marble and the other in black marble. Our producer friend said that she never used the giant pink bathtub. Before she left for New York, she explained that Michael Jackson, who the Menendez family bought the house from, surely used to bathe the monkey in that tub. She also pointed out that Elton John had owned the house before The King of Pop, so who knows what had gone on in there? There was just no way that tub could ever get "clean-clean" even with Maria's meticulous attention. She advised me to use one of the other nine bathrooms for my bathing needs. The fact that the tub disturbed her more than the patricide/matricide was kind of disconcerting.

Despite the fact that the house was a far cry from anything I had ever known, the mansion became just like any home after a while. I comfortably bounded up the grand curving staircase, taking the steps two at a time. The marble bathroom became less impressive as I realized that it was no more functional than the Formica I was accustomed to. I knew the exact timing of how to press the button and run out of the ten-foot-tall, mechanical iron gate before it slammed shut. Opening the massive entry doors became as routine as opening the hollow plywood doors of the Oakwood apartment 202 G. My suitcase was there, so I was home.

One day, I was stretched out on the leather couch, flipping channels on the theater screen that acted as a television. There was some Hollywood pseudo-news show that was giving an update on the ongoing trial of the Menendez brothers. Suddenly, a black and white photo of the murder scene flashed on the nine-foot screen; a body lying on the floor, one on the couch, covered in dark splotches of blood. The photos made me catch my breath and my skin got prickly. I started pondering the fragility of life...but, wait. Those windows in the photo...they looked familiar. I glanced behind me. Yep. It was this room. I looked down at the floor next to the couch I was sitting on. Sure, it was a different couch, but it was in the same position. They were right here. Bloody. Swollen. Dead. Massacred. I turned off the TV.

It had been easy to avoid information overload about the murders. This was in the blissful time before the Internet and 24-hour news networks, when getting information actually took some time and effort. I knew the murders had happened in the house, but seeing the details in black and white was something different. It was a little harder to sleep after that. I watched the protesters outside the gates of the house and wanted to invite them in to sit on the couch and look at that photo. I didn't know what the answer was, I didn't know if it was prompted by insanity or greed or self defense. All I knew was that something very, very sad had happened in the living room.

The producer had assured us that the house had been remodeled since the murders and somehow that really did make everyone feel better. I'm not sure why. That's a very L.A. mindset, thinking that a facelift changes the soul. There is an assumption that what something looks like on the outside is the important part. The content, the suffering, and the history don't matter.

So, we accepted the house for what it was: a place we pretended was home, while I went to work and pretended to be other people. We pretended that the remodel changed the house in a fundamental way while the people crying at the front gate pretended that there could be sense made of any of it.

CHAPTER 7

Becoming "That Girl"

The audition for *Mrs. Doubtfire* felt serious when they issued plane tickets. I was fourteen years old when Mom and I flew to San Francisco with a bunch of other kids and their chaperones for a screen test. There were a few kids for each of the three children's roles, and they kept mixing and matching, coming up with new combinations of us, like we were toppings at a frozen yogurt bar. Each new group would go into the studio and try to stay cool while we read with Robin Williams and then wait while the next trio of kids went to have their turn in front of the cameras.

Matt Lawrence, Mara Wilson, and I were grouped together early and instantly connected. We adored each other and I jumped at the chance to have siblings, if only for an afternoon. When we were on the mock-set with Robin and then with Sally Field, we went into professional mode, listening attentively to direction and trying to impress the veteran actors with the fact that we were all "off-book" and had our lines memorized. Robin and Sally proved what I was starting to believe about real movie stars: they are lovely. Legitimate stars have no need to pull rank and shoot others down. They are sensitive and collaborative artists who also mean business. They are as serious about getting the shot and landing the joke as the most hard-assed Fortune 500 CEO. Real stars are stars because they are good at both the creative and the business sides of the job.

While the other kids were screen testing, Matt, Mara, and I laughed and joked around and confided that we all really wanted to book this one.

"You've seen *Mork and Mindy*, right?" Matt asked me.

I confessed my obsession with Nick at Night reruns.

"But have you seen Robin's stand up? It's really funny. But like, *dirty* funny."

I thought Robin's only gig was playing an alien, so Matt was clearly more versed on the career of our potential colleague.

I didn't much care about anyone else's resume, I just held Mara's tiny hand a little tighter and decided that she was mine to take care of. I already loved her.

When the screen test was over, we all loaded up in a bus full of child actors and their parents and went back to the airport. A somber, emo-

Matthew Lawrence, Mara Wilson and me, in the school trailer of Mrs. Doubtfire.
PHOTO COURTESY OF THE AUTHOR.

tionally exhausted silence fell over the group. It's always hard to tell how these things go. You can feel like you totally nailed it, but politics or skin coloring or someone else who just nailed it a little more can leave you unemployed after even the greatest audition. All of us had done our best and now it was just up to the producers to figure out which pre-pubescent amalgamation would play the children of Robin and Sally.

As we reached the airport I saw a rainbow shimmering through the misty San Francisco sky. It was clearly a sign that I booked the gig. I guess my competitors could have seen the rainbow, too, but for whatever reason, I was convinced that none of them did. That rainbow was mine, and the job would be, too.

I went home to Canada and managed to attend almost ten whole days of 9th grade before I left to film *Mrs. Doubtfire* for several months. With my head hung low, I went to my teachers and told them the situation, apologizing that they would have to put together work for me to do while I was away. Some teachers put up a minor fuss, others were downright obstinate. I vaguely remember one saying something supportive, but generally it was the same old battle.

We arrived in San Francisco and Mom and I settled into our new home at the St. Frances Hotel. It was a historic hotel from the early 1900s, that was complete with gold-capped columns and a fancy art collection in the lobby. We dragged in our overused luggage, introduced ourselves to the staff, and settled in for four months of tiny soaps and prompt turn- down service.

On one of the first days of rehearsals, while we were still trying to find our way around from the school trailer to the craft services table, the director, Chris Columbus, introduced us to his mother. She had stopped by to visit the set and she joined Matt, Mara, and me for lunch. She was a sweet older woman, a bit eccentric, but nice all the same. The three of us felt like we had to impress the mother of our new boss and made as much small talk as we could manage at fourteen, thirteen, and five years old. After lunch, we shook her hand and attempted to say professional-sounding things:

"So nice to meet you," I said.

"Hope you enjoy your stay in San Francisco," said Matt.

"Bye!" said Mara.

We went back to the schoolroom to try to get a little educated before rehearsals resumed, and it was only when we returned to set that we found out that we had just had lunch with Mrs. Euphegenia Doubtfire. We had completely fallen for it—hook, line, and latex bosoms. Until that moment, the whole Robin-as-a-woman thing had seemed pretty far-fetched and had the potential to be an embarrassing career misstep for everyone. We all wondered if we were just doing a bad *Tootsie* rip-off. But maybe this drag thing could be believable, after all.

Even close up, Robin's makeup was phenomenal. It was the expert work of Greg Cannom, Ve Neill, and Yolanda Toussieng, who would rightfully win an Oscar for their effort. I was impressed with the fact that when Robin (a notoriously hairy man) was in character as Mrs. Doubt-fire, they went so far as to shave his knuckles and the backs of his hands. He once caught me staring at the stubble that grew by the minute on his fingers and called me out on it. I had never been good at being teased but I never knew how comprehensive the mortification could be until a professional teaser mocked me.

The biggest challenge was learning how to deal with Robin's improv on set. Ad libbing has never been my strong suit and I soon realized that I could not just look to the director with a panicked, wide-eyed expression every time Robin went off-script. Also ineffective was my attempt to just blurt out my line whenever Robin stopped for a breath, regardless of if it was logical or not. Eventually, I learned to ride that wave with him. I would never become a brilliant improv actor, but there were some good lessons in there about being flexible and embracing the moment. Learning to really listen and respond rather than just waiting for my turn to talk was a valuable skill, on set and off.

The whole experience was a blast and there were times I noticed myself, in the midst of this unusual situation, enjoying regular kid things. Matt brought his dog along to San Francisco and we would play fetch with Jack in the fancy ballroom of the beautiful and historic St. Frances. I'm not sure that the staff really appreciated a golden retriever bouncing off the mirrored walls but apparently no one is inclined to protest when a production company reserves entire floors of rooms for months at a time. Mara and I ordered butterfly chrysalides through the mail and kept them protected in a mesh tent until they were ready to be released. We opened the enclosure and squealed as our monarchs took flight and zigzagged through the trees in Union Square Park. Matt and Mara felt like the siblings I always wanted, and Robin and Sally could not have been more wonderful to us. Sally brought us games and books and smothered us with hugs every morning. Robin sang, "Lydia the Tattooed Lady," whenever I walked on set. The workdays were long, but no one complained because we knew they were always longer for Robin, who endured hours in the makeup chair.

Although we felt loved, I don't remember anyone treating us like we were particularly special. We were not put on any type of pedestal at work; people were not constantly telling us how wonderful we were. It was more like we were part of a large extended family and although people were looking out for us, I never felt a sense of being worshipped. We were there to do a job and although we were not expected to be perfect, we were expected to be prepared for work and do our jobs well. We always knew we'd have another take or could ask for an extra moment before an emotional scene if we needed it. When anyone flubbed a line, whether it was Mara or Pierce Brosnan, we all laughed it off and just went back to one to go again. The work was hard, certainly, but we felt supported. There was also a sense that being part of this production had the potential of changing much in our lives. People seemed to be trying to prepare us and keep us grounded because of attention that might come our way after the film was released.

By the time I was fourteen, I had been on catty sets, with weird, internal competition for screen time and the attention of the director. Older actresses who were losing the battle with time struggled with their age and took it out on me. There had been vicious attacks about trailer size and contractual perks. I had been on shows where kids were an unwelcomed addition, and our cuteness couldn't compensate for the underlying distain. I had been treated like an adult more than was necessary, being the object of inappropriate affections from producers who left gifts of cashmere sweaters in my dressing room and hugged me for too long. Those men told me how beautiful I was, and how I was so mature for my age, and they just couldn't talk to their wives the way they could talk to me. Even though I was dying to be grown up like everyone else I was working with, I was not ready for certain types of reality that tended to show up on set. On *Doubtfire* we worked with people who respected us, yet understood we were still children. It was good to know that there were ways to do it right.

Fuzzy: friend for hire

Film sets are large operations, with lots of trucks and trailers and other inconspicuous places for over-zealous fans to hide. *Mrs. Doubtfire* was a high profile shoot, so we needed security. Big, scary-looking security. Preferably with unkempt beards and an affinity for leather.

Like the other cast members, I was assigned someone to look out for my personal safety on set; his name was Fuzzy and he was a Hell's Angel. I didn't really know what that meant, but Fuzzy was a massive and kind-hearted man and I was incredibly fond of him. His job was pretty straightforward: walk all eighty pounds of me from my trailer to set and look terrifying. There were mobs of people behind police barricades; some brought coolers, prepared to spend hours, if not days, desperately trying to get a look at anyone who was working that day. Some actors find that kind of thing to be exhilarating: the clawing, screaming and crying at the mere sight of them. It's validating and encouraging, proof that their work matters to someone. To me, it was scary and simmering with unintended yet potential violence. I felt like a gazelle in front of a pride of lions who had brought their own video cameras and lawn chairs. When it was time to go to set, Fuzzy would pound on my trailer door, the assistant director standing next to him looking tiny. She adjusted her headset and looked up from her clipboard.

"Hey, Lisa. They're ready for you on set."

"You ready to go, kiddo?" Fuzzy would growl.

The teeming mass of fans was positioned just around the corner, amped and waiting. There would be a moment of wondering if it was feasible to just hide out in my minuscule trailer bathroom. Sure, your knees hit the wall as you sat and it smelled like an outhouse, but all that might be preferable to navigating that crowd. But just beyond the throng was set, comfortable, easy set, with the crew and my fake family.

As soon as I stepped outside, the group of people went crazy. This was not because they had any clue who I was, because there was no reason for them to know me at all. It was just that if a trailer door opened and someone emerged, screaming ensued, regardless of who they were. Seeing a person who was simply affiliated with the movie seemed to be sufficient for absolute mayhem.

When I heard the roar, my heart raced and my face burned with anxiety. Then I looked to my right and up, way up, and remembered that I was with Fuzzy. I was invincible. Or maybe it was more like I was invisible—because as we passed the crowd, he kept me on his far side, away from the mob and I could walk next to the hulking bear of a man and literally not be seen.

If anyone even came close to me, I imagined I would find myself swept high into the air. Fuzzy would hold me above his head with one hand like I was a waiter's tray, as he kicked aside whoever posed the slightest threat to my well-being. Then, he would run me off into the sunset, far from the maniacal movie fans, our long ponytails flapping simultaneously in the wind. We never had to test this, as no one was moronic enough to mess with Fuzzy. He was always kind and would slow his pace so my short legs could keep up. In that moment, I was safe. I was cared for. I knew that was really all I needed.

＊＊＊＊＊

The lengthy shoot for *Mrs. Doubtfire* was the last straw for my high school; a few months into filming they requested I simply didn't come back. They were frustrated by my frequent absences and felt that I was not giving my education the proper attention. This relationship just wasn't working, they said, my coming and going was a disruption to the classroom and created too much extra work for the teachers. It was my first break-up. They didn't even have the decency to try the whole, "it's not you, it's me," excuse. It was definitely me. At age fourteen, they decided to end my education.

It was devastating. While school had never been enjoyable, it seemed a necessary evil that needed to be survived in order to be a proper human being. What would I do now? I tried to just go to work and forget that I had been thrown out of school like some delinquent, but I was clearly distracted. When Robin noticed my sadness and asked what was going on, I explained the whole situation. He promptly asked for the principal's address and wrote an incredibly kind note. He spoke about me in embarrassingly glowing terms. He explained that I was attempting to get my education while pursuing my talent and the school should encourage and facilitate that. He respectfully asked for them to reconsider and help me in balancing my life.

It didn't work. Months went by and the school didn't acknowledge the letter and didn't change their mind. I was defeated and humiliated. My weird life had officially become too bizarre to be occasionally piggybacked into normal circumstances. Later, someone told my dad that the letter with Robin's signature was framed and hung in the principal's office. I wondered if anyone noticed that the letter was essentially a bitch-slap to the entire institution, or if they were blinded by the fact that it was on *Mrs. Doubtfire* letterhead. Sometimes fame can have unintended consequences. But at least I knew that in an industry notorious for back-stabbing, Robin was a generous soul who had been willing to stand up for me. My gratitude for that is eternal.

✳ ✳ ✳ ✳ ✳

When I went back to Canada after *Mrs. Doubtfire* wrapped, life was completely un-tethered. School had always been a challenge, but had also had a grounding effect. It was the one thing in my life that appeared to be standard and regulated. My parents worried about my social interactions, and rightfully so. Being an only child and an actor whose friends tended to be twice my age and/or in biker gangs, they were justifiably concerned.

In an attempt to keep me from becoming completely feral, my former high school granted me permission to participate in what might just be the most intense hour of high school interactions: lunchtime. My dad would drop me off in front of the school that had rejected me, so that I could eat in the cafeteria. By that time, I had gotten to know this one girl, Kathy, and she had introduced me to her group of friends.

The moment of walking into the cafeteria was always ulcer-inducing. If Kathy was busy with her last class or I arrived early, there was nothing to do but loiter uncomfortably in the cafeteria doorway and wait for her to show up. There was no way I could cross the threshold without Kathy acting as my membership card. I'd scan the room, searching for her blond hair. The cafeteria was always too bright and smelled like Clorox and old apples. Groups of kids huddled together in tight packs, sharing meaningful glances and bags of chips. They all knew the rules of engagement. All I knew was that in movies the freaky kid always got tripped in the cafeteria. The murmuring seemed to get louder as I scanned the clusters of adorable headbands and backwards baseball caps belonging to kids who all seemed to know their place in the system.

Finally, when Kathy found me pretending to read the class president nominee propaganda for the fortieth time, she would grab my arm and walk me to her table of friends, who would nod their acknowledgement and shuffle around backpacks so we could join them. I unpacked my peanut butter sandwich and a grape drink box and nodded along with her friends, pretending to know what the hell they were talking about when they complained about that social studies assignment and the new substitute teacher for French.

I played the part of "student" quite well, and some kids seemed to believe that I attended school there but we just didn't have classes together. Their mistaken assumption felt like a rave review in the *Hollywood Reporter*, but it was still disconcerting that even in what was supposed to be my real life, I was playing a role. I pretended to know my way around the large school, acting as if I intended to end up in the dead-end hallway under the stairs.

I pretended to fit in with the other kids, smiling like I knew who the Spin Doctors were even though I didn't because I had been on location and hadn't had time for teenager things like that. I didn't know which stuff to laugh at, not to mention the type of laugh that was called for. Did that comment about the "straight-edge kids" deserve a total crack up, or was a slight chortle with an eye roll more appropriate? Or had I completely misunderstood and it wasn't funny at all and a respectful nod would be best? I spent my whole work life studying people's facial expressions and I did the same here, mimicking their reactions within a fraction of a second so that I could blend in.

After we ate, we spent the rest of the lunch period sprawled out in the hallway, throwing things at each other and commenting on the fashions of the kids who walked by.

"I've got my ape class in the Ken lab this afternoon—which totally sucks," they'd lament.

"God, that's the *worst*," I'd commiserate.

I had no idea what they were talking about. I was too embarrassed to ask anyone, and it took me years to figure out they were talking about AP classes in the chem lab. Their short-hand reminded me of set lingo, except I was never that confused on set. Terms like Abby Singer and four-bangers and apple boxes were the foreign language that I'd learned along with English when I was growing up. It was such a luxury to understand everything that was going on, where to stand, what to say, and when to laugh. In that high school hallway, I'd think wistfully about the smell of lighting gels and the comforting weight of hitting a sandbag with your toes when you got to your mark. I missed being wrapped in the familiar routine that these high school kids seemed to feel here sitting on the scuffed, gum-stained linoleum. So, I just sat quietly with my back against a bay of lockers and imagined that my own locker was just down there on the left.

When the bell rang and students shuffled off to class, I pretended to walk to my imaginary locker and instead I snuck outside to wait for my dad to pick me up. Standing outside, the eerie stillness of a high school in session settled in around me. The chain clanked against the flagpole as I stood just behind the corner of the building so that no one could see me from the classroom windows. Within those windows, my peers were sitting in tidy rows and looking bored. I was desperate to be part of that, but it just didn't seem to be my path. Nope. My path was unusual and painful and involved packing a lunch for a school I was forbidden to attend. All the autographs I was starting to sign and the letters from Robin Williams couldn't make up for the fact that I didn't have a locker and I didn't know who the new French teacher was.

Billie Jean Is Not My Lover

Even though there were challenges, being in Canada had its perks. I loved canoeing on the river near my house in the summer and skating on it in the winter. It was refreshing to have a break from the constant industry chatter about movies. While my trips "home" were starting to be fewer and farther between, there was still a great sense of peace there. Although my accent would never again let on, I would always be Canadian.

On one of my trips up north, we got a dog. Mikki had passed away several years earlier, and although we still mourned the loss of our ill-behaved canine, we felt it was time to open our hearts to someone new.

Our Australian Shepherd mix was the most passive animal on the planet and we didn't see her walk for a month; as soon as she saw us, she would throw herself on her back as a show of appreciation for inviting her into our family. My little ball of gratitude needed a name. The dog was as beautiful as....as..... Marilyn Monroe. (I was still obsessing about old movies and scoffed at those who thought classic films meant *The Graduate*.) But Marilyn was a terrible name for a dog and way too on-the-nose to be cool. So I decided to be all "insider Hollywood" about it and name her Marilyn's real name. I began calling my pup Billie Jean. It suited her and the story made me sound cool and in the loop.

It only took a few weeks for someone to astutely point out that Marilyn Monroe's real name was, in fact, Norma Jean. But by then Billie Jean had learned her name and Norma was also a terrible dog name. So, my dog was named after Marilyn Monroe, but in my attempt to be all Hollywood insider and cool, I had failed miserably and inadvertently paid tribute to a tennis player.

Billie Jean started traveling with me on film shoots and spent much of her puppyhood in Star Wagon trailers. She chewed on exposed wires under the driver's seat and covered my wardrobe in dog fur. She stayed in a fancy hotel and occasionally peed under the grand piano in the lobby. She stayed in hotels in rough neighborhoods, too, carefully lifting each paw to step over the discarded Listerine bottles that kids had attempted to get drunk on.

I became one of those actresses that traveled with her dog and while it was a stereotype, it was about much more than that. Walking Billie Jean after a long day at work centered me and brought me back to myself. Her love was unyielding, whether we were on set or in our backyard. She was my constant and loyal companion who reminded me that to some, none of this film stuff mattered in the slightest, as long as I could still throw a Frisbee.

CHAPTER 8

You Owe Me

t was around this time that being recognized became a routine part of life. It had been an occasional occurrence before, usually by a few fans of independent films or after school specials. It was the most uncomfortable part of the job, but I would always try to be nice to people who approached me in random places. At least, as nice as I could be while trying to get my bra on/wipe food off my face/talk through a mouth full of dental tools.

In an attempt to cut down on all the recognizing, the hair had to go. My long mane fell below my waist. It might have seemed like a deliberate choice, but really, general physical maintenance didn't appeal to me. Getting a haircut fell under the same unpleasant category as getting a root canal, so something based in laziness and fear kind of became my trademark. But after a while, the locks became my albatross. People would notice the girl with the crazy long hair first, and then match up my face with that movie they happened to see last night. It became a liability.

I sat in the bathtub one night and chopped off my hair with a pair of kitchen scissors. I felt a resounding sense of hope as twelve inches of hair fell down around me. Maybe having shoulder-length brown hair would morph me into one of the mundane teenagers I saw loitering at the mall. Maybe I could finally blend in and move with stealth though the world, like those girls who felt free to giggle loudly because they always seemed to belong exactly wherever they happened to be. It didn't actually work that way, because as it turns out, I was still me. Just with shorter hair.

✳ ✳ ✳ ✳ ✳

I had a fearful respect for fans; without them, I would never have had a job in the first place, but it was a complicated relationship for a massive introvert who struggles with insecurity and shyness. Some people wonder how actors could possibly be shy, but they forget that we spend most of our lives hiding behind a character. It's the part where we have to be ourselves that is wildly uncomfortable.

Many roles involved me being angry, perhaps about the fact that someone put a chip clip on my head.

PHOTO COURTESY OF THE AUTHOR.

Ostensibly, it should be flattering when someone in the cereal aisle says that they like you. The problem was that I always felt on the verge of disappointing them. People would say that this chance meeting was important to them; it had made their day and they were going to tell their friends about it. I wanted to provide a story to live up to their expectations. I needed to be spontaneously witty and charming and provide them with details to make it worthwhile to come up to me. It was a pop quiz on my starlet abilities, but the problem was, I was flunking. I shuddered when people started to label me as a "movie star." I tried to correct them and explain I was just a working actor, but they waved away my words, mistaking them for humility. I couldn't explain that the term "movie star" felt like being stuffed in a pair of too-tight jeans that left me gasping for breath.

I had watched Sally Field interact with her fans. She was downright masterful. Sally had ease and grace that boggled my mind. She was the quintessential movie star in all the best possible meanings of the classification. The public aspect of the job seemed to come naturally to her —she never looked as if she felt the need to carve up a piece of herself as an offering, or put on a show to uphold a stereotype. Celebrity looked simple and pure on Sally. I tried to study her, to mimic her movements and her energy, but when it was my time I felt like I was trying to recreate Van Gogh's *Starry Night* with sidewalk chalk.

Whenever a fan approached me, the inner monologue went something like this:

Someone is coming over. Damnit, why do I always have to eat so much garlic? My breath is terrible and I bet I have something in my teeth. How the hell do I get it out before we take the photo? I should carry those little toothpicks. Oh man, I was doing that stupid Charlie's Angels imitation right before they came over. Did they see that? They are going to think I am such an idiot. Wait. I'm smiling too big. Tone it down. I really do look like an idiot. Oh, they just asked a question but I was thinking too much about my teeth to hear all of it. What was it? I'll say something about Robin Williams. People love hearing about Robin Williams. Photo time. I need to keep my head up a little because in that other photo I totally had a double chin. But now the shot is up my nose....a little lower. The flash didn't work. We'll have to do it again. Chin up. Oh, they want to hug me. I don't think I put on deodorant this morning. Wow, this hug is lasting a long time. I should let go. Or will that make me seem cold and unwelcoming? Okay, good, she let go. Now I have to sign this napkin. Napkins are hard to sign because they move all over the place and get little rips in them. Especially because I can only use this little tiny pencil she found. What is this? A golf pencil? Oh well, that's all she has. I really need to start carrying Sharpies. But then that would make me look like a self-obsessed moron, wouldn't it? If I pulled out my own Sharpie to sign an autograph? What did she say her name is? Shit. I can't spell that. She already spelled it once but she went too fast. I can't ask her to do it again. I'll just put "Best Wishes, from Lisa Jakub" because I know how to spell all those words. What do I do now? Are we done? Should I make small talk? Ask her where she is from? Go back to my garlic-infused meal? I'll just smile again. But I think I still have something in my teeth. Where do you even buy those little packets of toothpicks?

That was how it went. Every. Single. Time.

✳ ✳ ✳ ✳ ✳

Actors are afforded many unnecessary luxuries, like comped dinner checks and the first chance to get whatever thing might be the newest thing, but the luxury of being a real person is rare. Sure, you can say we are asking for it and are well compensated; however, it seems unfathomably cruel that actors are not often viewed as rightful human beings. Society tends to elevate actors, while taking away basic human dignity.

I was once in a pool at a hotel, when another guest recognized me and asked that I get out of the pool to pose for a photo with him. Not loving the idea of posing next to a stranger in my bathing suit, I politely declined, saying that if he could wait until I got some clothes on, I could do it then. He sighed deeply.

"I want to do it now. You are an actor. You owe it to me."

It was so degrading, so dirty. I had been reduced to merely one thing, and that thing needed to be performing for him. I was a rented human, here for mere entertainment, regardless of feelings or privacy. It says something rather unpleasant about society that this is acceptable, and in fact, normal.

After *Mrs. Doubtfire* was released, the extent of this phenomenon became clear. I had always thought of gossip magazines and tabloids as harmless entertainment, something charmingly amusing, like mini-cup-cakes or a tilt-a-whirl. At a certain point, it all became more ominous, more apparent that this was having a significant impact on our cultural norms.

We actors had always come into homes in an intimate way, show-ing up in the living room at the appointed time every week and making ourselves part of the family. But something was shifting. This ownership of celebrities, this stalkerish pseudo-journalism and entitlement was be-coming standard. This was no longer an era in which the film industry could keep Rock Hudson's sexuality or Marilyn Monroe's addictions pri-vate. Now, every time a celebrity took her kids to the park or ordered a latte, there was a stealth photo of the event, complete with commentary that took a decidedly disparaging bent. Actors' very souls belonged to the public, becoming their very own communal puppy to adore and then kick when they got bored.

But actors garner no sympathy in this regard, since we cooperated completely. We walked right into it, willingly dished up the core of our essence and agreed to never feel dissatisfied about that. It's all worth it, just to be famous. Isn't it? We agreed not to object to objectification.

Kind of Kidnapped

So, this one time I kind of got kidnapped. I say "kind of" because she didn't keep me for very long. I don't want to be too dramatic, and to an-nounce that there was a kidnapping, with no preface, just seems overly reactionary.

By the time I was fifteen, leaving my house had become significantly more challenging. My desperate desire to blend in became full-blown social anxiety in reaction to being swarmed and grabbed at in public places. Getting recognized in a busy public space can suddenly turn into something akin to a mosh pit. There is a shocking amount of physical contact. There is hair pulling, hugging that morphs into choking, and the thrusting of pens and cameras disconcertingly close to your eyes. Most fifteen-year-olds generally hate themselves and every inch (or, lacking inches) of their bodies, but being stared at constantly seemed to compound my typical teenaged angst.

I was working on location, and the show had its final wrap party at the home of one of the crewmembers, Pam. She lived on a farm and had acres of beautiful property. It was a perfect place for a bunch of over-worked, exhausted cast and crewmembers to talk about how the shoot had gone and wonder aloud when they would be seeing their next pay-check. Pam had a wonderful array of rescued animals on her farm. She had mountain lions, wallabies and one of those big dogs that take whis-key to people stranded in the Alps. For someone who always preferred the company of animals to people, her home was paradise.

My mom was inside, hanging out with the crew, but I was enamored with a wallaby in the yard. His creepy little rat hands grabbed mine as I fed him carrots. Just as I was considering the fact that the mountain lions hadn't gotten their due attention, a woman came up to me and said she was Pam's neighbor and a huge fan of *Mrs. Doubtfire*. Her kids loved it too, she said, and her little girl cried every time I cried in the film.

"Was it fun to make the movie?" Her eyes were wide.

I answered the questions in the standard format: yes, it was fun; yes, Robin was that funny; yes, Sally was that nice; yes, Pierce was that handsome. By this point, the words tumbled out like a well-worn mono-logue. All the salient details were covered, I smiled at the right times and with all the manufactured enthusiasm I could manage, while still keep-ing an eye on the wallaby, who had started digging through my pockets for more treats.

"Would you mind popping next door and saying hello to my kids? They would get such a kick out of you."

By that point, strange requests had ceased feeling strange. I was handed random babies to hold and would sign arms or shoes when people didn't have a piece of paper handy, so this didn't seem to be completely out of line. But I must have paused.

"I am Pam's best friend and I already asked her if it would be alright with your mom, and they said it is fine if you want to come over. I'll make sure you are back in a jiffy."

I took a quick look back at the mountain lion enclosure. They were lazing in the sun, the tips of their tails flicking slowly. They looked like they would wait for me. I agreed and started walking towards a nearby house.

"Oh no," she said, "I have a lot of property and it is too far, we will have to drive."

They say (and when I say "they" I mean Oprah) that everyone has an inner voice. Something inside you knows the deeper truth of a situation and will always guide you in the right direction. I had an inner voice, but it was shy, awkward, uncertain, and eager for acceptance; not that different from my outer voice. My inner voice said something like, *Wow, this seems sketchy and weird, but she won't like you if you don't go, so go.*

I felt the deep and constant pressure to be nice to fans, so that I didn't come across like a spoiled brat who thought she was better than everyone else. I wanted to be an accommodating good girl. It was also becoming clear that anything I did or said now had the chance to end up printed in a magazine article, fodder for "celebrity gossip." I didn't want to be labeled a bitchy little monster who wouldn't go talk to a fan's kids. They bought movie tickets and so I was obligated to perform, even when I felt the hairs on the back of my neck stand up.

I got in the car and allowed myself to be taken to the "second location," as any security expert would have called it. Fear rose up in me as we started to drive but I was also positive that my reaction was one of an overly dramatic baby, so I remained quietly scared. I decided to not put on my seatbelt, so I could jump out of the car if the situation required it. My hand stayed on the door handle to prepare for the leap, but we were in the middle of the country and there were no stoplights or signs. We never once slowed down.

I tried to remember where we were going, so I could find my way back to the farm with the security of the wallabies and my mom. I don't know how long it took us to get to her house but it felt like an hour. The whole time she chatted away, about the age of her kids and her husband's job but I only heard pieces of it, as my mind was mostly concerned with plotting my escape. When we arrived, I was shivering. She thought I was cold and gave me her sweater. Would a kidnapper give you a sweater? I was being ridiculous. This was embarrassing. Everything was fine. We went into the house and her three kids were sitting on the couch watching TV. They were all in their teens and had perfected the miserable teenager slouch. The coffee table was covered in cans of Dr. Pepper and the wrappers of whatever they had recently thrown in the microwave.

"Look kids, look who it is! Lydia, Mrs. Doubtfire's daughter!" She pointed at me and I wondered if I should clarify that actually, my name was Lisa and my real parents were not inclined to cross-dress.

Her kids reacted as if she were a stray cat who had presented a half dead mouse at their feet. They sort of snarled and went back to the program. They did not get a kick out of me. *This is fantastic*, I thought, *they don't care in the slightest so she will take me back to the farm and the mountain lions and this will be done.*

"I should get back to the party." I tried to be assertive but my voice cracked and I looked at my feet as I said it.

"Hold on, I have to call my husband at work."

She hurried to the kitchen and got on the phone. I sat on the front hall stairs and shivered, pulling my knees to my chest under the sweater she gave me, even though I worried that I might be stretching it out. In the TV room the kids were still mesmerized by the show, seemingly undaunted by the fact that their mother had kidnapped someone. She was fighting with her husband on the phone, trying to get him to come home early to see this prize of a child actor she had procured. He, from what I gathered, cared at the same level as his children and was trying to get her off the phone. She yelled back at him and that is when my tears started to flow.

The front door was right there, what would happen if I just bolted? But I didn't really remember the route back to the farm, my panic blocked out any sense of direction. All the farms looked the same, what if I stumbled into another farmhouse of obsessed film fans? Plus, I hadn't worn my glasses that day, as I thought they made me look bug-eyed, so my mediocre eyesight was not really up to a run though the rural countryside to safety. I ached with regret and fear.

She got off the phone and came over to me. My eyes were swollen and tears streaked my face. While I might have perfected the film cry with the one, slowly rolling tear on an otherwise unmarred face, I have never been a pretty crier in real life. It usually involves jagged gasping and shocking pink blotches. She seemed not to notice.

"My husband will be home soon, why don't you watch TV with my kids until he gets here? He will get such a kick out of you."

I started to heave, gasping for air and chocking out my words. "I want to go back, they are going to wonder where I am, please, I want to go back."

"Oh, but he will be thrilled to meet you. It won't be too terribly long. Why don't you go get to know the kids?" She shooed me towards the living room.

I heaved more and she sighed at me and shuffled back to the kitchen to call her husband back. Over my chattering teeth, I could hear her telling him that he really needed to come home sooner. They fought for a while, she screamed about other times he hasn't cared about her or supported the things she was interested in.

I was clearly going to die there. At my funeral they were going to talk about how it was my own damn fault for getting in that car. They always say don't get in the car. I deserved to get kidnapped.

I was reaching hysterics as she got off the phone the second time.

My legs were starting to get numb from holding my knees to my chest so tightly. She stood over me and looked disappointed. Her hunting and gathering project had been unsuccessful; no one was interested in her offering.

"Fine. Fine, let's just go," she yelled at me while she grabbed her keys and angrily marched to the car.

Did she mean it? I stood on my weak and wobbly legs and followed her like a stupid little lamb. We got back in her car and I wondered if we were really going back to Pam's or if I was about to be scalped and dumped in a landfill. She said nothing on the whole trip back, she just stared out into the fields that blurred past. Again, I kept my hand on the car door handle. My heart leapt as things started to look familiar. Maybe she really was taking me back. I cried the tears that come when you think things just might actually be okay.

As we pulled in to Pam's driveway I began to think that I over-dramatized this situation. Maybe she was just a really clueless movie fanatic who failed to notice that I was completely terrified. Maybe she just wanted attention from her husband and children and thought I might be able to get her that. Maybe she was just lonely and bored and I was something interesting that happened in the midst of her gloomy day, something she could tell the person behind her in line at the bank. When she pulled to a stop, I took off the sweater and got out of the car quickly, unfathomably saying "thanks" as I slammed the door shut. I saw my mother and Pam by the wallabies and ran over to them trying to hide the fact that I had been crying.

"Hey, I thought you were going to be here with the animals?" my mother said. She seemed a little annoyed that I was not where I said I would be. I was nothing but relieved.

Pam watched car and the driver as she pulled away.

"Who was that?"

Pam didn't know the woman or the car, the woman had not talked to Pam or my mother as she had claimed. I was not able to give a description of anything that was helpful. I had such stress-induced tunnel vision that I couldn't even describe the house, the woman, or even the kids very well. I couldn't remember where the husband worked.

I don't think she ever meant me any harm. She had fallen into the theory endorsed by the trash media: actors are not real humans. I had just been a little trinket for her to collect. She was so blinded by Hollywood that she didn't notice that I was just a scared kid who never learned how to say no.

This is what gets lost in the shuffle of gossip-fueled headlines and grainy undercover vacation photos—it's a big deal when the media doesn't treat actors as people. It might seem like a harmless distraction but the impact is significant. When we "otherize" people, when we look past their humanity and make them inherently different from us—it's a problem. We lose our sense of empathy and understanding. It allows us to be blinded by devotion, or unflinchingly merciless. When we turn people into infallibly divine kings or unrelatable, lowdown slime, we are doing some serious damage to our humanity. If we can just remember that people are all fundamentally the same, it doesn't make any sense to grab a kid from a party like she's a gift bag.

CHAPTER 9

Open Door Policy

After all those years of corporate apartments and murderous mansions, it was time to find a more permanent place to lay my head in Los Angeles. Age fifteen seemed a good time to get into the real estate game. The house my mom found was close to my favorite bagel place and had a gorgeous grapefruit tree in the backyard. So, I bought a tree, which just happened to come with a house.

It was the summer of 1994. The Northridge earthquake had hit in January and the city was still reeling. Rubble remained strewn about, as people tried put their lives back together while waiting for the insurance checks to clear. We had been in Canada for Christmas and missed the seismic event but my mother, always the opportunist, saw something positive amongst all the cracked drywall and crumbling roofs.

It was a simple one level ranch-style house with two bedrooms. It had been built in the 1930s and had all the charm and architecture of the era. It also had all of the crappy plumbing and electrical wiring of the era. It was a weird little place. The shower door was decorated with a frosted glass deer, eating frosted glass flowers in a frosted glass field. There had been clumsy and certainly illegal additions, meaning that there were random brick walls or windows that peered into adjacent rooms. Surprised guests would open a door, expecting a coat closet, and find themselves in a completely tiled room that served as a shower or a handy place to commit an easy-clean-up slaughter. Modern conveniences, such as temperature control, functional kitchen appliances, or windows that closed all the way were not part of the house's repertoire.

I lacked the motivation to fix those sorts of things, and without stable money coming in, those kinds of luxurious extras didn't seem financially feasible. The money in the bank was what I'd have until the next job, and if there was no next job, it needed to last until my actor's union pension kicked in. My actor friends always complained about their lack of funds, so, I tended to be in a constant state of panic that I was broke. Even though I was still a teenager, I was convinced that each paycheck might be the last one I would ever get.

The house had seen better days. Before me, it had been mostly inhabited, it seemed, by feral cats. The floor buckled in some places, pushing up cheap parquet tiles into jagged, threatening peaks. The ceiling was collapsing in other places, raining down insulation and rat droppings onto horrified Sunday Open House visitors. The house had a long line of short-term tenants in its past, who had no concern for sustaining its health. The earthquake appeared to be the final straw, the last owners had abandoned it and the bank became its reluctant owner. The house needed saving. It was awkward and strange and I absolutely loved it. We had a kinship. Mom and I did just enough renovation to make it livable, moved in, and made it our California home.

My next door neighbor, Paula, was an elderly German woman who loved to garden. She was short and sturdy and always moved quickly with intense determination, as if something behind her had just recently blown up. Because the house had been abandoned for such a long time, she had decided that she was responsible for it. When I first moved in, Paula kept telling me how happy she was that I was going to be living in her house. With her garden. She wasn't the type of woman that you could correct without getting something cracked against your knuckles, so I just said that I loved her house and was happy to be there. My meekness only seemed to encourage her, as she developed a habit of walking in my front door and demanding that everyone present identify themselves.

Paula's most helpful form of intrusion was caring for all the rose bushes that she had planted on my property. Since I couldn't keep a cactus alive, I was happy to have her wander around my yard, early in the morning, caring for the plants. She would get excessively emotional about gardening; she'd enthusiastically praise the rosebushes for their growth or yell impassioned threats towards the aphids that were chewing on them. This habit of hers, while undoubtedly beneficial to the flora, would become problematic later on. My Jewish boyfriend found Paula to be quite unnerving; he claimed that he had a genetically ingrained fear of anyone waking him up by shouting in German.

"The hill" separates the porn stars (San Fernando Valley) from the movie stars (Beverly Hills). My house was right on that hill, just on the sketchier side. The valley was populated with establishments where you could pawn something and then conveniently get some fro yo right next door. Delis, nail salons, and unsavory video stores were all slung together in long, low strip malls with flat roofs and large parking lots. Palm trees striped the streets, occasionally obscuring the billboards advertising liquor or TV movies. The smog settled in a thick layer between the mountains, giving the valley a golden radiance that you could easily delude yourself into thinking was merely a California glow.

My house was on Coldwater Canyon, essentially a two-lane freeway that snaked over the hill and delivered people from the Valley into the heart and soul (if it had one) of Rodeo Drive shopping and cosmetic dentistry offices. Most of the time the traffic was horrendous and people would sit in their cars, waiting to drive five miles per hour and sucking on fumes, because their convertibles were open so they could get both lung and skin cancer simultaneously. For three hours every morning and evening, a slow, New Orleans-style funeral procession of BMWs and Mercedes crept past, twenty feet from my front door. My bedroom was at the front of the house and inhaling those fumes for so long is why I don't understand geometry. I consoled myself with the fact that all those cars spewing noxious vapors in front of my house did the same thing in front of the multimillion dollar 90210 houses, just a couple miles and forty-five minutes later. If the acting work dried up, I planned to pay the mortgage by selling grapefruit to the commuters who were stopped in front of my driveway and hopefully in need of a low-carb breakfast.

I never felt shame in my love of the Valley. Sure, it is the porn capital of the world and is always ten degrees hotter than the rest of L.A. Sure, Valley Girls are known worldwide for being annoying and gagging on spoons sideways. But the place has the best vibe. It always felt like a true neighborhood to me. At my favorite hangouts, they knew my name and I would eventually date half of the wait staff. I was friendly with my neighbors and knew what they did for a living, or more accurately, which aspect of the film industry they worked in. I could walk to places, something nearly taboo in L.A. where the rationale is that if you can't use it as an opportunity to show off your car, there is no reason to go out.

I found myself in a dangerous situation: I was a teenager with a house and no personal boundaries. Everyone wants to come to L.A.; they have dreams of being an actor, a director, a screenwriter. They just wanted to be *somebody* and L.A. claimed it was the only place where that is possible. I said yes to everyone who might have asked and before I knew it there were fourteen of us living in my two-bedroom house, including Mom and I. Since I was so used to growing up in a constant state of disarray of home renovations, when I was setting up my own home at age fifteen, it made sense to continue the trend of chaos by turning it into as a refugee camp for creative types.

My very first boyfriend was the first to move in. He was eighteen years old and we met in Denver where he had been hired as my personal assistant on a project. He had driven me around, brought me endless cups of English Breakfast tea, and graciously put me out of my only-been-kissed-on-film misery. He was an aspiring actor/director and my mom allowed him to move in under the stipulation that he slept on the other side of the house and was never out of her sight. There was also an artist and her girlfriend. Various actors from Canada and their mothers/wives/mistresses/children cycled through. There were two backpacking Australians, and I honestly have no idea how they ended up joining us. You never knew when friends of someone who had sat next to my boyfriend at the movies might show up at the door, suitcase in hand. My mom operated under the assumption that we should help people out if we could, so everyone was welcomed in.

There was also an assortment of animals in residence. In addition to Billie Jean, we had gotten another dog, an eleven pound Italian Greyhound named Cleo, who had spindly legs and an impertinent manner. There was a stray terrier who we found running on the freeway who only understood Spanish and had an insatiable appetite for windowsills. Baby birds who had fallen out of nests were kept warm under towels and desk lamps in the bathtub until they were rehabilitated enough to be placed in the branches of the grapefruit tree. There were seven feral newborn kittens that had been birthed in the insulation within the wall of the dining room and then abandoned by their mother. After hearing pitiful mewing for days, we took a hammer to the drywall and rescued them. No one could be bothered to patch the hole, so we solved the problem by hanging a picture over it.

Everyone simply negotiated his or her own personal space. The couch and oversized chair were on nightly rotation, the Australians slept under the dining room table and the garage housed those who overflowed from the house. Did anyone pay rent, contribute to utilities or the thousands of dollars in phone bills every month? Of course not. Creatives don't sully themselves with such tedious logistics.

Did I complain? Of course not. I was an only child who always wanted to be part of a big family. I was a full and willing participant in this situation. If my parents thought it was strange, they never stepped in, and I would have likely resented it if they had. I opened the front door wide and welcomed in every stray dog/cat/artiste that wandered past.

We didn't have enough keys to the house and most of my room-mates were not the types of people who could rein in their inspired im-pulses enough to do something as mundane as keep track of a set of house keys, so we just left the door unlocked all the time. The house was populated enough with people coming and going at random hours that it would be impossible to burgle the place. A robber would have tripped over an interpretive dancer or a Canadian before they could get to any-thing worth stealing.

No one in the house had a real job, so there was lots of time to just hang out. A few people were musically inclined so they would write songs called, "The Coldwater Blues," on the old upright piano I had picked up at a garage sale in Beverly Hills for $25. I would attempt to sing with them, but since my one audition for a musical had not been encourag-ing, I usually just clapped along. (I auditioned for the part of Cosette in *Les Mis* under the pretense that they were "not looking for a singer." The audition feedback was that while it was true that they were not looking for a singer, they were looking for "more of a singer" than me.)

The roommates and I would spend hours in the woods staging pho-to shoots, thinking we looked subversive and misunderstood. We would strike poses that embodied our dark, esoteric natures. We would crouch at the base of the tree and examine a leaf with thoughtful, arty expres-sions on our faces. I waved away the smoke from my friends' hand-rolled cigarettes while we sat in 24-hour coffee shops and debated important, existential matters and read obscure plays. They claimed the title of "art-ist" with such fervor that I wanted it, too. No one balked when I used it on myself, so it seemed I could justifiably claim membership to that group. I filled spiral notebooks with bad verse and tried to channel the Beat poets.

It was nice to be considered an artist, but it felt more like I was doing a job that was second nature and that I had no memory of *not* doing. In fact, my job had been recently feeling more like the work of a ventrilo-

When creative people get bored, it results in photoshoots.
PHOTO COURTESY OF THE AUTHOR.

quist dummy than someone with artistic talent. I was someone who said what she was supposed to, while standing in the specific place she was told to, while wearing the chosen clothes and hair styles. Some days I felt I'd go limp when there was no one pulling the strings, falling to the floor in a pile of rote dialogue and contrived emotions. But the label of artist sounded nicer than puppet, and allowed me entrance into this group of charmingly tortured souls. So, we collectively shivered in horror at the thought of normal jobs with predictable schedules. We pledged allegiance to the craft and swore we'd never be anything but artists. L.A. was where it was at and we'd rather starve than leave the nesting ground for all that was inspired and worthy.

If we weren't skulking around a coffee shop, we were at the movies, critiquing other actors. Actors always think they can play a role. Even if it's a part that is thirty years older and of a different gender. Those are the roles that get nominations and so every single job felt like it was snatched out from under us. We'd elbow each other in dark theaters, pointing at the screen and loudly whispering, "I auditioned for that." We'd engage in long-winded, post-film dissections of why we would have been better in the role. When normal people get passed over for a job, they don't have to watch the person who beat them actually performing the tasks. It's harder to recover from the rejection when you have the opportunity to assess your competition's final contribution. All you can think about is how you would have punched up that line or held that meaningful glance a moment longer or totally would have rocked the role of Rogue in *X-Men* (or whatever). The failure lingers and gets very specific. We spent the majority of our time judging others while we waited for something exciting to happen to us.

When it did, that's when the real trouble began.

There is a limited amount of cheerleading available within the creative soul. There's a certain stage where that support is replaced with some serious envy-fueled mockery. It's grueling to be an artist; struggle is a prerequisite and in general, you are considered to be a society-draining slacker. It's painful to see someone down the hall doing well when you are not. The ensuing reaction is not intended to be malicious; it's just human nature.

I had an audition for the film *On the Road*, directed by Francis Ford Coppolla. I had made it past the casting director and was going to a call back to read for Mr. Coppolla. It was a major honor, and I was thrilled. This guy was serious; after all, he had almost killed Martin Sheen during *Apocalypse Now*.

When news of my meeting with the film legend spread through the house, it activated the simmering energy of our cast of struggling characters. I've heard that crabs will pull each other down when one tries to escape a pot, relegating the whole group to an inevitable demise. I'm not sure what that crab instinct is, but they might have learned it from a group of actors crammed into a two-bedroom house. The crab claws came out.

"Did you hear about Lisa's audition? She's reading with Francis Ford Coppola. I bet that guy just thinks he's the shit."

"God, I'm sure he's a total fucker."

"Ha! Yeah, what a fucker. Francis Ford *Fucker.*"

So, he became Francis Ford Fucker. That was how he was referred to in my house. For weeks.

"Big fucking deal," they said, "Go read with Francis Ford Fucker. You should say that to his face, just to see what he says. Say, 'Hey there, Mr. Francis Ford Fucker.'"

I did read with Mr. Fucker. It went fine. He seemed like a nice man, fairly quiet and reserved, although the whole audition was drowned out by my own thoughts. All I could hear when I walked into the room was the taunting of my freeloading housemates and my silent refrain of, "Don't say Fucker, don't say Fucker, don't say Fucker."

(I didn't call him Fucker, not that it mattered, as I didn't get the part anyway. The film got shelved and finally made it to production a few years ago. Kristen Stewart, who would have been about five years old at the time of my Fucker audition, played the part I read for.)

That one single audition seemed to ignite the prickly tensions at my house and people started to pick fights with one another. If an actor is not satisfied with his or her career accomplishments, at least they can taunt others in a way that expresses their creativity and passion in its most exquisite and cutting tenor. Our rock and roll photo shoots became rarer as I became the resident guidance counselor/therapist. People started writing me long, emotionally wrought, hand-written letters that they slipped under my bedroom door, complaining about the lack of respect from other housemates and asking me to fix it. I was fifteen and couldn't fix lunch. But I listened and said, "He didn't mean it that way," then made everyone hug it out while I went and paid the phone bill. I bought more bagels and the good cream cheese in the hopes that everyone would settle down and we could go back to our tight little community of misfits, debating the merits of the latest Lasse Hallström film.

Just down the street from the house, there was a vacant parking lot with a fence that faced the road and someone put a *Mrs. Doubtfire* poster on it, coincidentally right after I bought my place. Every time I went home, I passed that poster and wondered who had put it there. I'd see my face, demurely peeking around Robin's giant breasts and my real-life face would get hot and embarrassed. I'd run home and make sure the curtains were drawn tight and hope that my roommates had taken a different route. They would tease me about it, for sure. My boyfriend joked that he was going to get the poster tattooed on his ass and my roommates had all laughed and I had rolled my eyes and tried to not let my humiliation show. Why was that poster just out there? For everyone to see? The cast had never even posed for that photo. It wasn't real, they had just pieced together disparate parts of other publicity shots to make it look good. The rainy season came and that poster ripped and melted into a mealy pile on the asphalt and I could comfortably drive on that road again.

It soon became clear that even the good cream cheese couldn't soothe the drama that bubbled forth from the small house. People threatened to move out and never did. There were disproportional threats of violence waged when the last bag of microwave popcorn was gone. Phone messages from agents and managers may or may not have been delivered in a timely manner. When I got a job filming out of the country, our group home disintegrated; everyone moved out, going back to wherever "home" was, or to live with other boundaryless friends who must have also been lonely only children.

I packed for the shoot and locked the front door, leaving my weird little home to take a deep breath and enjoy the quiet. Paula kept up her constant vigil, keeping her house company, watering roses, and bullying aphids. All that was left of our commune was the smell of sit-com scripts left out in the rain, cheap cigarettes, and desperation.

C H A P T E R 1 0

Please Wait at the Bottom of the Ocean

My career planning tended to focus on the location of the shoot rather than the quality of the script. When I found out that a TV movie called *Bermuda Triangle* would be filming in Honduras, I was in. It was my first time traveling to a developing nation, and it suited me. We were staying in a simple but lovely hotel, and when we snuck out from the watchful eye of the production company to explore, that's when I saw the place for real and loved it. There was great comfort to be found in the ways it was so different from where I lived. This is not to say that there were no problems; poverty and corruption were clearly visible, but the place felt honest about the issues and didn't concern itself with further unnecessary obstacles like a fear of gluten or inadequate lashes.

The chances of getting recognized here were slim to none. Surely, in a place like this, people had other things to do than watch television. Most places were without electricity or even doors that closed all the way. It seemed that the entire male population napped on the beach between the hours of 2 p.m. and 4 p.m.; this was not a place that had been overtaken by American priorities.

In the US, life in public was becoming a blur of grabbing and hugging and signing and flash photography. The social anxiety that had hounded me since tape day of *Night Court* was reaching a fevered pitch as I was unfailingly mobbed in shopping malls and restaurants. It felt like I was being buried alive and I started to have full-blown panic attacks. Everything went dark and there was no air, just panic, sheer panic, and there was total silence other than the blood pounding, and there was shaking and gagging and praying that someone could make it end somehow, someway, very soon. It felt like I was dying, but death was welcomed if it could stop this avalanche of crushing dread. My armpits would start tingling at the mere thought of leaving my house and having someone ask me to sign their placemat, or go over to say hello to their cousin so they could take a photo of my sweaty, pale, panicked face.

This Honduran anonymity would be the biggest luxury of all, even better than the fresh mangos we had every morning. Here on a remote island off the coast, the rules were just different. We had to pay off the baggage handlers to locate our "lost" luggage. People boarded buses with a half dozen dead giant lizards, all bound together by the tail like a reptilian bouquet. Folks here had other shit to worry about. Better quality shit.

There were just a couple of restaurants in town, mostly just shacks on the sand with a couple of wobbly plastic tables. The roof of a bar near our hotel was thatched, and the warm breeze off the ocean made the grasses rustle softly. My mom and I were looking over the menu when the bartender glanced over at me. He was quite animated as he said a bunch of things in Spanish, and I offered up my confused, apologetic smile and the palms up gesture that indicates that you are entirely clueless. I hoped perhaps he was offering to crack me a fresh coconut with that machete sticking out of his belt but when I listened closely there was one thing he was clearly repeating—"HBO."

"HBO? Si?" he inquired, pointing between the bar's small fuzzy television and me. It was the only one for miles, and unfathomably, it was on HBO.

"Si, Señor," I confessed, smiling sadly. "HBO." My simplicity bubble was thoroughly busted. My charming little theory about happy, simple people with more honorable interests than us materialistic douchebags from the Northern Hemisphere turned out to be total garbage. I autographed a bar napkin for him.

That was how the locals came to know me as HBO.

"Buenos dias, Señorita HBO!" they hollered as I walked from my hut to the set for a day of filming. I'd wave and try to keep my head down. Even in the land of shoeless children and roaming packs of scrawny wild dogs, it seemed that movies were still king.

For my role in the television show, I was often shooting underwater. My character had a magical connection to dolphins that enabled her, within just a few moments of being in the water, to resemble a Shamu Show performer. The training area was in the ocean, but it was a large fenced-in area that looked like a giant underwater backyard. I spent hours training and learned how to do all that crazy stuff where the dolphins put their snouts on your feet and torpedo you though the water.

The first time I jumped in the training area, I was overwhelmed by the sheer size of the dolphins. I suddenly felt vulnerable and completely out of my element. This was their turf, and ecologically speaking, I was at a major disadvantage. The large school of barracuda that patrolled the fence line for abandoned dolphin treats didn't help me feel any more secure. I covered up my nerves because I was worried that the producers would give too much work to my stunt double, who looked remarkably like me, except for the fact that she was thirty years old and actually had muscles on her body. She was hired to do some of the more daring, fly-out-of-the-water-on-a-dolphin's-snout stuff. I told the producers I could do all of it, but they nodded, patted my hand, and hired a professional.

I liked doing stunts and when asked if I could do something, the answer would always be an unequivocal yes. As an actor, you always say you can do whatever the producer asks. Accents? Of course. Horseback riding? Sure. Work with explosives? Hell yeah. You always say yes and figure it out later.

This blind devotion to getting the shot tends to lead to some strange moments. I've been attached to a wire leash that was run through my pant leg and nailed to the ground, so that I wouldn't fall when the balcony of a movie theater collapsed inches from my toes. I've been placed in a harness and thrown over a railing dangling above a series of escalators in a mall. I've been almost hit by cars and have fallen out of a tree into the arms of a waiting crew member. It was all just another day's work. There might have been times that it scared me, but it's all about getting the job, getting the shot, getting the audience, getting the fans, and getting the next job. If you are worried about your personal safety, people start questioning your professional commitment.

A local Honduran fisherman caught a four-foot long black tipped reef shark and offered it up for a role in our film. It would be absurd to pass up an opportunity like that, so we had to come up with a shark scene. The dolphin wranglers took over and kept the shark still until we were ready to shoot. Apparently, a still shark is a "sleepy" shark. Everyone was more comfortable with a sleepy shark.

We were shooting a scene in a submerged airplane that had, as the script went, crashed in the Bermuda Triangle, stranding my entire family in an unbelievable paradise populated with attractive guest stars, who had also crashed, along with their own emotional baggage and B-plot storylines. I needed to dive into the plane, which had settled to the bottom of the ocean, in an attempt to recover the insulin that my brother needed. This was a no-brainer; put the sleepy shark in the plane at the bottom of the ocean. Sharks love being put into planes.

For this particular scene, I had been waiting on a bare bones pontoon boat in the middle of the ocean and keeping myself thoroughly occupied with trying not to barf. Finally, it was time for my scene and someone came to get me for filming. This meant that someone in full SCUBA gear popped their head out of the sea, yelled my name and I jumped in the water, clad only in my hot pink bathing suit. We then shared a SCUBA tank and descended fifty feet to the wrecked airplane set.

When we got to the bottom, the director swam over. He was also wearing complete SCUBA gear and communicated via a waterproof wipe-off board. It said,

Shark too sleepy. Scene taking longer. Just wait.

I nodded. I pointed up and looked towards the bottom of the pontoon boat with a questioning look on my face.

He waved away my suggestion and wiped off the message.

Sit here, the board told me. He pointed to the sand on the sea floor.

Some sort of oceanic assistant swam up and handed me an oxygen tank and a ten-pound weight. I sat on the bottom of the ocean and waited to shoot my scene. I placed the weight on my lap to keep myself from floating away and killed the time by doodling in the ripples of sand with my toes. I watched fish swim by. A little crab scuttled over next to my leg.

Sleepy Shark was being a total prima donna and took forever to get his scene right. He swam in the wrong direction and didn't look menacing enough. When he finally hit his marks and the director felt they got the shot, someone simply pointed the shark in the opposite direction of the set and he swam away. No one asked him to do interviews or publicity. He didn't need to recall his character motivation or what it was like to work with his co-stars. No one ever asked him for autographs or attempted to take incognito photos as he was eating dinner. Lucky shark.

Finally, we were able to shoot my scene and I swam around in a plane that the prop people had filled with rubber skeletons and long, tangled lengths of plastic seaweed. In this sequence, I was trapped in the plane when the door jammed shut. At the last moment before I drowned, a dolphin came to my rescue, shattered the cockpit window with his snout and I swam out amongst the floating shards of broken candy glass, to safety. Dolphin and I displayed a level of professionalism that had eluded Sleepy Shark and we got the scene quickly. He had clearly been an amateur.

(If you really want to see how this all played out, go to YouTube and search "Teenage girl underwater." It has an uncomfortable amount of

views. I don't think ABC intended the family-friendly show to be reduced to clips of me in my hot-pink bathing suit on YouTube, but footage lives on forever. We can never really escape. Even when it feels mildly perverted.)

Work vs. Prom

When *Bermuda Triangle* wrapped, it was time to trade in my bathing
suit for some snow boots and go back to Canada for a while. There continued to be this constant tension between trying to manage my career
and live a regular life. I was offered a scholarship to a private school
that had several other "non-traditional" students. They were athletes or
classical musicians who had to travel on occasion and the school said
they were used to making accommodations. I donned a plaid skirt, itchy
forest-green knee-high socks, and revisited my familiar school-related
intestinal issues.

I'd go to school for a week or two, then leave again, popping back
in a couple of months later. Upon one of my returns, I found that the
uniforms had changed six weeks prior and I was wearing the old clothes.
That was humiliating in the profound way that only a clothing-related
misstep could shame a teenaged girl. Out of pity and annoyance, the
principal finally offered to let me write my locker combination on the
back of his office door, because after months of traveling I would never
remember it and the janitor was sick of sawing the lock off. My sojourn at
this new school was brief, as I was told once again that my absences were
just too frequent to be workable. High School Number Two was a fail.

While it still hurt, at least it was less shocking than being thrown
out of high school the first time. It seemed clear that this whole idea of
getting educated was just futile, and it seemed ridiculous to attempt to
pursue it. My life had simply moved away from that stage and there was
no way to regain it. Many of my co-workers had dropped out of school
and become emancipated, so high school seemed like something that

was just dragging me down. It was best to cut ties before I got rejected anymore; the only thing that could be worse than being thrown out of two high schools would be getting thrown out of three.

I was still convinced that it was possible to manage both of my lives, the actor one and the normal Canadian one, though it often involved having to make choices in which one thing or another was inevitably sacrificed. Every decision felt like it would make an epic impact on my career, for better or worse, and people were counting on me. There was a whole domino effect of paychecks that started with my paycheck, and I felt a huge responsibility for that. Blame it on my Canadian-ness or just my massive capacity for guilt, but if I turned down a job I always felt badly for my agents and managers, who got a cut of my earnings.

I was offered the lead in a pilot for a television series. It looked pretty good and the chatter was that it would get picked up and turn into a regular gig. There was only one problem; it would be filming when my new boyfriend had his prom and I had already bought a dress. This would be my only chance to have this experience; girls that get thrown out of two high schools don't get proms. I turned down the series, and disappointed a whole team of people. But I went to prom.

My memory of it all streams like a movie montage. My boyfriend and I piled in a limo with a bunch of his friends. I kept my mouth shut as the girls giggled about it being their first time in a limousine. We arrived on a small cruise ship that was decorated in cheesy prom stuff, with terrible food and loud music. Colored lights flashed and moved around, throwing a red glow on the boys who were in the corner, reaching into the pockets of their rented tuxes to retrieve the flasks they had smuggled aboard. An *Ace of Base* song shook the dance floor as the girls moved in clusters back and forth to the bathroom. I tried to dance, too, but the bent pin in my corsage kept coming loose, leaving the white rose to flop around upside down on my dress. My boyfriend and I had a fight about something, so I slow danced with his best friend to make him mad. But later that evening, in his parents' basement, we apologized and made up, in the traditional manner of teenagers on prom night. I could not have scripted a more classic experience for myself. It was perfect. The normalcy of it all was luxurious.

Of course, there were times when I thought back about the TV show and worried about my career path. As it turned out, the pilot didn't get picked up anyway, so it was unlikely that it would have been massively career-altering. Regardless, I felt like the luckiest girl in the world, dancing to "I Will Always Love You" on a boat that never left the dock, as my wilting corsage fell apart on the dance floor.

CHAPTER 11

Professional Pretender

For many years, I carried a vintage lunchbox from the 1950s as a purse. It was made of tin and depicted cartoon vignettes from a school setting on the front. A marching band strutted across the top, and beakers bubbled in a science lab. On the inside lid of the lunch box, I taped a cartoon showing a different kind of classroom. A teacher stands at the front as attentive students lean forward in their seats. The sign on the door indicates that this is "Evelyn Wood's School of Acting." The teacher holds a pointer and gestures to a single word on the blackboard. It reads, "Pretend."

This is very funny. Like most things that are funny, the reason it is funny is because it is true. Actors get a disproportionate amount of reverence for our craft. Personally, I think there should be Oscars given for coal mining. Or to those people who search for dead bodies in swamps. Those jobs are demanding. There should be a red carpet night for 911 operators and orphanage employees. A drug treatment counselor should be dripping with diamonds and answering, "Who are you wearing?"

Nevertheless, at some point, slowly and without my awareness, I submerged myself in L.A. life. Going out and hearing, "Hey, you look like that girl from that movie," followed by a realization and screaming, became the norm. I went to have coffee with three different people, in three different coffee shops, on the same day. It was considered productive to spend the entire afternoon driving to an audition and reading just four pages of dialogue. It became acceptable to not immediately remember if today was a weekend or a weekday. My work responsibilities included going to parties where I pretended not to notice when Cher walked by on her way to the coat check. I kissed everyone on both cheeks and used the word "brilliant" to describe a lot of people who might or might not have been deserving of the label. My car was full of half-read scripts and parking passes for film studios. Going to the movies four times a week was considered research and a tax write-off. I did all the things I was supposed to, but I always wondered if the L.A. lifestyle was an acting challenge that I wasn't quite up for.

I wasn't happy, but happiness wasn't something that it occurred to me to desire. Who expects to be a happy artist? I assumed the job required me to be brooding and morose. I was doing what everyone else around me was doing, and they all seemed—if not quite content—at least deeply devoted to this existence. A non-movie life was the consolation prize to those who didn't make it here, so clearly this was as good as it got. Life in Los Angeles became the accepted delusion.

The prom boyfriend and I didn't make it much beyond prom, so I went on a date with an unbelievably hot guy who worked at my neighborhood Mexican restaurant. We sipped non-fat soy lattés and pretended to accidentally bump our legs into one another under the metal café table. He was very skilled at talking about himself, and I was fascinated to learn that having a Native American father and a Swedish mother resulted in an Abercrombie and Fitch model. He wanted to be an actor (no shock there) and talked about movies with the same dreamy, Vaseline-lensed tone that everyone in L.A. did. I was finally able to offer up some of my autobiographical information and mentioned that I was Canadian.

"You're Canadian? Whoa! Man, your English is really good."

I spent a very long time considering whether or not we should have a second date.

* * * * *

Everyone knew *Independence Day* was going to be big. It had a big budget, big actors, a big director, and we blew up a lot of big buildings. It had to be big. This created additional pressure for the actors in the film because there would be a lot of press and we needed to speak coherently. As always for me, the best part of shooting was that feeling of community, which even included off-set opportunities to make out

With James Duval and Giuseppe Andrews on the set of
Independence Day.
PHOTO COURTESY OF THE AUTHOR.

with 90s heartthrob Andrew Keegan. But sadly, actor hook-ups are not appropriate interview stories. I was supposed to talk about the magic of movie-making and my personal acting motivation, subjects that made me even more tongue-tied than Andrew and I ever were.

There is such a thing as media training. This was not something that I ever had, but it exists, and should be mandatory for all young actors. If you are not trained on how to answer reporters' questions properly, in a manner that is polite but still retaining a sense of your own self, interviews tend to feel like you are being filleted and offered up on a platter. The words, "I'd rather not talk about that," didn't exist in my vocabulary. I was terrified of looking like some entitled Hollywood brat. I felt the compulsive need to be nice to everyone and answer all their questions like a good girl. I was far more concerned about making interviewers like me than I was about protecting my soul. Therefore, interviews felt scary, unpredictable, and completely out of my control. Anyone who had the slightest interest in seeing my most sacred guts was welcome to get in there and poke around. They could even move in if they wanted to, and rearrange the place to their liking. As long as it felt like they would give me a hug when we were done, anything they wanted was fair game.

Even deeper than my desire to people-please was my concern that during an interview they would find out the truth; I was not a real actor. Real actors were passionate and dedicated and never felt like they were just puppets. The film industry expected me to be one thing, but my heart always had doubts. I was an impostor. When I spoke honestly about being uncomfortable with the concept of fame, it only elicited confused looks from reporters. So, I said the things I heard other people say. *This is a dream come true.* I attempted to talk romantically and wistfully about my job and give people the impression that under my straight teeth and shy smile was an ingénue, primed for worshipping.

The *Independence Day* premiere was just as big as the movie. There were fireworks and multiple screenings in multiple theaters and streets were closed for hours to accommodate the parade of Hummer limos.

The party was so chockablock full of excessively cool people, that no one building could contain all the hipness. The screening was at the Mann Plaza in Westwood but the party continued outside, where the streets were equally decked out with carefully thought-out mood lighting and attractive servers.

My mom was my date. Having spent much of my childhood sharing a Murphy bed with her, she was still pretty much my best friend and constant companion. Our relationship was definitely unusual—part friends, part business partners—so I knew I could count on her to be a good premiere date and not drag me into any of the drama that came with bringing a boyfriend to these sorts of work events.

My insecurity was enhanced by premieres. I'd watch Faye Dunaway effortlessly pose for 200 paparazzi and then I'd hear Billy Crystal's laugh as he entertained the crowd behind me. How was I ever going to be comfortable at these things? I held my mom's hand as we turned sideways to shimmy through the masses and get to some freer space away from the bar. I realized that I was clinging to her like a small child, but it helped me somehow. I was eighteen years old, but holding Mom's hand at least made me felt a little more protected. This did have the unintended consequence of leading people to think that my young-looking mother and I were a couple, but creating a lesbian rumor was the least of my worries at these things.

While Mom ordered us food at Johnny Rockets, one of the restaurants that had been closed to the public for our premiere, I waited out on the balcony where there were only a few people milling around. My feet hurt, and I was running through the list people I needed to say hello to, so I could go home and put on some sweatpants. A man walked out and leaned on the railing, apparently needing a quiet moment, too. I looked out into the sky and reminded myself that this was just part of the job, there was more networking to be done; I didn't have my next show booked and premieres were filled with producers on the look-out. I took a final deep breath and calculated the exact amount of time this would all require, when:

"Hey, want a smoke?"

I looked up and said that I didn't smoke but thanks. I was immediately regretful of my healthy habits as I registered his face. It was PeeWee Herman.

Paul Reubens was offering me a cigarette and once you say "No, thank you" it's really hard to take it back. I'd never had a cigarette before, since even being in the vicinity of a smoker sent me into a coughing fit. I doubted my ability to look cool even holding one, since my instinct was to hold it like a pencil. I was trying to figure out how to make small talk, when he turned around and started chatting with someone else. Someone who, presumably, knew enough to not hold a cigarette like a pencil.

I had grown up watching PeeWee's playhouse. He had been my constant, non-judgmental friend. I'd watch him when I was home and the other kids were out riding bikes. I'd watch him when I traveled to location shoots and was spending long hours waiting around to film my scenes. He was predictable. I was never the weird one in the company of PeeWee, Miss Yvonne and Chairri. Their weirdness eclipsed my own and they reveled in it.

And now I'd passed up the chance to have a smoke with PeeWee. Almost sharing a smoke is not nearly as good of a story, but it will have to do because I'm not trying to get sued. "I love your work," was a thoroughly unoriginal line at these things and there was really nothing else to say. I simply took a long last look at my childhood hero and went back into the fray of the party, wishing I were a smoker.

✳ ✳ ✳ ✳ ✳

At a certain point, right around my PeeWee moment, although not necessarily because of it, some people might have called me "successful." This concept is deserving of quotes because success seems to be the Bigfoot of the entertainment industry. People are convinced that it is out there somewhere, lurking just out of reach, but no one has ever really seen it or felt it. *Mrs. Doubtfire* broke box office records and I got mobbed upon leaving my house. *Independence Day* was widely adored for the fact that we punched an alien in the face, and I had the honor of being the trailer girl who didn't want to die a virgin.

However, like many actors I knew, I failed miserably at *feeling* successful. When we signed autographs we worried we would be failures if we never signed another one. When we were auditioning, we worried we would never work again. When we were working, we worried that the film might be terrible and could ruin our careers. When the film came out, we worried about publicity and what our next move should be and wondered if the public was getting tired of us. Then, we'd start auditioning again and the whole vicious cycle would repeat.

It was awful to incessantly worry about what came next. Not for one moment did I sit there and go, *ah! I did it. I'm successful.* When I bought real estate before I could drive, got recognized, or worked consistently, all those things should have made me feel like I was doing it right, but the system is not set up that way. That insatiable hunger for more is the thing that hooks you, that lodges itself deeply and painfully under your ribs and keeps you coming back. You are so desperate for the next hit, and surrounded by people who share that frenetic striving, that you don't bother to question your motivation for getting on this roller coaster in the first place.

This cycle appears to be the same, whether you are doing walk-ons in commercials or if you are legitimately "famous." That is the dirty truth that no one tells you; that is the hamster wheel that is Hollywood. The people walking down the red carpet and looking fabulous in front of the Step & Repeat are all terrified that we are currently in the act of committing career suicide. The movie could tank, the dress could be unflattering, the statement could be misinterpreted, the date could be wrong. The number of possible fatal missteps is endless, because the industry really is that fickle and the desire for money and fame is a bottomless pit. The poverty mindset becomes ingrained—never working enough, famous enough, paid enough, perked enough.

It made me wonder if satisfaction was possible in regular life. Did people feel successful when the new dinner recipe turned out well? When they graduated from high school? Made their partner laugh? Or did everyone, everywhere, feel like they had to constantly do more, be more? Was the whole world consumed by this crazy, competitive, dissatisfying vortex?

Then again, maybe this was all just me. Maybe other actors found a way to feel content even within the narrow definition of success in Hollywood. I hope that they did, because it's a soul-grinding thing otherwise. I never could manage it.

CHAPTER 12

Playing with Danger

Although my tendency towards being an authority-fearing goody-two-shoes is strong, working in the film industry exposed me to all kinds of things that opened my eyes to the world. Some of those experiences were on screen, some of them off. And I'm grateful for every one because they made life so much more interesting.

My phobia of guns continued from my early John Malkovich days. Thirteen years after that first film in which I lost my mind in the presence of a gun, I did a TV movie called *Dream House* in which I had to shoot one. And the only thing scarier than shooting a gun is shooting yourself with a gun because you don't know how to use the thing.

When you read a script, it's always tricky to know what the end product is going to be like. The script for *Independence Day* seemed so crazy that I didn't bother to finish the whole thing before my audition. The budget is often a factor, but it mostly has to do with the passion and vision of the production team that either lifts a show up, or damns it straight to hell. Creative passion can be hard to judge from just the bare-bones outline that most scripts provide. There were other reasons to accept a role, even if the project looked less than stellar. If you rejected too much work you looked like you were getting a big ego. There was always the risk of pissing off the wrong people, or the siblings of the wrong people. Throw in the fact that there was a mortgage to be paid and there were many contributing factors that made me say yes. Even if the project was about a demonic house.

It was kind of like HAL in *2001: A Space Odyssey*, except for the fact you have heard of *2001*, unlike my movie. Our technologically advanced house took on a will of its own and attempted to kill my whole family. Low-budget special effects and overly dramatic music seemed to be the vibe we were going for. Towards the end of the ordeal, my character takes matters, and a firearm, into her own hands and gets some shit done.

The gun handlers showed me the gun I would be using and upon seeing my panicked reaction, they promptly sent me to a shooting range to learn how to hold a gun without shaking and tearing up. It turned out the only shooting range in the small town where we were filming was in the basement of the police station.

On my day off, a police officer escorted me down to the depths of the building and taught me about guns. He showed me various holds, my personal favorite being the "teacup hold," which both sounded adorable and allowed me to use both hands so my shaking would be less obvious. After listening to a lecture about the anatomy of a gun and general safety rules (don't point it at anyone, don't point it at yourself) the officer set me up in front of one of those paper targets shaped like a body.

He stood behind me, held my shoulders and told me to just take a deep breath and squeeze the trigger. Just like that. Just shoot something. So, I tentatively compressed the trigger and felt it catch. The gun bounced back in my hands, causing my elbow to ache as the bullet flew. The sound caused a primal fear in my pacifist vegetarian body, but my aim wasn't half bad. Each time I actually hit the black silhouette, I instinctively apologized to it. Sorry, I hit the shoulder. So sorry. I nicked an ear. The officer laughed at me and reloaded the firearm.

The day we filmed the gun scene, all I could think of was Brandon Lee's heartbreaking death. He was killed when a gun backfired on set, severing his spinal cord. He was rushed to the same hospital in North Carolina that I went to when I broke my back. Post-1994, everything changed for actors using firearms on set. Before that, there was always this feeling of invincibility. Our industry was smoke and mirrors, but they were smoke and mirrors that we trusted implicitly. We never thought that the smoke could be toxic and the mirrors could slice us open.

The scene went fine. Despite the anxiety, I managed to remember my lines and the proper teacup hold. The gun went off as planned and we only had to do one take. I gladly handed the gun off to the handlers as soon as the director yelled cut, holding it out by the handle, barrel pointed down, like a dead, stinking fish. I made a mental note to never take another role where I had to work with firearms. I'm just not a good enough actor to look anything but terrified while holding a weapon.

Whenever a film wrapped, the depression hit pretty hard. After a few months of being part of that family, returning to the vast spaciousness and loneliness of being an unemployed actor is disheartening. Life is once again flooded with the physical insecurities, wondering when the next gig would come, going to promising auditions with the inevitable disappointments when the producers decide to go "a different way" with the role.

So, I looked for entertaining distractions and there are few places that were more distracting and entertaining than the Hustler Store on Sunset Boulevard. This was no dark, sketchy shack of fornication; it was the Gap of porn stores. The store was bright and cheery, with lots of windows and bubbly salespeople. They sold everything from conceivably modest massage oils, to far-from-innocent apparatuses that were almost beyond my imagination. There was even a café inside the store, providing a place where you could take a break from leather and chains shopping by enjoying a nice caramel macchiato and Danish. This was sex the way Walt Disney would have wanted it.

I had gone to the Hustler Store with a girlfriend who was in need of a bedside companion. That was the kind of thing you did at the Hustler store, take a friend with you to shop, as if you were picking out new linens and wanted a second opinion. Except instead of debating thread count, we were researching the differences between Master Cock Model #200 and the #300 series.

As my friend wandered off down the aisle to compare speed options, I noticed a woman tiptoeing around the corner, clearly mortified by her surroundings. She was utterly adorable and undoubtedly an actress. There is no reason anyone should be that good-looking and not have a camera pointed at them. At my own 5'3, I seemed to tower over this pixie-lady. She had a button nose that had been recreated in Hollywood countless times.

She was obviously not a frequent porn store shopper and she looked as if she was going to implode as her wide eyes scanned the shelves of naughtiness. Suddenly, a man came over from the café, circling her like a starstruck shark. He was about as non-threatening as you can get; dorky and slightly puffy, wearing a sweater his mother probably bought him.

He approached her. Was she really who he thinks she is? Yes, she is, she admitted. The actress slid her hand behind her back, attempting to hide the bottle she had clutched in her humiliated grasp. Alas, her ninety-pound frame was not blocking much. She blushed an endearing pink color and I could hear her silent prayers for the floor to open and swallow her evil, porn-perusing self. The man was clueless to her discomfort and kept pressing her to recite her resume for him. Oh my God, he loved that scene in the last episode with that guy. She nodded as she frantically searched the store for a random sniper or a runaway llama that might cause enough of a commotion to distract her fan. The moment of truth.

He wanted her autograph. She needed both hands free.

It was like watching a turtle lay helplessly on its back in the brutal desert sun. I couldn't take it anymore. I walked behind her and discreetly removed the bottle from her white fingers clutched behind her. Playing along, she released her grip and never looked back at me. She took the pen and Hustler flyer from the guy's outstretched hands and looked up with her gigantic baby blues.

"Who can I make this out to?"

I placed the bottle back on the shelf and went back to my friend, who was waving a hot pink phallic monstrosity at me. I realized that it was okay that I was currently unemployed and it was okay that no one was going to watch my HAL rip-off of a TV movie. Fame came with a price, and it was more than the cost of even the extra-large bottle of Self Heating Boobie Oil.

Red leather, yellow leather

My other unemployed friends spent their ample free time doing something more valuable than hanging out in porn stores; they took acting classes. Oh, how my friends loved acting classes. They took them with renowned teachers, visiting teachers, teachers who had taught famous people before they were famous people. They went to little spaces in strip malls next to doughnut places and they stood on a stage and cried and laughed and pretended to be in rowboats. They shared intimate details of their own lives so that they could release suppressed emotion. They told strangers that their dad smelled like whiskey and yelled at their mom and how that one time their cat ran away while they were on vacation. They unearthed their most tender and feeble parts in order to embrace their humanity and experience the universal pain. Then, they stood up and read someone else's words and crawled around, wallowing in someone else's pain while other people sat in folding chairs and watched.

When my friends stopped gasping at the fact that I didn't have an acting coach, they said that I HAD to meet theirs and they threw around glowing adjectives and guru terms. I was promised that my life and career would be changed and that I needed to clear my calendar for the next Wednesday night from 7-10 p.m. I would patiently explain how it was just not my thing and they would patiently explain that I just didn't understand. Attendance was mandatory.

Then, of course, my friend bailed on me. He had to cover someone else's shift that night, but he made me promise that I would go anyway. His teacher was expecting me. It sounded like a horrible way to spend a Wednesday night, especially without my friend to walk me through it, but undeniably, I held a small flicker of hope. I went because perhaps this class, this brilliant acting sage, could infuse me with passion. Maybe this person could convince me that this was the right career path for me, that this was something that could be fulfilling for the long haul. Maybe this person could be my light and lead me through the dark periods of unemployment and the growing restlessness I was starting to feel, even on set.

When I arrived at the class, there were actors milling in the hallway of every body-type and psychological intensity. There was the pretty waifish girl who existed solely on brown rice. There was the broody boy with dark eyes and dirty fingernails who wrote bad poetry. (Those were the boys that I wanted to lay around in bed with, listening to them analyze *Waiting For Godot* while I caressed their long, scraggly hair that smelled vaguely of goat's milk.) Then, there were the people that the film industry cruelly termed "character actors," which meant they were there to fill the role of the cranky neighbor or the hunchbacked bridge troll. They would all be standing around, drinking water from paper cones, touching each other lightly on the arm, saying, "Your monologue last week? It, like, moved me. From some deep place."

It was uncomfortable, not being able to agree that the troll's monologue had indeed been a monumental experience, so I went to the bathroom to kill time before the thing started. Looking in the mirror, I re-did my ponytail and wondered why I couldn't get emotional about this. I would sob about accidentally stepping on a snail, so where was my connection with this career that I had devoted my life to?

When class began, the teacher stood in front of the stage as we all took our seats in the audience. She went over some general news; class was cancelled for next week, as she had to travel to New York (murmurs from the class speculating which famous client she was going to coach in New York) and then she announced that there was a guest in class today.

All eyes turned to me and I panicked, being singled out and examined by this room of strangers. They wanted me to talk. As myself. There was no character to hide behind, no scripted lines to memorize. It was just me, with the clothes and words and ponytail that I picked out myself. Wearing around other people's choices was so much easier than this.

I felt a hand under my arm, pushing me to stand and be welcomed as my face burned and I swallowed down the bile that had risen to the back of my throat. I heard my voice introduce myself and say how long I had been acting. When the guru prodded me further, I rattled off part of my resume, to the nods of recognition from the other students. I ran out of air before getting to the end of my sentence and took an awkward gasp in the middle of a word. It was not a good beginning. Then my mind went blank so I just completely lied and said that I was happy to be there and thank you so much. As I collapsed into my seat, one of the brown rice girls waved her arm maniacally, her bony elbow flying in her neighbor's face.

"Stephanie? You have something to share?"

Stephanie stood up with much more grace and poise than I could even imagine and announced that she got a callback for the TV movie with Scott Bakula. You would have thought that Stephanie was receiving the Peace Prize by the audience reaction. Apparently, she had worked on her audition scene in class the week before and the entire group felt invested in her accomplishment.

When the excitement died down, it was finally time for class to begin, and we were asked to stand and do some group warm-up exercises. We stood in a circle, Brown Rice holding hands with Troll who was holding hands with Dark Poet, who, electrifyingly, was holding hands with me. We then launched into voice and tongue exercises that included saying "red leather, yellow leather" over and over again. I tried to give a cute smile to Dark Poet but he was intensely focused and had no interest in The Guest. He was only here to pursue his craft.

We sat for hours and watched talented and devoted actors get up on stage and pour their guts out for all of us to see. They pantomimed and improvised and cried until spit dripped from their mouths in long, slow strings. They got angry and threw things and collapsed to the ground in exhaustion. They laughed and kissed one another. They changed their postures and walks and facial expressions. They lived other people's lives and they thrived there. It was beautiful.

The guru asked if I wanted to prepare a scene. I declined as politely as possible but I might have been yelling as I said, "No, thank you." Dark Poet did a dark scene, Troll did a quirky one and Brown Rice worked on her Scott Bakula callback material again. I wondered why I couldn't just jump in the thespian waters and be like them. Why could I not feel excited about going to the acting studio in a strip mall and dissecting the motivation for a scene pulled from *The Godfather*? Why couldn't I work on creating a whole background and history for a character? Why couldn't I get in there and dig deep and decide that in 7th grade, my character's best friend had kissed the boy she liked and now she was scarred for life? Why could I not join this group, be like Dark Poet and just become one of the real actors? I wanted that. It seemed legitimately rewarding for them, but all I knew was that every time I tried, I felt like a wolf in sheep's clothing.

I went home and realized that I had been cast in the perfect role: The Guest. That was not the right club for me; it had felt just like being back in high school. I was not a member of that tight-knit group that discussed Stanislavsky's theories on emotion memory and modes of inquiry for character building. The problem was, I wasn't sure a place existed where I could be anything other than The Guest.

Actors On Ice

"Is someone boiling dirty laundry on set?"

I was about eight and Mom and I were walking down the hallway of the production offices of some TV show. I fanned my hand in front of my face.

"Yuck. It's so smelly."

"That's marijuana," Mom said. "It's gross."

All kinds of pharmaceuticals are easy to get when you are an actor. On some sets, they were practically lying out on the craft services table next to the bowl of Gummy Bears. I attribute my lack of drug use to that accessibility. It would be nice to say that I just possess a great deal of personal character and inner strength, that I saw it ruin the lives of co-workers and I made a life-long vow to shun destructive substance, but it just didn't go down that way. My lack of drug use isn't profound and it doesn't make me heroic. I have never done drugs. I have also never eaten a Fig Newton. They were both around and neither looked appealing.

In fact, I have a certain amount of shame about the fact that my mother's rather casual assertion that pot was "gross" was enough to keep me away from it entirely. It feels as if I have somehow not lived up to my reputation as a child actor, like I couldn't even do that part right. But some other actors like the drugs. There's no judgment, but I tend to extricate myself from the area when they partake because of my unrelenting fear of getting in trouble.

I was working on a show in which a couple of the other actors were looking for some recreational substances. They zeroed in on a local girl who had been hired as background for a crowd scene and apparently had some sort of drug hook-up. This girl was more than happy to oblige the guys, who had presented themselves as The Next Big Thing movie stars. That was not at all true, but she was easily convinced otherwise and did the thing that people do for actors: offer favors.

People seem unfathomably eager to do favors for even vaguely famous people. It's truly absurd. Actors are one of the few groups of people who can afford to have no favors done for them. They have the money to buy stuff and the time to wait in line and yet they are the only ones who never do. However, favor-givers seem to whole-heartedly embrace the role of giving more stuff to the people who already have access to everything.

Local Girl had agreed to meet one of the actors in the lobby of the hotel we were staying in and deliver the drugs. I didn't know that a low-level drug deal was going down when I agreed to get dinner after work with the guys. It was presented as, "I just need to pick up something in the lobby before we go," as if he was going to grab one of the complementary cookies from under the glass dome at the front desk. Local Girl was waiting in one of the puffy upholstered lobby chairs, just thrilled to be part of it all. After a quick but undoubtedly thrilling hug with the actor, she clandestinely handed him the goods. In return, he offered her some crumpled bills. Oh no, she refused, it's on her. Apparently it was enough of an honor just to help this B-level actor get high; she couldn't possibly take money, too. With thanks and a kiss on the cheek from the actor, Local Girl giggled and was on her way.

"Let's go back up to my room for a second," he said. "I need water."

We went back up to his room and he distributed the spoils with the other two actors who had joined us. I must be honest and admit how much of a loser I am: I don't know what kind of drugs they were. They were little pills, they were white and you needed water with them. I was offered my share.

"I'm good, thanks." I waved him away.

They divvyed up my portion of the Drugs You Need Water With. There was only one sink and one glass in the room so the three actors lined up one at a time to take the pills. They looked like little boys waiting to brush their teeth. I wondered if it was smart to be in a hotel room with three stoned men I had only known for a couple of weeks. They had always given me a protective, brotherly vibe, even the guy who spent his lunch breaks kissing me, so there didn't seem to be cause for concern.

I sat on the couch and tucked my feet under me. The situation was slightly uncomfortable but more than anything I was hungry. It had been a long day of work. I was wondering if the restaurant would be busy and if there was a wait, maybe we would sit at the bar and order mozzarella sticks or something. Suddenly, there was a loud banging on our hotel room door. The boys stood up tall, their eyes wide. Only two of them had swallowed the Drugs You Need Water With and there were still several pills on the counter, along with the bottle. We all looked at one another.

"Maybe it is the maid or something. Did you request extra towels?" I offered.

"We know you are in there. Open up." A booming voice demanded from the other side of the door. He didn't sound like a maid.

"OhShitOhShitOhShit." The boys raced around the room like they were in a Buster Keaton movie.

"Flush it. No, wait, don't flush it, they can't search without a warrant."

"Is that true?"

"I dunno, I think so."

"Put it in your pocket, they can search the room but not you."

"Is that true?"

"I dunno, I think so."

(Never ask people who watch too many movies about the nuances of the legal system.) More banging. Fists were about to bust through.

"Open the fucking door!"

My heart raced. They were swearing. They were mad. They were going to yell at me and take me to prison. My one phone call would have to be to the Assistant Director to tell him that we might be late to work the next morning. I hate being late. Something told me that I would hate jail even more.

"We know you have the fucking ice, open the fucking door!"

Apparently, the Drugs You Need Water With were actually "ice," and I was definitely going to jail. This was just like it happens in the movies. I stood up on the couch and flapped my arms uselessly, as the boys started to get cool and collected. I was not sure if they were calm under pressure, or if the ice was starting to take effect.

"Guys, chill. They can't do anything without a warrant." One of them slowly walked to the door.

My heart was pounding in my ears and I couldn't hear the first thing the actor said when he opened the door. I grabbed a decorative pillow and clutched it to my chest like some sort of tasseled bulletproof vest. A cop and a hotel security guard stood on the other side of the door. Both large men, physically appropriate for their chosen careers.

"We know you have the ice. Where is it?" The two men started searching the room. Flipping the comforter off the bed, kicking the bottom of the curtains.

"You can't do that without a warrant," said the guy I liked to make out with.

"Bullshit."

So much for mounting that defense. This cop was having none of that legal mumbo jumbo.

They continued walking as the actor spouted off what must have been one of his lines when he guest stared on NYPD Blue. Another actor interrupted him and started to explain "who we are," and offered to call the producers to vouch for us. The cop ignored him and started moving the furniture. They were serious. The other guys paced the room, saying whatever they could think of to convince the cop there was nothing going on. I started to tear up and rubbed my wrists, wondering how much handcuffs really hurt, when the security guard's radio crackled. He took the call, and proceeded with a short exchange that contained more static and numbers than words.

He then looked up at us and smiled. There was a certain levity in his face that had been lacking until this point.

"Sorry about this folks. Someone has been throwing ice out the window and hitting people walking on the street. It turns out it was in the room directly below yours. They got the kids now. A couple of twelve-year-olds, if you can believe it. Sorry for the inconvenience." He patted one of the actors on the back and he and the cop left.

When the door closed, the guys burst in to laughter as I just sat there, eyes full of tears. My not quite Next Big Thing friends washed down the rest of the pills, and put on coats. They handed me mine.

"Ready to go?" they asked me.

We really were untouchable. Just like we thought.

"Love"

As I pondered the possibility of going to jail with my castmates, it occurred to me how quickly actors create a strong bond on set. It's a phenomenon that was so eloquently explained in the film *Speed*; when people experience a traumatic event together, they tend to be drawn to one another due to the shared experience and unique level of understanding. A deep connection is forged and the combination of anxiety and adrenaline causes an avalanche of emotion that may or may not be truly appropriate for the couple involved.

Every film is like its own little traumatic event. You have very little freedom on set. Your time, your body, and your words don't belong to you. You are working long hours, often in a foreign land. By the end of the shoot it's likely that you'll end up in a passionate embrace with at least a couple of fellow captives. Yet, at the time, it never feels like a temporary hook-up. We are convinced that this is *Love*. This is someone who finally understands this insane life, and by all its extensions, you and the essence of your being. I have found this love with an assistant director in Prague, a camera guy on the windswept plains of Alberta, and costars of various films on three continents. Every time, I thought it was real and we would live happily ever after once the credits rolled. Emotions are amplified in the way that the camera adds ten pounds.

It's not about sex. It's about having someone who gets it. Someone who gets that your "weekend" is actually just a Wednesday afternoon, because you are switching to nights so you have to be at work at 10 PM on Wednesday, even thought you just finished at 2 a.m. on Wednesday morning. It's about someone who knows that the most romantic thing they can do is sit with you at the local Fluff 'n' Fold while your one pair of jeans circles the dryer, because they are the only thing other than 18th century gowns that you have worn for the last three weeks. Someone who knows that here, in this strange location where you don't know anyone and don't speak the language, walking three hours to find the closest pizza place is a high-quality use of time.

This can be especially challenging for the on-camera dynamic. On one show, I was spending all my free time falling in love with the guy who was playing my brother, which made the on-set energy a little creepy. At one point, the director called cut because he said the glances between us in a scene, which were supposed to be evoking sibling rivalry playfulness, were looking "slightly incestuous." That's where you really need to exercise those acting chops.

I fell in love with the sort of reckless abandon that was never possible in the rest of my life. It was the one place I was totally irresponsible. I purchased earthquake insurance and got my teeth cleaned, then, I fantasized about how I could save the alcoholic I'd just started dating. He was a sweet, charming guy who was just a little too fond of bingeing on Sam Adams and watching puppet porn, which is exactly what it sounds like. In hindsight, I might have benefited from partying more and falling in love less.

This kind of love only lasts for a few months, yet has all the attributes of actual love. It is intense, it is compassionate, and it is understanding on a deep level. It's a way to feel like yourself when you spend every day becoming someone else. It's the most basic way to keep a handle on your humanity. To give and receive love reminds you that even though you are doing something that seems so strange and fascinating to the rest of the world, you love just like everyone else. Your heart leaps when they walk in the room, and you cry when they don't call. It's simple. It's normal. And sometimes, normal is the thing you need most.

Then, inevitably, when a show wrap is called and the set is broken down, that love flies into the stage lights like a moth, and dies in a puff of smoke. Quickly and cleanly.

CHAPTER 13

I'm Not Your Actress

There were many, many roles I didn't get during my career. Usually I got over the loss pretty quickly, but there are a few that still sting (I'm looking at you, *Scooby-Doo*). I did a screen test for *Boys Don't Cry* which was being held at a famous hotel in L.A., Chateau Marmont. The place drips with Hollywood. It was the hotel where F. Scott Fitzgerald had a heart attack, John Belushi died, and Jim Morrison almost died.

I had a customary outfit for going to auditions. Well, "outfit" makes it sound more put together than it actually was. It consisted of jeans and a dark grey t-shirt with my hair pulled back in a ponytail and only enough makeup to cover any zits that might have erupted that day. This was not because of any filmmaking rationale; it was just that I knew nothing about putting on makeup or managing my own hair. Since I was four years old, it had been someone's job to take care of those details, so I never learned girl things like how to straighten my hair or use an eyelash curler. So, I went to auditions with curly hair and straight lashes and just hoped that the producers had vision. This didn't really work when I auditioned for *Clueless* looking like a dull little house finch while everyone else got the secret actor memo to dress in shimmery little pink things. Unsurprisingly, I didn't get that job either.

For the *Boys Don't Cry* screen test, I once again donned my blank slate clothes; baggy jeans, a t-shirt and black Chuck Taylors. I found my way to the imposing, castle-looking hotel and wrote my name on the sign-in sheet that sat on an ornately decorated side-table in the lobby. I grabbed a chair next to the other girls who were also auditioning and smiled my hellos. The curved windowsills and wood-beam ceiling were a nice change from the florescent-lit hallways of film studios that we normally waited in. Actors are used to sitting on the floors of office buildings and tucking our feet under when the lunch delivery guy comes through, so having a high-backed chair to sit in while we gazed out the huge windows to the glistening pool was quite luxurious.

Film auditions are not like *Toddlers and Tiaras* or something where there is backstabbing and maliciousness, all under the guise of friendly competition. There are many nuances involved in casting, so there's no point in trying to take down the girl in the next chair. Producers are considering if you look similar enough or different enough from the people who have already been cast. Are you going to make your co-stars look really tall or really short? Did the producer's niece recently show an interest in becoming an actress? Besides all those casting details, you end up auditioning with the same girls all the time, so you might as well be nice because next time you might need their help navigating the sweltering labyrinth that is the Twentieth Century Fox backlot in August.

Hillary Swank was auditioning, too. We tended to be up for the same types of roles and had auditioned together several times. I didn't even recognize her when she walked into the hotel, because she had absolutely morphed herself into a boy. She was dressed in her then-husband Chad's clothes, wearing a plaid shirt and dark jeans into which she had stuffed an assortment of balled-up socks. She had her hair slicked back and tucked into her collar. I complimented her bold and impressive look, and she showed me her "guy walk." She had a deeper voice that she had been working on for days. We examined the profile of her crotch and chose the most realistic, yet empowering, sock combinations.

Finally, they called my name and when I walked in to the room all I could think was—*please, just give Hillary this role. Let's just get this audition over with so you can get your real actress in here.* I did my job and read my lines and they smiled and said they were glad I came in. I shook their hands and thanked them for their time and wondered if I should grab dinner and wait out the traffic that would be winding its way back to my side of the hill. I had no desire to fight Hillary for this. It was clear that the place where was my passion should have been was empty. I was just going through the motions.

They did give Hillary the role and she perfected her guy voice to the tune of an Oscar win. You always want those people to win. You want to know that those balled-up socks did their job and revealed the hard work and commitment. Because then we get to see actors up there, their souls lit up from within, knowing that they are in the zone, doing the thing they were meant to do. And whenever you see someone living out their soul's true purpose—it's magic.

There are no small parts

Being overly emotional is an occupational hazard. Actors are required to instantaneously tap into every possible emotion, so it's necessary to keep those feelings right up top where you can reach them. It's challenging to turn that off and be a regular functioning adult human who hides her moods when it's appropriate. Sometimes it's just more than we can handle.

Often at a casting session, the producers will be seeing people for several different roles at the same time. At one particular call-back, I was waiting with several women in their early forties who were auditioning for the role of the mother, when suddenly, a flustered woman blasted out of the casting room with tears in her eyes. It obviously hadn't gone well. That feeling of failure was familiar to everyone in the room, and we all lowered our eyes as a respectful acknowledgement of her pain.

She grabbed her bag from a chair, almost dumping the contents on the floor, walked up to the receptionist and slapped down her ticket from the parking structure.

The receptionist glanced up from her *People* magazine.

"We don't validate."

"You don't validate? Are you serious? I came all the way down here and they barely paid attention during my read and now you are telling me you don't fucking validate?"

I tried not to stare, but it was horrifyingly mesmerizing. This was a glimpse of my future. This was the life of a working actor; we would always have to stand there, emotionally exposed and begging for validation. Rejection and heartbreak were just built in to the job description. Was it worth it? Was I willing to fight for a job on a crappy TV show and feel like an invalidated piece of meat when I was forty-two? That scenario was feeling likely, as I had just been rejected for a role I had gone on three call-backs for. Their feedback claimed that I was great, just too "ethnic," which is Hollywood code for being brunette and occasionally in need of a good waxing. It was not the first time it had been said, and I was starting to feel sorry for myself. My poor, ugly, ethnic self.

To add insult to injury, I was insanely jealous of my friend who was all floaty and in love with a man who wrote songs about her and massaged her feet in public. Meanwhile, I had recently rolled over in my boyfriend's bed to get a glass of water from the nightstand and noticed a card signed, "with love from your fiancée." As I hyperventilated, he attempted to reassure me.

"Sweetie, calm down. It's fine. Rebecca is very open-minded. She has a girlfriend, too, so she totally won't mind."

He flashed his dimple at me, which proved to be deep enough to convince me to be the #2/straight girlfriend for a few weeks. Needless to say, being labeled the ugly chick by the film industry was not a hit I was poised to take at that moment.

But every time life became seriously dissatisfying, something would always happen to hook me back in.

Like the mail would arrive.

Opening up an invitation to a premiere was always exciting. It meant you were included. Important. Sometimes the invites were elaborate and expensive, ramping up the level of prestige even more. My friend Dean Devlin invited me to the *Godzilla* premiere, and the invitation roared when you opened it. The invite acts as a sly little wink, indicating that you are a member of the club and you can relax for just a moment. There would be a card with a map on it for your limo driver so he would know where the drop off was. Your name would be put on a list at some front door, in the hands of a bulky man whose job it was to decide if you were in or out. Premiere invitations would always have this notable weight to them, because they contained a tangible sliver of affection and approval inside the shimmery envelope.

But this delivery was soon followed by the realization that I now had to go to the damn thing. Sometimes it was a premiere of a film I had been in, other times it was a film that a friend or co-worker had produced. Regardless, I needed to prepare to say glowing things about the project that may or may not be true while inflating egos in a thinly veiled attempt to get my next job. That was just what you did at those things. It was just like any other work dinner in corporate America. No one needed to explain those rules to me, the air would once again be heavy with uneasiness and grasping—and it would just be obvious. It was much more about impressing the big wigs and networking than having a good time.

So, I'd stand in my entryway wearing a fancy dress that I felt awkward in, hand on the front door, and give myself the speech. *This is going to be fun. It's just a party and parties are fun. Everyone enjoys parties. You'll be fine. There is no need to freak out.* I'd push the Breathe Button on my palm. I'd will my hand to turn the knob and force my feet in my wobbly heels to walk out the door. *This is going to be fun. Really fucking fun.*

The theater was always swarming with energy and camera flashes and security guards. Some people live for the yelling of the paparazzi, the hands-on-hips pose all ready for publication. Personally, I always assumed the red carpet was red because it was actively flowing lava—it certainly felt like walking on hot coals.

I had a small role in a film called *A Walk on the Moon*. I was surprised to be invited to the premiere and couldn't come up with a good reason to get out of it. Mom acted as my date again and I wore a plaid skirt with fishnet stockings and a Gap sweater purchased for the occasion.

The film was a 1960s period piece and some of it took part at Woodstock. I was curious to see how our recreated hippie wonderland had translated to the big screen. For the shoot, we had spent hours out in a field, smoking fake joints and grooving to Jimi Hendrix as they blasted *Freedom* through giant speakers. Still not knowing how to hold a cigarette, let alone a marijuana cigarette, I copied those around me and pretended that being completely naive was a character choice. The whole Woodstock sequence was an awesome experience for me, a budding hippie who had the crummy luck of not being born until 1978.

Mom and I drove to the premiere in my Toyota and parked in a lot that was massively overcharging as they cashed in on the event. Large crowds were stuffed behind police barricades all straining to get a look at something. Mom and I started to make our way in to the theater, when a publicist stopped me.

"Lisa, glad you are here! Come on over here and walk the line."

Mom gave me a quick hug and dashed into the theater, leaving me to deal with the cameras. She always dodged them; even in the few family photographs that exist of my mother she is hiding behind someone's shoulder or holding a bottle of green olives in front of her face. She hated having her photo taken because she said that the camera would steal her soul. I had asked her once about the state of my soul; it had been overly-documented since I was four years old. She said she was sure that mine could survive it just fine, but honestly, I was beginning to wonder if that was true.

The publicist was pulling my arm and calling out to reporters that I was available. There were legit, big deal actors in this film, it had not occurred to me that the press would even glance in my direction when they could be talking to Diane Lane. I expected to watch the film, wince through my fifteen minutes of screen time, eat some toothpick food, and be in bed with a book by 10 p.m.

"The line" was an actual line of men and women with fat microphones and bug-eyed cameras. They were from *E!*, *Access Hollywood*, *Entertainment Tonight* and various foreign press. They tend to ask convoluted questions like—"if you were kidnapped by aliens and they wanted to know what this film was about, what would you tell them?" You have to lean really close to these reporters and awkwardly tilt your head down because it's hard to hear with all the people screaming. Then you have to wonder if your neck veins are visible at this totally unflattering angle.

"No, no. I don't need to walk the line." I protested, but the publicist took my completely unprepared reluctance as false modesty and made introductions as she pushed me towards the cameras. It was quickly evident that these were serious reporters. They wanted to actually talk substantively about the film. I had worked on this movie for about a week, many months prior and was woefully ill-equipped to answer any questions about it. My most distinct memory of filming was the fact that the director, Tony Goldwyn, would occasionally direct us shirtless, much to my delight. It was hot during the Woodstock recreation filming and when the spirit moved him to strip down, I was not inclined to complain. However, there was only so much mileage I could get from the, "I thought my boss had nice pecs," storyline. There needed to be something else to entertain these reporters and give them a decent sound-bite.

A reporter, who was dressed far better than I was, shoved a mic in my face. Now *she* looked like a movie star. She had a shock of blond hair with a perfect wave, each individual strand ebbing and flowing on cue. Her lips were a shade of red that made me feel like nature had been mistaken in not making that the standard color. I was shamed by her flawlessness and the fact that she looked like that, even though she wasn't even in the shot. The camera was ten inches from my face, staring defiantly at me. Everyone was acting like I was in this movie for more than fifteen minutes.

"Who do you play in this film?" Ms. Perfect asked me.

I went blank. I could not remember my character's name. The babbling began.

"Well, you know, she...she is so strong and so...independent."

Words kept spilling forth without my consent. I realized that this was being recorded and would last forever. My voice kept going up a little at the end my sentences, as if each answer was a question in itself. I pulled all my responses out of my ass and waited for someone to call me on it. No one corrected me and I moved on to the next serious reporter who had done more homework than I had.

"Lisa, tell me about Myra." The reporter said into her microphone.

Myra! Of course, that was my character's name. It all came flooding back to me. Well, not really flooding. I was not in the film enough for anything to flood, but at least now I had a name to go with. I made my way down the line, doing a terrible job talking about the movie to one put-together journalist after another. Thankfully Viggo Mortensen was there to distract the reporters from my incoherent rambling, and they quickly moved along to him. After surviving my firing squad, I met my mother in the lobby of the theatre. She had gathered theater snacks, her arms overflowing with Diet Cokes and popcorn while she waited for me, having dodged the cameras with her soul firmly intact.

"Hey, how'd it go on the line? Oh...umm." Her face fell a little.

"What? What umm??" I was a little edgy after my reporter encounters.

She cringed and pointed to my chest. I had not removed the sticker from my Gap sweater. All the way down my right breast in that long, distinctive Gap labeling, it read "SMALL SMALL SMALL SMALL"...

I don't know if anyone noticed. I'm not sure if they would have been more offended by the fact that my breasts were a size small, or that I was wearing Gap to a star-studded Hollywood event. Sure, Sharon Stone had pulled off that move three years earlier and had made headlines but I was no Sharon Stone. Plus, she had paired her Gap shirt with a Vera Wang skirt. My skirt had cost $19.99 at Express and that wasn't even a sale price.

The film was good, the Woodstock stuff looked cool, and I managed to make it appear that being a total naive tool was a character trait. Once the SMALL sticker was removed from my chest, I could relax a little, knowing not much else could humiliate me that evening. I was able to pull myself together enough to be witty in front of Tony Goldwyn, who sadly decided to remain in his clothes for the evening. At the end of the night, I took what was left of my increasingly photographed and tattered soul and we drove back to the Valley. I swore that I'd remember this feeling when I opened the next invitation to the next premiere, but it turns out it's kind of like labor. How quickly I forgot about the pain when the next fancy envelope arrived.

CHAPTER 14

It All Comes Down to a List

As I neared my twentieth birthday, an uncomfortable truth was dawning—I felt like my life no longer resembled me. The creeping feeling of self-betrayal was becoming palpable and anxiety attacks frequently left me sobbing on the floor of my closet, curled up on a pile of shoes. So, I made a list.

I loved the work. I loved:

* walking to set and seeing the people, my cohorts, with whom I had gotten so close

* starting work at four in the morning, getting breakfast at the catering truck and watching the sun come up

* understanding the rhythm of a scene set up and learning about light filters and having lunch at long tables with the teamsters, who have had my heart since they taught me how to play craps as a preschooler

* the sharp clap of the slate and that brief, breathless moment between that sound and the director's cue, where you know you are in the zone

* making rounds to say good night to my friends before going home, although I knew it was only a few hours before I'd see them again.

There was a lot to love in my job.

There was also much that I hated. I hated:

✳ when the film came out and the reviews, good or bad, sent me on a nauseating emotional rollercoaster

✳ when people recognized me and I had to answer any manner of questions even though I was on a date or watching a movie or late for my pap smear

✳ having my physical appearance harshly criticized in the name of "art" and then losing the job to a "Britney Spears type"

✳ that no one liked my glasses even though I thought they made me look like Lisa Loeb

✳ the press interviews that always felt like a trap

✳ the calls from my agent…and waiting for the calls from my agent

✳ driving all over Los Angeles for an audition that was really just a courtesy because the director already knew that the producer's daughter would be hired

✳ the politics of knowing the casting director wants to hire you but the director doesn't because he didn't like my last film

✳ hearing the subtle suggestion that the character might be a little thinner than me

✳ the fact that I would fall in love with every one of my costars and then be heartbroken when we wrapped and I realized I had done it, yet again

✳ feeling like I wasn't really being creative, I was just acting out everyone else's creativity

✳ that I just never, ever, felt good enough.

It's pretty clear that the cons list is longer. It's sad to realize that the thing you have based your life around is leading you in a miserable direction. It's terrifying, actually. Because you have two options: pretend you are not realizing it and hold off the misery with the parts that are still somewhat satisfying, or, get out of the situation and try to figure out what the hell would make you happy. Both of those options are really scary, but the first option sounded more likely to make me an alcoholic.

I was doing a job that many people in the world wanted to do. They longed for it. They became starving artists for it. Here I was, not being grateful for it. In truth, I found the whole thing embarrassing. It felt shameful to have something so socially valuable when I wasn't sure I really wanted it. It was like a vegetarian trying to eat a ribeye in front a starving kid. I felt awful about it and just wanted to hand my career off to someone who was interested in it. I tried forcing myself to like it. I tried to read acting books and tried to intellectualize my way in. My eyes glazed over the words "method," "motivation," and "character development."

I fantasized about being a social worker. A librarian. A farmer. A dog trainer. One of those people who works for aquariums and dives into the big fish tanks to clean the insides. I thought about working in an office, filing things in alphabetical order and wearing sweater sets and heels that clicked on the linoleum. I fantasized about carrying a briefcase and my lunch in a paper sack. How wonderful, to go to the same place every day, see the same people, and do the same, structured, repetitive work. I envisioned myself learning how to make a casserole, the kind with a can of mushroom soup in it. I dreamed of the suburban nightmare.

But what was "fulfillment" anyways? Wasn't it a myth? Wasn't everyone just accepting of the general unsatisfactory nature of life? Was there ever really going to be a job or a life that I liked more than this? Maybe the grass really was greenest in Hollywood, even if it was just all special effects that made it seem that way.

I went to work on a project where the director hated me. He told me that he hated me. He had these long bony fingers that he would poke in my face, and tell me that I was a terrible actor and that the producers forced him to hire me. During read-throughs, when all my castmates sat at a round table going over the script, he made me sit on the floor.

"Like a dog," he said. "You don't deserve to sit with this talented group of artists."

I sat on the floor, saying nothing and suspecting that was where I deserved to be, anyway. My silent tears fell and wrinkled up the pages of my script.

Whether this was supposed to be motivational or some sort of creative exercise to toughen me up remains a mystery. In a small, windowless production room filled with script revisions and old coffee cups, I quietly begged the producers to fire me. At least allow me quit. They wouldn't let me out of my contract. They claimed it would get better, his anger would burn itself out. So, I trudged through work, heaving over the toilet bowl at 6 a.m. as the driver knocked at my hotel room door, ready to take me to set where my boss called me an undeserving hack and pointed those long gray fingers. When we wrapped the show, I got so sick I couldn't get out of bed for three weeks. The cruelty finally over, my body throbbed with fever, shame, and unresolved anger. I just needed another job to get over it. Hair of the dog.

My friends didn't notice how broken and disconnected I was becoming. I was an actor, after all, specializing in the facade. A sane-looking person looked back at me from the mirror and I wondered how I could look so normal. It was surprising that my face wasn't in jagged pieces and that my arms were still connected to my body. They didn't feel attached. I went on another shoot, slept with the assistant to a Baldwin brother, and felt more broken than ever. I walked like a zombie through my life and didn't question what came next. More of the same came next, of course. I went to parties and talked about how good the script was for the new Russell Crowe movie. I pretended it wasn't killing me.

The passion beneath the passion

Desperate for a reprieve from my own darkness, I once again fell in love with my costar, so I could walk around in the blinding love glow. We met for rehearsals, and within the first three minutes I would have died for him. I loved him with the type of force generally reserved for planets that are collapsing in on themselves; it was unreasonable to assume any human could survive it. My love for Michael was reciprocated on about a ¾ scale, which proved an acceptable ratio for me at the time. I immediately broke up with my current boyfriend with a quick and unceremonious phone call. I would have texted him had that been a thing back then. My blissed-out love state made me completely numb to the pain that I caused while plummeting joyfully into my new relationship.

Michael was tall and willowy and even though men aren't supposed to be willowy it looked mighty fine on him. He seemed darkly fragile and just broken enough to be relentlessly attractive. Never one to be thwarted by minor details, I persevered even though my new boyfriend had just separated from his wife, was nine years older than me and was mourning the recent death of his mother. I decided that all could be overcome, even the fact that I was clearly more in love than he was. He just needed time, that was all. Gigantic red flags flapped in my face but I slapped them away and proceeded to coach him, word by tortured word, into professing his love for me.

Michael did some acting, but really he was a writer. He was introspective and emotional, and had wild hair—all important attributes for a writer. He was committed to his writing process, sitting alone in the apartment he rented over someone's garage, tapping away during his designated writing hours. This was a new concept to me and I was slightly baffled by the idea that anyone had working hours that didn't involve being away on location. Most of my friends were available to hang out whenever we saw fit, because (being generous) an actor's schedule is non-traditional or (being less generous and more realistic) pretty much everyone I hung out with was chronically underemployed. The idea that Michael was unavailable at 11am on a Thursday made him even more exotic and desirable. I had such respect for this dedication that I accepted being kicked out of his apartment so that he could write.

Writing had always been an important part of my life but it was something that gushed forth of its own volition. It was an unruly creative geyser that would simply overtake me—often in the middle of the night when an idea would send me scrambling out of bed, searching for a pen like it would save my life. This was not something that could be funneled into the hours between 8 a.m. and 1 p.m. My journals and attempts at fiction and screenplays had piled up over the years, lingering under my bed, surrounded by lost socks, and firmly categorized as a silly hobby. This was the first time I had seen someone take it so seriously.

Michael was a member of the Writers Guild of America, and they would hold events around town that would be of interest to their members. He invited me to a screening of the pilot for a new television series and a talk by the creators.

The place was crammed with writers, yet I felt a surprising element of comfort there. No one cared about what you were wearing or who you showed up with. It was an electric creative environment and there was a substance to the air that I normally found sucked out of the events I attended. We found two seats in the audience and the lights dimmed. The music swelled and it sounded like a movie.

"Seriously? This is for TV?" I whispered.

The opening credits of *The West Wing* came on. It was like nothing I had ever seen. It was fast-paced and funny and smart. I was far from being a political junkie, but the show still captivated me. I was interested in those characters and longed to know more about them. This was what great writing could do. Mere words, just some letters strung together with some negative space in between, could create something truly thrilling. Beauty and compassion and agony and life—it could all be created with nothing more than a pen and a healthy dose of commitment. There was great writing in the world; you just needed to work for it. It startled me that my first thought was not, *I want to be on that show*, it was, *I want to write like that.*

After we watched a few scenes from *The West Wing*, Aaron Sorkin took the stage accompanied by heartfelt applause. I had clapped a lot in my life. I had clapped for actors in small, dark, poorly attended theaters and I had clapped while sitting on the floor in someone's living room after a Pepsi commercial during the Super Bowl. I had clapped out of respect for their effort and enthusiasm. I had clapped out of obligation because other people were watching and needing me to clap. I had clapped to clear the air of neediness. I had clapped so that others could relax and breathe again.

This clapping was different. I had to physically remind myself to stay in my seat and not run to the stage and embrace the man who had just cracked open my world. Sorkin talked about his writing process and inspiration. He talked about the characters like they were friends of his. And I thought, *yes, I get this.* When actors sat around to talk process, I picked at my cuticles for a while and then went to get a Jamba Juice. This gave me goose bumps and I scribbled notes on the back of a flier because Aaron Sorkin was speaking to my soul.

Suddenly, a light was shone on everything that I had suspected was missing. I had no enthusiasm for acting. I had just assumed I was a passionless person. But, creating a whole universe, pouring your heart out on the page, finding the exact right word and putting it in the exact right order with the breaks in the right place; that was electrifying. Not being a puppet to someone else's vision, someone else's shot, someone else's editing whims. Words burrowed into my guts and made a home there. Words lightened my heart and jolted my soul.

But there was a problem. I was not a writer. I was an actor. It was too late for me to be anything else. So, I shelved the thought and buried that fire and distracted myself with my all-encompassing relationship.

My love proved to be somewhat contagious; Michael caught it and we became the kind of intense couple who sicken the world at large. He spent hours stroking my hair, outlining my birthmarks, calling them, "the places where the artist signed his masterpiece." We had our own secret language and fourteen nicknames for each other and never included anyone else in our plans. We'd spend long summer afternoons with the curtains drawn to shut out the world, sitting on the floor listening to Bob

Dylan, and he'd tell me which songs were important and I'd believe him. We lay draped across each other at 3 p.m. on a Wednesday like we might have been victims of a carbon monoxide leak.

When Michael went to the gym, my eyes wandered to the top shelf of his closet, wondering if any of the bound books he kept stashed away were his wedding album. Was there any sign of apprehension in his face? Were there candid photos of him nervously fidgeting with cufflinks and a tie that felt too tight? Were there people in the pews thinking that he would be better off marrying a petite Canadian? And what about her? The faceless woman whose voice I tried to ignore on his answering machine when she called about lawyers and paperwork, was she apprehensive? Even more horribly, maybe they were both just thrilled to be together. Maybe they were as thrilled as I was, as I found myself in his bed with his old t-shirt pressed to my cheek. When I left for a location shoot in Canada, I took that shirt with me, and for the first time, I didn't search for an on-set playmate.

When the shoot wrapped and I went back to L.A., Michael was waiting at my house. The second I saw his face I knew. He threw words at me, and I only caught some of them.

"...not even divorced yet..."

"...too much...too fast..."

"...I love you, but..."

My eyes glazed over. All those movie scenes of women being left flashed in my head. All the wailing and falling to the knees. All the false claims of pregnancy or threats to fling herself into a rushing river. I remember very little of my actual reaction, but I remember wishing that I drank. Michael gave me a hug and looked deeply into my eyes.

"Call me if you need anything."

If I needed anything other than him, I suppose. The next day, with a puffy, tear-stained face and a credit card, I stumbled into an electronics store and bought a gigantic TV to console myself. I named the television Michael, in honor of my lost love. I dared the flickering screen to distract me from my agony and immersed myself in a world of Sex and the City reruns.

Just to make the grief even more excruciating, after a few weeks Michael and I would pick at the scab and start talking again. We'd get back together, try to make it work, and only succeed at destroying each other a few more times over the next year or so. I'd leave, not trusting him; the next time he'd leave, feeling trapped. Then we'd both apologize and recommit to figuring out how to be together. The love and misery seemed inexorably entwined. For a while, that felt tolerable. Maybe that was just another concession of life, another thing that should be endured, because it looked so lovely on the outside.

We ended up walking away, both of us with claw marks on our hearts, since being together was slightly more painful than being apart. I will always be so grateful to him for many things. Everyone should fall so recklessly in love and have their heart shattered into bloody splinters. Everyone should sit sobbing in the driveway, watching their beloved drive away for the last time, just to know what that essential human experience is like. Because until you are truly broken, you'll never fully understand your ability to put yourself back together again. Most of all I'm grateful because he taught me what it was to be a real writer. He showed me how to use authentic passion and discipline to bring out the best in myself.

Michael broke my heart and those cracks let in the light and set me free. He freed me to find all the beauty that came next. He freed me to embrace the writing that was my true purpose all along. Could I have written in L.A.? Sure, but I wouldn't have. In Los Angeles, I was an actor. It had been stamped on my forehead at age four and I didn't have the strength to do the amount of reinventing that would be required of me. I had almost eighteen years of career precedent behind me. There was no starting over there.

You're never as great or as terrible as they say you are

"It's a spoof. A mash-up of *Star Wars* and *Shakespeare in Love*."

"Well, that sounds...odd."

But Joey was a friend and he was asking a favor. With this group of friends, weekends would often be full of student films, amateur productions, and guerilla filmmaking. Generally, I found reasons to be "busy," choosing to stay home instead of running from the cops because we were filming in a restaurant where we didn't have a permit. But the script for this short film was actually really good, and I'd get to wear Princess Leia hair buns. I wasn't currently employed and had no plans for the week and so I agreed.

George Lucas in Love ended up going viral, at a time when going viral meant that everyone handed everyone else a VHS tape of the movie. When something like that happens to an actor, you get calls. You get calls from people who want to tell you that you are fabulous. It's important not to believe them, because if you do, your life gets considerably more complicated.

Filming George Lucas in Love. With Martin Hynes.
PHOTO COURTESY OF JOSEPH LEVY.

I got a call from the William Morris Agency. Everyone said I should listen to those kinds of calls. William Morris is one of the oldest and largest talent agencies and is incredibly well respected. They have represented everyone from Katherine Hepburn to Matt Damon and they wanted me. It was beyond flattering.

I had been changing agencies more often than I changed boyfriends, always thinking there was someone out there who was better. I tended towards the boutique agencies. (Remember how if you talk about a role being small you have to say how pivotal it is? It's the same deal with agencies; you call the small ones "boutique" so that they seem exclusive.) I was wooed away from my boutique agent and signed with William Morris. My resume was reprinted on fancy paper stock with their striking letterhead. I had my headshots retaken, with my slightly smug smiling face beaming at the fact that the WM logo would be printed along the bottom.

William Morris thought that the popularity of the short film earned me the right to be "offer only." I should skip the auditions because filmmakers should already know who I was and should just give me work. They were sure that Hollywood would be clamoring for the girl in the the hair buns, so my agent's responsibility would shift from getting me auditions to "fielding offers."

However, my field was proving to be a pretty lonely place. I had been in some popular films but this offer-only move was not warranted. It was a classic little-fish-in-big-pond situation. When the offers were not pouring in, I got that awkward call from my big-time agent. The call where they say that it's just not working out. That I was not the right fit for them. That I might be better suited at a different agency. It's the call where I got off the phone and cried, hating myself a little more and feeling like a failure, feeling like that elusive "success" had been there just within my grasp and had slipped away.

Like a flickering flame that I was inexplicably drawn to, I began again, crawling back to the boutique agencies, telling them I made a mistake and petitioning for representation. They had a need in their roster of actors for an "ethnic type," so I was back in. Right back where I was. Begging to do a job I wasn't sure I wanted anymore, but feeling too scared to know what other options existed. I just waited for the inevitable burn.

CHAPTER 15

Love. No Quotation Marks.

had done the Hollywood dating thing. Men with private planes had taken me to restaurants that boasted Michelin stars. We had our photos printed in tabloids, more because of him than me. We had done the hand-in-hand walk down the red carpet. But somehow it was not a surprise that the relationship with the true love of my life began with a kiss next to a dumpster in a Ralph's grocery store parking lot.

When I was seventeen, I did a movie called *The Beautician and the Beast*, and became friends with the actor who played my boyfriend. Tim had just graduated from the University of Southern California theater school and kissing me on screen was his first job out of college. Kissing me off screen was not technically part of the job, but it came with the territory. Eventually we realized that it wasn't a relationship suitable for real life, so we morphed into friends.

I quickly joined Tim's large social group, all film and theater people from USC. Most of them had stayed in L.A. after graduation to pursue some branch of the entertainment industry, with varying levels of success. It was the kind of crowd where birthday parties and New Year's Eve celebrations would inevitably include an enthusiastic group rendition of "Summer Nights" from *Grease*, complete with complex choreography and slightly cutting post-performance critiques.

Tim's roommate, Jeremy, worked in management for a group of theaters in L.A. This fact alone made us utterly incompatible. I hated theater. With the promise of a good meal afterwards, I could be reluctantly dragged to go see it, but I was completely terrified to do it. Over the four years of our friendship, Jeremy had tried to convince me to do several plays for his company; he was particularly insistent when they were trying to cast the role of Juliet. I tried to be polite in my repeated rejections of his offers, but kept wondering why this guy had no clue who I was as a person.

The fact that an actor can be afraid of theater might seem confusing, but doing a film is nothing like a live performance. Yes, there are a lot of people on set, but none of them are really looking at you. They are looking to see if the light is falling on you in the right way. Or if your hair is curling in the right places. Or if you lifted up that glass on the same line that you did when we shot from the other angle. They are watching details of you; they are not watching you as a whole person. Thus, film acting was never stressful, it felt intimate—like the director and my fellow actors were the only ones in the room.

A dauntingly beautiful makeup artist named Kelley was part of this new group of friends and we quickly bonded over the fact that we each had a parade of disappointing relationships. Kelley and I decided to get tattoos that illustrated, in a stylish and sophisticated manor, the concept of, "Fuck you, men." It seemed a good time to declare our feminine independence, since I had finally given up on my latest boyfriend, who had a frustrating habit of telling me he was out with the guys when he was really out banging either the girl from *The Real World* or the girl from *Survivor.*

Kelley and I sat in the Barnes & Noble going through symbol encyclopedias and tracing the ones that best signified our autonomy. We chose a tattoo shop in Venice Beach because it was the first one whose neon "Open" sign was lit, and it didn't look like the kind of place were our chances of contracting tetanus were unreasonably high.

While the tattoo guy traced the Celtic knot onto my ankle, I stared at photos of bare-breasted mermaids and skulls biting roses and pretended it didn't hurt like hell. It only took ten minutes for my tiny tat but I was proud of it. It was the most controversial thing I had ever done, aside from reading *Fear of Flying* when I was sixteen.

A tattoo is defiant by definition, but as an actor, it was a particularly insubordinate choice. Every image decision I had ever made, from eyebrow shaping to daily food selections, had been with the initial thought of my career. What would make me the most visually acceptable for the widest variety of roles? Would a particular hairstyle limit me for period pieces? If I was a little more muscular could I be considered for action films? My body had been a time-share situation since I was four years old. This tattoo ruined me as a blank canvas.

With this decision, I had claimed my body as belonging to me first. It felt bold and although I was seemingly staking my independence from men, it was really more of an independence from the ownership of the film industry. For the first time ever, my career was taking a backseat to my life.

The next day, I wanted to show off my new ink. The first person I showed it to was my friend Jeremy. We had recently become closer, due to the fact that my parents were in the process of separating. His parents had separated when he was in his late teens so he could relate and advise me on how to navigate these painful waters.

"I've been there." He'd say that phrase, that has no practical purpose, but offers a world of comfort.

My parents' marriage crumpled into a heap of lies and neglect. I felt responsible. This is a typical kid reaction to parents separating but I had evidence to back up the claim. When I ran into an old set tutor of mine at a shopping mall, she asked about my parents. I lowered my eyes and shoved my hands in my pockets and told her they were separating.

"Oh, I'm sorry," she said. "But, in a lot of ways, that makes sense. You know, because of you. All that traveling your mom had to do with you for work. It's tough on a family."

I remember this moment even more vividly than the moment that my parents told me they were separating. It felt like being hit in the temple with a pick axe. Someone's white Keds squeaked by along the bleached tile floors and nearly blew out my eardrums. The bright lighting of the Macy's makeup counter sliced through my eyeballs and I had to hold on to a rack of discounted necklaces to stay on my feet. It actually *had* been my fault. I had destroyed my family.

People would tell me that divorce is common among the parents of child actors, as if this might be a comforting fact. It was true that my mom had been dedicated to my career from the beginning. She dropped everything on a moment's notice to go on location while my dad ran his business at home. Sure, flying to Rome to visit his wife and daughter for a week might have sounded exotic, but we could all have benefited from more quantity over quality. Apparently, the break-up of their marriage was a *fait accompli*—another hidden cost in this acting career contract I had signed when I was four.

For seventeen years, I had been an inevitable wedge, taking my mother away and leaving my father with nothing more than a few good stories to tell at the golf club. I felt guilty and angry with both my parents for not stopping it sooner, for not putting our family first, for not getting a chaperone to travel with me so that they could care for their marriage. Maybe if my mother had stopped all the gallivanting with me, and if my father had stepped up and put his foot down. Maybe if I had had rules and boundaries and someone had thought about this career of mine in a larger context, things could have been different. There were consequences to being a child actor that went beyond the now seemingly minor seeming issue of being repeatedly thrown out of high schools.

I was pissed off. My career, my relationships, and now my family—they were all unraveling around me and there was nothing I could do but stand there in the mall, clutching a rack of cheap necklaces, feeling completely responsible and completely helpless at the same time. Once again

I was a passive participant in my own life. I went home and punched the tile walls in my shower until my knuckles bled.

For the first time I understood the emotion behind the teary-eyed teenaged girls that approached me and wanted to talk about *Mrs. Doubtfire* and how it helped them through their parents' break up. Divorce was rarely dealt with realistically in the media and it was groundbreaking that that the film didn't throw in a bullshit Hollywood reconciliation at the end. My angry character Lydia meant something to these kids of divorce, which I only truly understood after being wounded by separation myself. I always defended Lydia when people said she was mean, because I loved her and really felt that she was just misunderstood and hurt. After my parents separated, I understood her emotion on an even deeper level. I wish I hadn't.

My friend Jeremy and I would talk about how painful it was, even in the pseudo-adulthood of your early twenties, to watch the dissolution of your parents' marriage. It might be easier than when you are a little kid, but then again, when you are a little kid, your parents don't ask you for dating advice, so, in some ways it was worse. Worse or not, it was agonizing and Jeremy got that. At a Super Bowl party at a friend's house, we sat on the floor in a corner and he listened to me. He actually listened. *While there was football on.*

✳✳✳✳✳

Kelley and I decided to cook dinner. This was huge. We didn't cook. It was just about as daring as saying we would skydive into a swimming pool. We figured someone else should witness this monumental event, so we invited ourselves over to Tim and Jeremy's apartment where we would cook for the boys, drink wine, and stay overnight so that we weren't driving. There was nothing illicit about it; the four of us were close friends—crashing at one another's places was not unheard of.

I had attempted to sleep on the couch, but the crick in my neck had become unbearable. So, emboldened by one and a half glasses of wine, I climbed into Jeremy's bed. Not to make myself sound too innocent in the whole thing; I had admittedly begun to see him differently. He was no longer merely the sidekick of my former hook-up buddy. He was a man who related to me, listened to me, and made me laugh the kind of laugh where it's hard to catch your breath and you have to put your hand up on your chest. I started to notice how smart he was. He was scary smart, actually. But it was balanced out by the fact that he made adorable blunders like saying "drownding" and never remembered if an albatross was a bird or a fish.

So, I ended up in his bed where we talked and shushed each other's laughter. I kissed him first because I knew he never would, since the roommate code dictated that Tim had dibs on me. The whole night we kissed and talked and nothing more. And that's when I knew it was something real. It was enough to just be next to him and feel him breathe in the stillness that only comes at 3 a.m. after you've been peeling open your heart for the past four hours. I draped my arm over his chest and rested my hand lightly on his neck. That was all I needed. Everything beneath my skin melted into a warm swirl.

The next morning we snuck out of the apartment to hide our guilty consciences from Tim and Kelley and he walked me to my car, which was parked next door in the 24-hour grocery store parking lot. Behind the grocery store dumpster, he kissed me, a real Hollywood kiss—had it not been for the dumpster. At home, I curled up on the couch, with swollen lips and a sleep-deprivation headache and wondered what the hell I was getting myself into. Another boy was not going to fix anything. My parents were proof that this film life could destroy any relationship it touched.

Within four hours, Jeremy called me for a real date. I was confused and exhausted by the night of enamored gazing, plus there was the looming fear that Tim would kill me for dating his roommate, but I was still intrigued. Could there really be something here, with this guy who had been just a friend for more than four years? This guy who I don't remember meeting, but who I always remember being there?

While getting ready for our first date, I made a list of things we could talk about and slipped it in my back pocket. There had never been a problem with conversation with Jeremy but spending hours outlining the contours of someone always changed the dynamics. I drove to the restaurant to meet him and prove my status as an independent woman and make the statement that things hadn't changed that much. Dinner was the most fun two hours I ever spent with someone and the list stayed in my back pocket.

We moved on to the next part of the date, the theater portion. We were going to see a play at the Mark Taper Forum, the smaller of the two venues that Jeremy worked at. Before the play began, he wanted to show me the Ahmanson theater, which was dark, meaning there was no current production there. He swaggered around as we went backstage, past all the costumes and lights, which were all much larger and grander than the ones I was used to working with for film. It was endearing to see him in his element, he was confident in a way that I never saw standing in line at a movie opening or at large group dinners at Hamburger Hamlet.

Jeremy took my hand to guide me through the darkened halls, lined with musty costumes and abandoned props. I kept wondering if he was going to sneak me into a dark corner and kiss me, passionately pushing me against the heavy ropes that lifted the curtains. It seemed there were endless numbers of romantic situations we could find ourselves in back here. We turned a corner. Suddenly, I was on stage. We had walked through the wings and there were two thousand empty seats, staring back at me, full of judgment and anger. Any hopes of romance drained out of me. I snapped my head to look over at him, terror in my eyes. He was so proud of himself and totally misread the look.

"Cool, right?"

I began hyperventilating. His face dropped.

He dealt with our first panic attack together quite well. He rubbed my back tried to make it better. I gasped and turned purple and tried to stop my hands from shaking. When I could finally breathe again, he helped me up off the floor as I wiped my nose on my sleeve. A guy inducing a panic attack on the first date is not a great sign, but it gave Jeremy a chance to do something absolutely heroic. He took my hand.

"Can you tell me what I can do to help you when that happens? Just so I know for next time?"

I knew at that moment that I was going to keep him.

In the past, I had always fallen for the latent possibilities I saw in someone. I loved what they could be, if I could only get my hands on them for a while. The battered and broken men, the ones that looked like they could have been set out on a folding table at a garage sale, were the ones that drew me in. I always hoped that once I shaved off a slice of my soul to close up the gaps, then I could glue them back together and make them whole. The more broken they were, the less broken I felt.

But Jeremy appeared to be a complete human person. He needed no mending, no saving. He didn't need me to prop him up and make him stable enough to stand on his own. He was just fine. It was both intriguing and disconcerting. What would I do with a man who was not a project? I was usually the one who swept in and made it all okay, I was the knight in shining armor. In past relationships, me and the shattered man that I had rescued would ride off into the sunset upon *my* horse. But, he didn't need that. He just wanted to love me. There was actually a delineation where I stopped and Jeremy began.

The beginning of our relationship involved some challenging moments, since I have read too many scripts and had too many tumultuous relationships with guys who thrived on drama. I was accustomed to having fights until dawn that culminated with me sleeping on the couch in my own house while some moron slept in my bed with my dogs. I tried to evoke such delicious drama with Jeremy, but he never bought into this idea of true love requiring sob-filled misery.

Nevertheless, I attempted to goad him. An itch would appear down in my soul that could only be scratched with a salty comment. A scowling glance. A roll of the eyes. There is always that really good fight in the movie, that zinger that accompanies the turn on the heel and strut out the door. Yet anytime I would try, Jeremy would refuse to play this dangerous game with me. The most he would give me was a calm look and a firm, "I love you. Please don't be mean to me."

This just made me want to kick him in the head. He was so right. So calm. So reasonable. He couldn't comprehend my desperate desire for him to hate me just a little; that is how the good love story always starts.

I wanted to leave a note that was vague, yet poetic. I wanted him to hear my voiceover reading the letter to him in a sad, yet sultry voice, and then he would run out into the rain and down the street yelling my name in a desperate, yet masculine way. I wanted him to catch me just before I was about to board a train and throw my baggage aside as if it were empty. I would be wearing a hat. As he grabbed me in an arched-back, bended-knee kiss, my chapeau would blow away and down the track.

To me, this narrow, black and white representation was real love. It was the only true love. If we didn't break up in the second act, how can we make up in the third and live happily ever after? Jeremy thought this was ridiculous. When I told him that we should break up so we can make up again, he looked at me like I had slain a cat with a kitchen knife. What was wrong with me? Why did I think movies were better than reality? Jeremy didn't think that life had to be like a movie to be good. There didn't need to be one dramatic, conflict-filled scene after another to make it all worthwhile and keep people's attention. He thought that I could stop worrying that the audience would get bored and walk out.

Even though I made so many mistakes, there was something there that was so significant and so different than anything else. My fear of a real relationship, a real commitment, made me try to set it on fire and watch it burn. But he wouldn't let me. He held me so close that his arms seemed to wrap around me twice, like he knew that was the only way I'd finally feel safe. He told me he loved the thing that was deep down, the thing that never changes and isn't defined by any label.

This was reassuring, because my label was about to get very murky.

The death rattle

As a final, desperate attempt to find happiness in the film industry, I

tried moving behind the camera. Perhaps I was just more of a crew type of person than a cast type of person. A friend had written a short film and he needed a producer. I didn't really know what I was doing, but I had spent my entire life on set and saw what the producers did: they did a little of everything.

It was a small project; the crew was working for the credit and experience rather than the money, which was perfect since we had none. We were quick and efficient because we couldn't afford to buy more film. Our actors were talented, and while I waited for the jealousy to well up inside, I never once envied their position on the other side of the lens. I ate orange Tic-Tacs without worrying that they would dye my tongue an unnatural color. I wore no makeup, my ugliest cut-off jeans, and a t-shirt with toy trucks on it. I went to work wearing my glasses and with my hair stringy and unwashed. No one cared how I looked as long as the shots were running smoothly and I broke us for lunch on time. Not being an actor was downright luxurious.

When the shoot was complete, I fell into my predictable post-wrap depression. *What the hell do I do now?* Everything had gone well, but that gaping hole was still there. It didn't take long to realize that what was wonderful about that experience wasn't the craft of filmmaking; it was the fact that I was being productive and not being an actor. I loved being creative while having the freedom of not acting.

As we worked with the editor and finished the short film, we realized that our director of photography was even more talented than we thought. The film looked gorgeous and expensive. It was beautiful enough to get the film into a showcase at the Cannes Film Festival. We would not be competing but we would be shown in a smaller theater during the festival.

This "work trip" to Cannes was a perfect opportunity to show off to my shiny new boyfriend and invite him to come to France. It was also time to test drive Jeremy in more serious, off-road conditions. I had taken boyfriends to my work events before, and many of them failed spectacularly. They either:

* were starstruck and spent the evening stalking Mel Gibson
* were clingy and couldn't take care of themselves when I had to talk shop with someone
* pouted in the bathroom because I talked to my co-star too much (likely with good reason)
* took the open bar too seriously and then fell down
* met the producer and immediately launched into the pitch for the screenplay he was working on.

There were a plethora of ways a boyfriend could go wrong and it was time to make sure Jeremy had game. What better way than to throw him into an international film festival? It was sink-or-swim time, and he claimed to be up for the challenge.

Hotels in Cannes cost more than our entire film budget, and were booked months in advance. So, Jeremy and I spent a few days before the festival in Nice, a short train ride away, in a little family-owned hotel with tons of charm, no elevator, and a room that was only two feet wider than the bed. We wandered cobbled streets, ate mountains of cheese, and drank beautiful wine until we were bursting. Then we ate whatever we could find that was smothered in Nutella.

Jeremy and I took the train into Cannes for the festival and toured the sweet little beach town until the screening. My film was shown during the day and there were maybe a half dozen other people in the theater. With none of the glamour that you would associate with Cannes, it was kind of perfect. There was no "line" to be walked and none of the fancy-shmancy uncomfortable stuff. There was a party afterwards, under tents that were set up right next to the sea, where there was prerequisite chatting with film people.

Jeremy navigated the crowds with me, keeping a hand lightly on the small of my back to let me know he was still with me. He made easy conversation with a random collection of people and asked interesting questions. He was good. Very good. I watched him step up when I needed him and hold back when I didn't. When I gave him the "let's get out of here" look, he immediately whisked me off to the train station and back to our hotel.

We climbed the five flights of stairs to our tiny little room, and lay in bed listening to the clinking of silverware that wafted up from the café below. I tried to use my old high school French to translate the music that the street performers were crooning. The movie adrenaline (or was it anxiety?) finally dissipated, and every cell in my body relaxed. We held hands in the dark and fell asleep with the windows open.

CHAPTER 16

When Even Work Wasn't Working

After Cannes, we returned to normal life in L.A. Jeremy went back to his job at the theater and I went back to auditioning. The scripts all seemed to be painfully trivial contributions to the moronic roar of popular media. L.A. was enamored with the ditzy, the blonde, and the curvaceous, and my acting skills simply didn't stretch that far. I was tired of reading for the role of the overly sexualized tramp. I read the first and last ten pages of scripts while watching reality dating shows, and then I told my agent I didn't want to audition for it. Then I'd spend the evening crying in the bathtub, my tears mixing in with the French lavender bath salts that were supposed to bring me peace.

I wanted to be like those bath salts and quietly dissolve into nothingness, like I had never existed at all. If all the work dried up then no one could blame me for quitting. But I was working just enough for people to think that I still wanted it. I got a small role in a film with Christopher Walken. I signed the contract mostly because I was dying to know if his vocal intonations were as inexplicable in person. (I can't find this movie on his IMDB page or mine, so I'm not sure it even got released. By the way, his voice is truly inexplicable.)

We filmed in a strip club during the day, while the dancers who worked there were sleeping or taking care of their kids or attending law school. This was not a "funny" strip club like a place you go and giggle with your girlfriends on a dare. It was gross. Sad. Lonely.

During rehearsals, the director of photography was setting up the shot when his contact lens fell out. We all crouched to help him find it. Since strip clubs are not known for their ample lighting even in the daytime, we were crawling around with our faces just inches from the floor that was sticky from I don't want to know what. When we finally located the contact, he instinctively popped it in his mouth to wet it before placing it back in his eye. When he realized that he just picked up something from the floor of a strip club and put it in his mouth, he had the look of a man realizing he had just contracted hepatitis C.

I trudged to work, did my job, and went home. Even the on-set part was feeling lifeless. There was nothing peaceful or energizing to be found there. I became a clock-watcher, trying to calculate how long the next set up would take, what time we would wrap for the day. I became someone who sighed a lot. I'm sure many people feel empty in their work but when so many other people would have loved to be in my situation, it felt selfish to not just quit.

The shoot was so unsatisfactory that when they offered to write me into some additional scenes that they would be filming the next week, I lied and said I had a conflict. My pay rate for a day's work would have been enough to cover the mortgage for a couple of months and yet, I just couldn't bring myself to do it. Everyone on set was nice enough, and it's not as if my bank account was overflowing, but going back there sounded about as appealing as sticking my hand in a blender.

I tried to explain this to friends, hoping that they would admit to secretly feeling the exhausting emptiness. I asked if they felt like they were just sleepwalking from one thing to the next. I'd spent so long disguising myself as other people that I didn't even know if I'd recognize my actual self anymore. Everything felt like a costume. Did they feel like that, too? They looked at me and wrinkled up their foreheads and told me I was just having a bad day and made me eat a brownie sundae.

No one seemed to understand. Hope was what separated us the most profoundly. They had faith that a life in film would make them happy; they could see such a satisfying life just up ahead. They were committed to seeing this thing through and living their dreams. I couldn't remember what my dream ever was. I had seen that no amount of acting work would make me happy. So, I stopped trying to explain how I felt. I did what I did in interviews when honesty wasn't going to fly—I said what sounded right. My hair started falling out in clumps.

I booked a guest star appearance on a TV show called *Jack and Jill*. My character was in medical school and one of my scenes involved walking through the living room spouting medical terms while balancing a textbook on my head. I would love to place some blame for the disaster that followed on my terrible balance, since that seems consistent with my lack of bike riding skills and the whole falling-out-of-a-chair-and-breaking-my-back thing. However, it likely had more to do with the fact that I was not committed to the job in the slightest.

I didn't prepare as well as I could have and it showed. I went up. You know what that is; it's when fully functioning humans get brain freeze so badly that they are unable to remember their own name. It's amusing to watch, but for the person who is going up, it feels like a slow motion car crash. Things were going horribly awry and there was no way to stop it. Sure, my lines were medical terms that were complicated and walking with a textbook on your head is no picnic, but I should have been able to get a handle on it. Since I was four years old, I had been known as "One Take Jake" for my ability to come on set and nail it on the first try. But clearly, Jake wasn't there anymore.

Slowly and painfully we got through the scene and I could feel the crew alternatively cringing for me and wondering why I was not better prepared. I left the set, exhausted and humiliated and confused. Never once in my eighteen-year career had I gone up. This just wasn't something that happened to me. Why was it happening now?

When the show wrapped, I sat in my car on the Warner Brothers backlot and cried. This wasn't working. Even when I was working this wasn't working. It was like the past eighteen years had been for nothing. My life was not where I wanted it to be, but I had no idea what I wanted. I just knew I wanted out. When I turned the keys to start my car it made this terrible chugging sound and then it just clicked. Unfortunately, more crying and punching the steering wheel did nothing to fix the car. After wandering down a street that was supposed to look like a wild western town, I finally found a security guard in a golf cart to help me. I went sniffling back to my car and waited for my jumpstart.

I waited for someone to get me the hell out of there.

The wok

If I was looking for drama in my relationship, I was sure to find it. Before we upgraded our friendship, Jeremy had committed to a MBA program in Virginia. We had agreed to do the long distance relationship thing: he'd come back to visit and I would go down there for long weekends. It was only eighteen months, anyway.

But with his busy class schedule and my habit of going out every night, we didn't get to talk much. We emailed and I missed him, but the rest of my life just took over. I was not a good long-distance partner; my need for constant attention and reassurance was too strong. My career was making me unhappy and I was stagnant and lost. I still got dressed up and went to parties and tried to be young and fun and all the things people told me I was. My panic attacks persisted; the slightest trigger would completely possess my body and leave me gasping for air and on the edge of fainting.

I went to auditions but barely prepared for them. Although my dialogue would be memorized, I had no interest in finding the character or the emotion within the words. The self-sabotage was exquisite. But wasn't this just a bump in the road of my career? You didn't get divorced just because you had one little fight. I came to California in 1990 to be an actor. Wasn't I one? Wasn't this why I sold out to KFC when I was four years old? So that I could live in Hollywood and audition for bigger, better things to which I could sell out?

Besides, the idea of being a *former* child actor was more terrifying than anything. It scared me to think that I was going to end up like Baby Jane, or be laid out on a fainting couch somewhere, begging Mr. Demille for my close up. It never goes well for former child actors, does it? Don't we all OD on dirty sidewalks or try to reinvent ourselves in our thirties when we are no longer cute but can play the parents of cute new crop of child actors on a Fox Family sitcom? A former child actor was a tragic figure. A cautionary tale. That couldn't be me.

I bought a wok. That would make it better. This simpler life I longed for was possible in L.A., I just had to figure out how. I didn't know if I needed to buy a pot or a pan to learn to cook with, so I bought a wok because it kind of looked like a combination of both. This wok represented the new me, the self-sufficient grown up who could have a real, normal life. I made a grilled cheese sandwich in my wok. I could learn to be normal.

The Tuesday the World Blew Up

Little did I know that everyone was about to have their idea of normal altered forever. I remember not knowing what to call it. I referred to it as The Tuesday the World Blew Up. I tried to call Jeremy in Virginia but he was two hours from Washington D.C. so I couldn't get through. I'd just clutch the phone, the hollow recorded voice telling me over and over to please hang up and try my call again. I shivered on the couch with my dogs as we watched people jumping out of the Twin Towers.

I flew to Virginia on September 20th. I was desperate to see Jeremy and would have walked across the country if I had to. At the Los Angeles airport, soldiers stood on guard with guns. I prayed for John Malkovich to step out of the Duty Free Shop and take that Uzi apart and guarantee my safety. But he wasn't there. There was no such assurance for anyone. Behind a pillar, a flight attendant was trying to console her coworker who was sobbing about not wanting to get on the plane. It was suddenly very obvious that their jobs were not about offering passengers the whole can of Diet Coke.

Once on the plane, I took a Dramamine, eager for the drowsiness to take effect. The flight attendant woke me and flipped down my tray table to give me lunch. As I opened the napkin packet I noticed that they had provided me with a silverware fork and a plastic knife. I took another Dramamine, not wanting to think about what could be done with a butter knife.

The few days I was able to spend in Virginia were delightful. It was reassuring to be back in Jeremy's arms and the bucolic college town offered a break from obsessing about my career. We walked around the university that Thomas Jefferson built and I lost myself amongst musty stacks of library books and ornate Corinthian columns. There was so much peace to be found in Jeremy's one-bedroom basement apartment. We intertwined our fingers and I got reacquainted with this man, who reminded me that he loved me, regardless of any labels or job descriptions. It was just on the cusp of fall in Charlottesville and you could see the season changing by the hour. I had lived in L.A. for so long that I had forgotten about seasons. But here you could see that nature was continually reinventing itself.

On the flight home, the heaviness returned as the plane descended through the golden smog over L.A. The city was reeling from the terrorist attacks. L.A. feels a certain kinship with New York that I am not confident is reciprocated. Los Angeles is like the ditzy cheerleader younger sister who is constantly searching for approval from the all-black-wearing, don't-give-a-fuck-older sister who is actually really embarrassed to have any association at all.

The film studios were on high terrorism alert because al-Qaeda must care about the entertainment industry. I went to auditions and opened my purse, offering it up for bomb dogs to sniff. Men crawled under my car with little mirrors, searching for explosives. One panicked thought consistently raged through my head: *I don't want to die doing this job.* Friends of mine would gladly have their lives end on the Twentieth Century Fox backlot, in front of those fake New York street brownstones, but I always kind of wanted to be a goat farmer. If I was going to die I wanted it to be in the fresh air surrounded by animals and fields of wheat. I didn't want there to be a blurb in the Associated Press about how I perished going to a screen test for *Boston Legal.*

Many people made life changes in the wake of this staggering tragedy. When the end of the world felt imminent, it offered justification to do something people would think I was crazy for. I wanted to build a new life. I hadn't the faintest idea what that life should look like, or even who I actually was. All I knew was that I felt like an empty shell, with just a few grains of dry sand rattling around inside. I wanted to talk about what was on sale at the grocery store and have a hobby that didn't involve buying a movie ticket. I wanted a relationship I was not willing to abandon in exchange for making out with my co-star. I didn't want my worth to be based on who I had worked with when I was fourteen years old. Everything and everyone could be dropped at a moment's notice to go to Europe for three months to film something. I wanted to be tied down. Needed. Responsible.

It occurred to me that I could leave. Leave L.A., leave movies and just do something else. It was a revelation, like the prisoner realizing that the cell door had never been locked. I could just choose to be done. Couldn't I? Didn't people change jobs? But it's not like I had my engineering degree to fall back on. What was I going to do? I had always been too busy working to come up with a backup plan.

I told a friend that I was thinking of retiring from acting. Maybe I'd move away. Start over. He laughed at me.

"It's just a phase, it'll get better. This is what you do—you get restless and want something new. But you're living the dream, baby. Why would you give all that up? And for what?"

I didn't know. But I kept dreaming about airplanes.

"Welcome home"

Jeremy was getting his MBA in Virginia and I was...well, I had no idea what I was doing other than having a complete breakdown, but it couldn't happen in L.A. anymore. It had to be possible to escape the centrifugal pull of Los Angeles, although I had never seen it happen. A few of my friends had been talking about leaving for years. One had always wanted to be a teacher and would talk wistfully about how much he wanted to stand in front of a chalkboard and get middle-schoolers excited about reading *Animal Farm*. But then he would get a call for a job. The sparkling film industry with its plentiful bankroll kept him in the gravitational field. My emotional state had the fortitude of a twig, so it seemed unlikely that I would be the one who had the strength to say no and really mean it.

Absence does not make producers' hearts grow fonder and I worried that this was a huge mistake. But spinning my wheels wasn't fun anymore. This ungrounded, unfocused life was exhausting. At twenty-two, I was, quite simply, too old for this shit. It was time to fling myself into the dark, hoping that this reckless act, finally, would make me feel alive.

There was a problem. I had lived in a bubble for much of my life thus far and there was little evidence that I was equipped for regular life. There were things you learn while growing up that had been missed while hopping from school trailer to school trailer, from country to country. I couldn't convert measurements to metric, for example. I was a terrible speller who couldn't ride a bike well. I didn't know what it meant to sauté something. I didn't know that a car could be paid for in monthly installments and that laundry should be separated into like colors. I didn't know the difference between Catholics and Protestants or that college football had different rules than professional football. The common sense that I possessed was restricted to the uncommon life that I had been leading. Knowing exactly how many steps it would take me to get to a mark on the floor or which syllables to emphasize while doing an Eastern European accent was not exactly practical.

Money was also something that had to be considered. I was abandoning the only thing that I was qualified to do, which happened to be fairly lucrative, when it went well. My financial plan had never been savvy; it was simply to save as much as I could while assuming that I'd get another job before it all ran out. Since money had never been the rationale behind the job, it seemed ridiculous for it to be the reason to stay. I had a small amount saved, but this was far from a set-for-life situation. With the naïve optimism and blind faith that only a twenty-two-year-old can have, I just figured that it would all be okay and it would work out somehow. I wasn't proud. I could be broke and eat Ramen noodles—except for the fact that I didn't know how to cook them.

I told my friends, family, and agent that I was leaving L.A. My parents covered their surprise well and said I should do whatever I wanted. Most people figured that it was a bluff and predicted that I'd be back sitting in a Paramount studios casting office within ninety days. I was tempted to agree with them. It was comforting to know that whatever happened, it would all still be there. L.A. would remain its Botox-injected, unchanging self, and I could come back and pick up where I left off; dating wanna-be actors and reading over-written scripts.

I was also throwing myself headfirst into a relationship that for all intents and purposes was about six months old. Sure, we had been friends for four years before that, but this new version of us as a couple was barely old enough to eat solid foods. We were still working out the kinks of melding together two lives and two very different personalities. I had always jumped from one boy to another, enjoying just the early parts of the relationship, when it looks the way it does in the movies. Now, I'd be committing to the monotonous parts that rarely show up on film. It's hard to sign up for the grocery shopping that is not in the form of a fun montage with peppy music and playful food fights. A real relationship involves gastrointestinal issues and passive aggressive attempts to get the other person to take down the Christmas tree. If you see those unsavory parts in a movie, it just means that there is either an affair or a divorce coming. Probably both. But if there was anyone who I wanted to go to the grocery store with, it was Jeremy. More than anything else in my life, he felt like home.

I rented out my house and packed all my furniture into the garage. I collected my actor's union t-shirts and jackets from various films and shoved them in a giant plastic tub. I didn't know much about where I was moving to, but I figured wearing an *Independence Day* crew jacket in central Virginia was not a good way to blend in. I packed one suitcase of clothes and another of books and figured that was all I needed for my new life. Maybe intentionally losing everything was the best way to find something meaningful.

My friends were so convinced this was temporary that they mostly said, "Bye, we'll see you soon." Someone joked that I'd be barefoot and pregnant in some hillbilly kitchen in no time. I handed over my house keys to the renter and sobbed as I fed the dogs drugged spoonfuls of peanut butter and loaded them into the cargo hold of a plane. On the cross-country flight, I put the blanket over my head and convinced myself that this was not career suicide. It was a break from films. Not a break-up. Eventually, maybe I would realize that I really was an actor who couldn't live without films and I would make my triumphant return. The return of the ethnic girl.

At the Dulles Airport in Washington, DC, the dogs and I stumbled into our new lives. We were all equally traumatized by our cross-country flight, but as we saw Jeremy waiting for us, our hearts settled. The dogs slowly wagged their sedated tails as they sniffed his face, and I managed a tired yet deep smile that seemed to come up from my toenails.

"Welcome home," he said.

I felt it. From that first moment, everything behind me was truly the past; the slate had been wiped clean. My life wasn't about L.A. and being an actor anymore. I was not sure what it was about, but I knew it wasn't about that. Doubts still lingered in the back of my mind, but it was all covered with this blanket of peace. If you had just ruined your life, wouldn't you feel like you just ruined your life? Wouldn't you look behind you and see it all ablaze like some apocalyptic nightmare?

It didn't feel like that.

It felt like we were finally home.

CHAPTER 17

We Do It Different
Round These Parts

When I moved to Virginia, being out in public became much easier. There were, I believe, three main reasons for this.

1. People are polite. They considered it rude to interrupt dinner simply to inform me that I was on cable last night.
2. People don't really care. They had interests other than movies. I might have been hanging out with a guy who just got back from building schools in Haiti, a chef who was nominated for a James Beard award or Thomas Jefferson's five-times-great-grandson.
3. People who are legitimately famous live here. If someone really was stealing glances in my general direction, chances were good that Sissy Spacek, John Grisham, or Dave Matthews was behind me.

I settled into our nerdy, hippie college town and it suited me. There was an annual festival celebrating books and another celebrating vegetarianism/stray dog rescue. There were seasons, glorious seasons, a full four of them. It was not just fire season, pilot season, earthquake season, and awards season, either. These were real seasons that demanded a change of wardrobe.

The place was also a writer's paradise. There were almost more used bookstores than there were drunken freshman. Writers from Edgar Allan Poe to William Faulkner had chosen this place, in the shadows of the Blue Ridge Mountains, to find themselves and lose themselves and write it all down.

Our Charlottesville social circle consisted of people with far more degrees than I, which admittedly, was not much of an accomplishment. The last thing I had graduated from was a two-day class on producing short films from The Learning Annex. It did come with a diploma though, which I framed, since it was my first since 8th grade. Jeremy's cohorts were all MBAs-in-training, the classic polo-shirt wearing, educational elite that I feared would rain their judgments down on my high school dropout self.

Most of them didn't. A couple of them did. Generally, I got a lot of questions about why on earth I would leave acting. I was clearly an outsider and there were times I wondered if I was not better off in the environment I had just left. In L.A. no one scoffed at a high school dropout. It was a badge of honor; a metaphorical middle finger salute to the establishment. It indicated that you were such a brilliant artist that nothing so inconvenient as a formal education could hold you back. Here, people heard I hadn't graduated from high school and they looked like they wanted to contribute to some sort of fund.

I bought a cookbook and made veggie stir-fry in the wok I had brought in my suitcase. I managed our bills, clipped coupons and delivered our rent check to the landlord on time. I learned how to use the coin-operated laundry facilities that were down the hall from our apartment, and usually got the stuff out of the washer before a college kid threw our clothes on the linty laundry room floor. I did normal. And I found a staggering beauty in all of it. This was the real life that I had once scoffed at while sitting in coffee shops with my actor roommates? What had I been so afraid of?

I obsessed over those multiple-choice career quizzes. They unfailingly told me that I was an artist—usually an actor. This was not reassuring. It made me wonder about the chicken and the egg-ness of it all. Was I simply born to be an actor? Or had my experience crafted my personality so strongly that every multiple-choice test was forced to come to the same conclusion?

The MBA program had a "Partner's Association" organized to boost the morale of the lonely mate of the exhausted graduate student. These women (male partners didn't seem to join) were very kind, but seemed to be from another planet than me. Many of them had kids and threw dinner parties that included a soup course and they decorated their homes using the rule of threes. They made New York-style cheesecake using the recipe on the back of the Philadelphia cream cheese container. They didn't exactly know what to do with a broken-down former actor recovering from an eighteen-year career. I tried to politely extricate myself from the tennis parties, book clubs and the cookie swaps. Besides, I was a girlfriend of nine months, decidedly not a wife. Along with the complete abandonment of my entire life, career and identity, that level of commitment made my throat tighten.

✳ ✳ ✳ ✳ ✳

As I tried to branch out from the graduate school world and make my own friends, I faced a surprising problem; I was not quite famous enough. You wouldn't think this would be a problem for someone who leaves L.A. and doesn't want to be an actor, but it makes things awkward.

I was not rightfully famous. It's not like when I walked in a room, everyone knew who I was. They were more likely to squint at me and wonder if we went to high school together. I considered this to be a massive blessing; however, it's tricky when you are beginning to be friends with someone. There was this period of psychological stress, wondering if they knew I used to be an actor, either by recognizing me or hearing it though someone else. If they already knew and I told them I was an actor, then I looked like a self-obsessed asshole. Because really, what kind of regular person meets a new friend and announces what their job *used* to be? Can you imagine? "Hey, I just wanted to mention, just to get it out there, that when I was eighteen, I worked at The Olive Garden. I hope that doesn't make things weird now."

So, when I tried to make new friends by taking pottery classes filled with newly divorced ladies, or agreeing to be a judge in the neighborhood Halloween pumpkin carving contest, I just wouldn't say anything about it. Then I seemed sketchy and suspicious because when my potential new friends asked about my childhood or where I went to school, I looked as if I would rather bolt from the room than discuss my past. A friend once told me that I behaved like someone who had killed her entire family and moved out of state.

Whenever I finally confessed to being a former actor just to explain my scattered history, it always involved stumbling over my words, staring at my own feet while red blotches crept slowly across my neck. Then, the nice women sitting across from me in Introduction to Quilting Techniques would ask why I left L.A, with an inevitable look of astonishment. I would stammer out my diatribe of, "I started when I was really young and I feel like there are other things in the world that I am interested in..." They would look as if they were hoping for a better story. "My eating disorder counselor recommended that I take some time off..." or "I had an affair with a famous actor and his wife had me blackballed from the industry..." Even my story of leaving L.A. felt like a colossal disappointment.

All this nervousness was well-founded; people were often thrown off balance by my past. They tended to respond as if I had just removed my jacket to reveal that I was actually a winged Pegasus. The next part would proceed in one of two ways:

Outcome #1—My potential new friend knew my films and felt embarrassed about that,

or,

Outcome #2—My potential new friend didn't know my films and felt embarrassed about that.

They apologized either way because they were nice southerners, then there would be this long silence. I knew what they were doing. They were trying to remember what the poster of that movie looked like, and then do one of those age progressions like you see on fliers of missing people and make it match up to the face sitting across from them. I'd just wait, watching that familiar movie-induced distance creep in, creating an opaque fog between us. Sometimes those friendships didn't go anywhere because apparently being friends with a former actor can be strange. I am not nearly that special, but some people seem to think, thanks to tabloid fantasy projections, that actors are fundamentally different from everyone else and can't possibly be quality friendship material. A few brave souls waded through the fog and reached out a hand, but more than once, I found myself grasping at nothing, all alone in the haze.

Not fitting in together

All around me, adult people were getting their lives sorted out in a calm and orderly fashion. They seemed to be following a path that had been nicely manicured and they didn't publicly weep at the mere thought of their future. It looked so nice. I decided to try to fit into this mold of the "educated adult." I vaguely thought about college, but with such a disastrous educational background, who would accept me?

The fact that I hadn't completed high school was something that haunted and shamed me. A GED could rid me of that particular insecurity and prove that I could have graduated high school had circumstances allowed. My lack of experience with standardized anything meant that I tended to freeze up during tests and even the thought of a Scantron form made me hyperventilate. But I needed to prove my worth beyond just being a film actor. At least I hoped there was worth there.

I took a GED prep class, which was held at an elementary school on the other side of town. The halls were decorated with hand tracings made to look like dinosaurs. I dodged little kids, struggling with backpacks bigger than they were and made my way to the strangely miniaturized bathroom with the foot pedal sinks and powdery green soap. I tried to remember if my elementary school was like this but I had absolutely no recollection of it.

My GED-prep classmates and I were riddled with the same insecurities; all of us were just hoping to have that piece of paper to prove that we were not complete failures at life. We all craved the same thing, a stamp of approval that told us that we were just as good as everyone else, even though our paths had not been the norm.

I liked my classmates. During breaks I hung out in the hallway and shared a bag of Doritos with a sixteen-year-old girl who sat near me. She was tired and her stringy hair wouldn't stay behind her ears, no matter how many times she tucked it back. The day before she had gone home after a double shift at the fast food place to find that her baby was inconsolable. It turned out that the neighbor, who had been watching him, hadn't bothered to change his diaper in more than twelve hours. My friend worried that she'd need to find some money to take him to the doctor to tend to the sores he had, since they didn't seem to be clearing up. Another guy had dropped out of high school to help with the family farm when his father was diagnosed with cancer. Someone else had just been released from juvenile hall. Since I didn't volunteer the information, no one asked why I was there and no one told me that I "looked like that girl." As we sat and went over workbooks of scientific equations, we all realized that we were not alone in not fitting in. There was a whole world of us, with our stories that made people cock their heads sideways at us.

Our teacher came to me the last day, holding the completion form for the prep class. It had some general demographic questions as well as questions about my experience of the program. She had looked over the form and wanted to make sure that I had checked the correct box for my annual income range for the previous year.

"Is this right, dear?" She asked, pointing to the top box.

"Oh. Yeah. It's right."

She looked at me with a questioning look on her face.

"I used to be an actor."

It was the first time I had said that. Using the past tense had never felt so profound. I was also pretty sure that would be the last time I would check the top box.

She smiled and patted my hand.

"Well, that's nice, darlin'. I just wanted to make sure that you understood the question."

She ensured that I had my #2 pencils and sent me off to the local high school to take the GED. There were maybe fifty of us, all gathered to take the seven-hour test and prove something to our parents, our friends, our former teachers and ourselves. We were armed with Red Bulls, granola bars, and frayed nerves. It was our chance to prove that we were just as good as people who had that high school diploma. Weren't we? We hoped we were, despite the surreptitious routes that had gotten us there. We filled in the bubbles completely.

When the test results came in the mail, I tucked them under my arm and locked myself in the bathroom. If I had failed, I didn't want to have to deal with that in front of my soon-to-be-MBA smarty-pants boyfriend. If I had failed it would mean that I really wasn't cut out for the real world, I wasn't smart enough to do anything but be an actor. If I had failed it would mean sucking it up, going back to L.A. and admitting that I made a mistake. I'd have to go back to pretending.

I didn't fail.

A little, tiny, porthole-sized door opened to my future. The light streamed in. Maybe there was an alternate life available. Maybe the real world would accept me. Maybe I could adapt and learn how to do this thing. The GED results came with a certificate, which I framed alongside my two-day filmmaking class diploma.

CHAPTER 18

I Get That A Lot

I get that a lot," is one of my favorite phrases. It's a classic, like, "carpe diem," or, "this too shall pass." It gets me through a multitude of uncomfortable situations in which I am recognized by someone who thinks they know me but are not entirely sure. It tends to follow the omnipresent "You look like that girl..." It is not a lie and yet, it sidesteps the obvious question of whether or not I am in fact, "that girl." Most of the time, people squint a little harder, nod slowly and then move on, without further interrogation. The evening can then proceeded. No one is uncomfortable or overly excited and nobody pulls out a cell phone camera.

Jeremy took me on a date to celebrate my GED: drinks at a trendy local bar. We sat in a cozy booth amongst the glowing, happily inebriated people wearing hip clothes and cowboy boots. When the waiter came to take our drink order, he gave me The Look, that some might interpret as *Can I get your number?* In my case it tends to mean *my cable package includes HBO.*

"Hi?" he asked. The greeting was a thinly veiled question.

"Hello."

"Why do I know you?"

"Oh, I don't know. I come here a lot."

That was not entirely true; I had been there twice. Eager to change the subject, I asked for an apple martini.

"Sorry, what did you just order?

"Apple martini."

"With a twist or olive?"

That particular combination didn't sound terribly appealing, so I just asked for an apple slice.

"We have an apple martini, would you like that instead?"

"Great idea, thanks."

Jeremy ordered a beer. We were brought two apple martinis. When he asked for it to be changed to a beer, the waiter apologized to him.

"I am totally distracted by your lady friend. Did you see *Mrs. Doubtfire*? You look like that girl."

The set up was perfect.

"Yeah, I get that a lot."

He nodded and left and came back with the beer a few minutes later. We enjoyed the drinks and I was attempting to hold up my side of the conversation with Jeremy, but it was clear that the hunt was on. The waiter was lurking behind the bar, peeking out from behind hanging wine glasses, conferring with coworkers and looking concerned that I might take flight at any moment.

It was starting to get uncomfortable, so I slammed my martini and gave Jeremy the raised-eyebrow-head-nod that all good partners understand. He asked for the check. Another server, who had been enlisted to investigate further, brought it over. She put down the bill and stared deeply at my face.

"Here's your...check," she said.

It was a dramatic read of the line, full of pauses and brimming with underlying meaning. It turned out that we had been charged for two martinis plus the beer. When Jeremy gently asked for a revision, the waiter spasmed into a flurry of apologies and I cringed. He was flustered and claimed the title of worst waiter in the world. The guilt was overwhelming; I needed to confess and reassure him. My intent had not been to upset anyone, I was just trying to fly under the radar and have a quiet night with my boyfriend. When he arrived with bill number two and a barrage of further apologies, I leaned forward and quietly said, "Don't feel bad, you were right."

"Oh I know, you totally do look like her."

"No, I mean, I am..."

He waved his hands in front his face in an attempt to silence me. "No, I get it, it is just you look SO MUCH like her. Sorry for the screw ups."

I tried to clarify again but he ran away. I don't think he ever got what I meant. Because when I went in again a few weeks later, he said,

"Hi?"

✳ ✳ ✳ ✳ ✳

An acting career is kind of like herpes; it never really goes away. Most of the time it is manageable, I can live my life normally, but then there are flare-ups. I was listening to the radio one day while I was driving to the post office. They were playing an hour of music from the 90s and had a canned intro that said, "Remember baby doll dresses? Pagers? *Mrs. Doubtfire*?" It was strange. I was a relic. Like a Slinky. I was a moment of nostalgia. It was a time in my life that felt so personal, yet it was shared with enough people that it was a common enough societal reference to put on the radio.

I cut my hair in another attempt to change my life. I went with bangs this time. Maybe they could be my Clark Kent glasses, the thing that would make me invisible to everyone. All it did was make people stop me in the street to say that I looked like Zooey Deschanel.

Job-job

Jeremy was entrenched in business school and had precious little free time when he wasn't absorbed in a Power Point presentation. We managed dinner together every once in a while but I saw him so infrequently that it was laughable whenever someone gossiped that I had left L.A. "to follow a boy." But what was I doing? At least when I was awkward in L.A., I had context for it. I knew *how* to be awkward there. Now, here I was being awkward in a place where people had a twang and gave directions like, "turn right onto that li'l pig path about a half mile before where that barbeque place used to be." A place where something called "greens" came with everything and there was such a thing as "good" mayonnaise.

This was a long way from the Menendez mansion or my arty squatters commune in the Valley. I thought back to the days living at the Oakwood Apartments. My insomniac mother and I would share the Murphy bed and I would fall asleep nightly to reruns of *The Beverly Hillbillies*. The flickering black and white screen and the Standard American accent tape playing on my walkman would lull me to sleep. Now, life was *The Beverly Hillbillies* in reverse.

I came up with the novel ideal of getting what my actor friends called a job-job. Wasn't that what normal people did? But doing what? No one had bothered to ask me what I wanted to be when I grow up; it would be a silly question to ask a four-year-old who already had a career. Besides, what could ever compare to a profession that places you, twenty feet tall, on the screen and in the hearts of the world? How would the devotees of online fan sites feel about any other occupation? What about the boys who hunched over keyboards, trying to calculate my date of birth from information gathered from *Tiger Beat*, August 1995? They would shake their heads in glow of the screen, awash in disappointment in me. They'd report to their equally disappointed friends, "Dude, she couldn't cut it. That chick with the hair is a total has-been."

I had never had a job-job. Sure, there had been a career, but I had never had one of those things where you go every day and sit in a cubicle or carve little smiley faces into the latté foam. How did a person get one of those? Could I just show up with one of my leftover film resumes, still on the fancy William Morris letterhead? And where could I really work? While I was definitely getting recognized less, it was still frequent enough that asking someone if they wanted whipped cream on their mocha would inevitably be followed with questions about what Will Smith is really like. I would be a liability for the efficiency of a Starbucks line.

Then, there was the issue of not being qualified for anything. Sure, I had some skills but nothing that had any relevance in the real world.

Here is a list of the completely irrelevant things that I am good at:

✳ **Finding my light.** This is a skill that is immensely important as an actor and means absolutely nothing in real life. Sometimes I still do it; it's an unconscious thing. In a restaurant, I will adjust my body so that I am lit well and not sitting in a shadow. It has nothing to do with vanity. It is simply where I am supposed to be. It's like Rainman counting toothpicks—involuntary yet immensely satisfying. It's like being bathed in love and acceptance. It's like hitting the sweet spot in golf or tennis. It is the one time in life when you know you are in the right place. You can close your eyes and when you have found the light, it holds you.

✳ **Sleeping upright in a folding chair without messing up my hair or makeup.** This is really vital because the hours on set are long and you need to get all the rest you can. Plus, the hair and makeup people are critically important and you don't want to piss them off by creating more work for them to fix. You make them happy—they make you gorgeous.

✳ **Looping dialogue.** This is something that happens in post-production. If the sound on your line is not clear, maybe someone talked over you or you mumbled a word, you need to loop it. This involves going into a little booth, putting on headphones and saying your lines in time with yourself on screen. It's a hard thing to do, because you need to get the timing right to a millisecond while doing some legitimate acting. There were three beeps and when the fourth beep would be, that's when you start talking. Thanks to my early days with *The Care Bears*, I could rock that.

How do these things help me in the rest of the world? They don't. Not even a little bit. Not anywhere.

There was one last reason that working at a real job felt terrifying and it was the one that was hardest to admit to. My exit from the film industry would be final and official the second I took another paying job. Cue the exit music. Fade to black. Roll credits.

✳ ✳ ✳ ✳ ✳

There was a radio station in my new hometown that played some great music. It was the stuff that was familiar to me, a far cry from the thing called "bluegrass" that seemed to permeate this part of the country. Incubus, No Doubt, and U2 were all a part of a soundtrack that carried over from L.A. Those songs had accompanied me on my long car trips to horrible auditions in horrible traffic. Although they were not great memories, there was something in the continuum that was comforting.

Radio seemed kind of connected to the entertainment industry, so perhaps someone could be convinced that I was qualified. I called the radio station and spoke with the "Drive Time" guy. I expressed my interest in learning about radio and asked if he could use a volunteer. He seemed legitimately confused by the question; I wanted to work for free? He told me to come in the next day to meet with him.

I tried to dress like a professional for my meeting, but a professional what, I wasn't sure. Riffling through my wardrobe, I tried to emulate the mannequins in the Banana Republic window, as it seemed like they all worked in offices. As I walked into the station building, it became clear that I had totally overdressed. Everyone was in faded jeans and promotional t-shirts with car dealership logos all over the back. My shiny black dress pants and button-up blouse made me look like I intended to audit them.

Cameron was in his late twenties and was cool the way DJs should be. His office had stereotypical DJ décor: it was overcrowded with boxes of CDs and promotional stuff intended to be given away after it had been thoroughly played with and enjoyed. On the wall was an award he had won, something about having "good ears" and being able to predict the popularity of songs.

I explained my desire to learn about radio and told him that I was happy to help out, in exchange for learning the ropes. I quickly ran through my past in the film industry, just to explain my lack of education or a resume and to justify that I could be a hard worker. He asked some questions about the film specifics and when he heard the answers he pointed at my face.

"Oh my God. You're that girl!"

"Yeah, I guess so."

"I don't know why I am pointing at your face."

"Everyone reacts differently."

"Is it weird to be pointed at?"

"Well, you've been pointing for such a long time, that it's starting to become kind of strange."

"I'll put my finger down now."

"Thanks."

With all that pointing, I worried that my point had gotten lost, so I reiterated my interest in learning about production.

"Do you want to be on-air?" he asked.

"Oh, no. Not on-air, I don't do live. I just want to learn production. The technical stuff. Like...you know...the buttons."

"Well, I don't need a volunteer but I will put you on the payroll. We will start you off with production and then we'll talk about getting you on-air. I really need someone on-air."

"I don't want to be on-air. But the production stuff sounds good."

It seemed that we had some sort of deal, but I left not really knowing what I had agreed to.

I was cooking dinner when Jeremy got home from school that night. He started setting the table and using a gentle tone that would be appropriate if you were speaking to someone who was walking through a minefield and is prone to seizures.

"Do you want to tell me about your meeting with Cameron?"

I moved ineptly around my new kitchen, salting the water for pasta. "It went okay. Cameron is really nice and the offices are cool. The studio has a giant sound mixing board and there are a million CDs just lying around everywhere."

"That sounds interesting. How did you guys leave it?" He got the plates down from the cupboard.

"Well, he said that he would put me on the payroll."

"Wow. That's great! How do you feel?"

At that point that he must have noticed the tears gathering in my eyes because he started to back-peddle.

"I mean, it's not great unless you think it's great."

"I don't know what to think," I took a breath and displayed my shame. "I don't know what 'on the payroll' means." I laid my head on the cutting board and burst into humiliated tears.

He put the plates down and picked the chopped garlic out of my hair. "It means you are going to get paid to do a job-job, babe. It means you did well."

Jeremy showed incredible patience and zero eye rolling as he gathered up his mess of a girlfriend into his arms and kept her there for a long while.

Somehow, I ended up on a payroll. The job paid about $150 a week and I'd never felt richer. That was about what I earned per hour for my old gig but that didn't matter. We went out to dinner and celebrated my first real job and spent three days of my pay.

Finally, there was something to fill my days and provide me with a purpose. On my first day of work I learned how to "rip" shows. Basically, I downloaded CDs of syndicated programs, like *Rick Dees Weekly Top 40*, into the computer so that our station could play them. It required putting a CD into a big machine, tapping a few keys, and then I'd read J.D. Salinger for twenty minutes until it was done. Next, I'd go into the program and insert the local commercials for tanning salons and mattress sales in to the syndicated material. I parked in the same place every day. I carried the same travel mug filled with English Breakfast tea. I learned how to fill out a timesheet so I could be paid my $8 an hour. It was official and ordinary and wonderful.

After a week of ripping shows and Salinger's entire literary catalogue, I was ready to learn something new. I started bugging Cameron to teach me how to work the mixing board with all the sliding bars on it. He still wanted me to be on-air with him, as his drive-time partner. I just wanted to play with the buttons.

With the latest Ryan Seacrest countdown loaded into the computer, I went into the recording studio and sat across the desk from Cameron to watch him work. It was exhilarating to listen to him, to see someone so perfectly in his element. He had been doing radio for years and he had a wonderful rhythm and ease. The way he seamlessly hit the post was magical; he stopped talking the moment before the lyrics started.

When Jack Johnson and his strumming ukulele started to fade out, Cameron turned up the volume on his microphone and promoted a local car show that was coming to town the next weekend. He followed that up with,

"I am also happy to announce that we have a new afternoon DJ here at Mix 107.5, let me introduce you to Lisa."

I saw a button on the mic in front of me glow red. It was on. I was on. My eyes got big and my throat closed. It occurred to me that if I just yelled, "Oh, fuck no," Cameron would be forced to turn off the mic and save his listeners from a flurry of filth, but I decided that is not what one does in a real, eight-dollars-per-hour job.

"Hello?" I croaked in to the glowing monster before me. It sounded like I was answering a phone. A phone that had a serial killer on the other end of it.

With that, Cameron made me a DJ. With a combination of grooming and manipulation, he got me to agree to being on the show every afternoon with him as his drive-time co-host. Slowly and with great uncertainty I became more DJ-ish. I choose my DJ name, Lisa Bailey, paying homage to that hot nerd, Bailey Quarters from *WKRP in Cincinnati*, a show I watched religiously with my dad when I was a kid. The anonymity of radio allowed for a little more bravery. We attempted witty banter and discussed current events. I ventured into old territory and did a voice-over commercial for a local carpet company. The headphones fit better than when I did *The Care Bears* gig.

To manage my live-performance nerves, I convinced myself that no one was listening, which was not a difficult thing to believe in our small town. Our low audience numbers were confirmed by our contests and giveaways. We would announce that a car wash gift certificate or free lunch at Red Robin would be given to the 7th caller, and inevitably the one and only caller would receive the prize. One time, not a single person called in response to a trivia contest and out of fear of total embarrassment, I called a friend, gave him the number to call back with instructions to say "Harrison Ford." For his trouble he received a Trivial Pursuit 20th Anniversary Edition board game.

Occasionally, we went out into the community to try to drum up more listeners by giving away free stuff. We did "remotes," where we would set up a tent plastered with our logo at cell phone stores, hot tub sales, and charity 5Ks. I wore my Mix 107.5 baseball cap pulled down low over my eyes and distracted passers-by with free t-shirts and magnets so that no one even noticed my film face. I drove the radio station

Jeep, wrapped in the colorful logo, and took pleasure in knowing that if people were staring at me, it was for completely different reasons. They wanted free CDs, not autographs. I was Lisa Bailey now.

That morning when I walked into work, I knew things would be different. The US had invaded Iraq and the radio station went "wall to wall," meaning we didn't play music or do our regular silly banter, we just streamed the latest information from various news sources. I sat on the floor under a poster of Pink and listened to the first days of Operation Iraqi Freedom. The television in the studio displayed MSNBC on mute and showed endless lines of deployed men and women, obeying orders and bravely sacrificing everything. Leaving their families and their lives and their dogs. I suddenly felt ashamed for ever thinking I had ever given up anything. Our previous radio fodder critiquing *American Idol* contestants felt both pathetically trite and adorably quaint. I stacked and alphabetized CD cases, hoping that the war would be over as quickly as they were predicting.

Outside of the radio station, Jeremy and I had managed to collect a tight circle of friends who had never stepped foot on a film set and didn't care about the new Screen Actors Guild guidelines for insurance coverage. Friends who came over to play board games and called to ask me if a clove of garlic meant just one of the little segments or the whole big thing. I even met some actual Republicans. My mediocre famousness was fading blissfully into the background, and when people asked what I did, I said with mock confidence, "I'm a DJ at Mix 107.5. Would you like a magnet?"

CHAPTER 19

La Dolce Vita

Marriage had always seemed so contrived. It felt like government bureaucracy and a way for the wedding industry to rake in bazillions of dollars from brides who care more about the dress than the marriage. It was about Cuisinarts and getting a bigger diamond than your friend did, and I wanted no part of it.

Until one day I did. I woke up, looked at the man to my left and confessed that I wanted to be his wife. I wanted him to know he was different. I wanted to be different. He was the best person in the world for me and that needed to be officially announced in front of people that I loved. Turns out most people call that a wedding. Jeremy had been ready for this commitment for a while and had patiently waited for me to clue in.

We invited twenty of our favorite people to stay with us in a villa in Italy for a week, and watch us get married in the garden on a Thursday afternoon. In a surprising Hollywood ending, after six years of separation, my parents reconciled just before the wedding. Suddenly, they were fused back together, that single parental unit I had known in my childhood, making me wonder if any of it—their separation, my film career, anything in my past—had ever really happened at all. All I knew for sure was this moment in front of me.

As the ceremony began and my dad and I walked down the path together, the sight of our guests filled my heart to overflowing. On either side of that aisle, beaming in the soft Tuscan light, stood the community that I was always searching for. Our families were there, as well as old friends from L.A. and new friends from our non-L.A. life. We were all one cohesive family, and we had come together to celebrate love.

I walked my father to his seat, between my mom and Grandma, then made my way to Jeremy, who was standing in front of the rolling countryside, wearing a light linen suit with sandals and waiting for me. When I arrived at the end of the aisle, I leapt into his arms for a hug, even though I was supposed to just stand there and play the role of the emotional-yet-composed bride. We wrote our own vows and Jeremy's were funny even though I told him not to be funny, because funny vows are never actually funny. But somehow, offering yet another reason it was a good idea to marry him, he pulled off the elusive funny vow and I spent much of our ceremony doubled over and cracking up. We didn't bother with a bridal party, a garter toss, or wedding presents. We focused on tiramisu and ill-conceived drinking games with limoncello.

We danced until even the Italians thought it was time to go to bed. It was so much fun, it didn't even matter to me that a friend of our dog-sitter posted on an Internet fan site that I was getting married in Italy and that my new husband had forced me out of the film industry. We just laughed.

After our wedding, we stayed in Italy for a while. I get a high from traveling that can't be found anywhere else. The opportunity to step out of my own life and attempt to see things from the perspective of another culture is intoxicating. Put me in a place where I don't speak the language, I'm relying on unreliable public transport, and a pickpocket just stole my map; I'm in heaven.

Travel was always high up on my list of reasons to take a film project and I was overjoyed to learn that traveling is possible even without signing a movie contract. You can just go! You need a passport and a little money, but it's all out there, that big old world! You can see it for yourself! You don't have to work long hours and promise the production's insurance company that you won't rent a scooter!

We cruised over gently sloping hills lined with olive trees and tried to figure out how to put diesel fuel in our teeny-tiny rental car. We saw ancient ruins sitting comfortably next to the neon signs of supermarkets. I sat in the shade of a pergola, writing and meditating. A little stillness had entered into my life. It was easy to credit that happiness to being in Italy or my newlywed status but it was so clearly deeper than that. A sense of quiet replaced the restlessness that was deep in my soul. It had been planted the moment I stepped off the plane in Virginia, and it was now a steadily creeping ivy, covering everything in a blanket of rich stillness. It finally felt like I was living a life that fit. I was no longer looking for the next thing, the next job, and the next compliment from Spielberg. I decided to be delighted with whatever life I found right in front of me. I had finally woken up.

New role: student

Back home as a newlywed, it was time to figure out what the details of that life really looked like. Continuing to work for $8 an hour at the radio station was tempting, but the fact that the University of Virginia was in my backyard felt like some sort of sign that I should try to get this educational chip off my shoulder.

Before moving to Charlottesville, college seemed like a great thing for other people. With my education placed firmly on the backburner, it just never seemed like the right place for me. College was an environment where you learned theoretical things, out of context and without getting your hands dirty. The ivory towers of academia seemed wildly irrelevant to this real world I was trying to experience. But when higher education was right there, flaunting its beautiful, cavernous libraries in my face, I swooned and confessed my all-encompassing desire to attend school. Current students, all enthusiastic and exhausted, rushed around carrying teetering stacks of textbooks. I longed to be stressed out about exams and panicked about research papers, too. I gathered together my GED, my pitiful N/A high school record and some random college credits. I held out my moldy crumbs as an offering and I applied to the University of Virginia.

I had gotten quite adept at sidestepping my history but for my application I had to face it straight on and explain my life. I even came clean about being thrown out of two high schools. My personal essay was bursting with my love of books and my longing to be part of something big, something with pride and deep roots. Something with a crest and a fight song that involved synchronized hand gestures.

It worked. I was accepted to the University of Virginia and became one of those students who stressed about papers and who napped on the Rotunda steps during breaks, and then ran across grounds (we didn't call it campus, it's not the Jeffersonian way) because I was late to class. I went to fair wage rallies, found the quietest nooks in the library and choked down the cafeteria food. For the first time in my life, I was really a student, I didn't have to sit in the hallway and just pretend that I belonged.

Beyond needing to learn about APA grammar, I needed to learn how to learn. Sitting in a classroom, taking notes and reading stacks of crooked, photocopied PDF files was all incredibly foreign. But exams and research projects filled my days, and at some point, when I looked around, I realized I was actually doing this thing. In an attempt to fill in the gaps in my education, I studied everything from the History of Southern Africa to Introduction to Statistics. Textbooks about Buddhism and feminism and physics covered my kitchen table. I became one of those people who knew things about the works of Simone de Beauvoir and the basic laws of entropy.

The break-up with my old life was official. It was a no-fault divorce, to be sure; we separated amicably and without throwing dishware, but it was a divorce all the same. It had been a complicated, painful relationship, yet I found myself avoiding any kind of "entertainment news" because I didn't need to hear how Claire Danes and Acting made such a happy couple. That was when the good times flashed back, the fun sets, and the rush of positive feedback from auditions. There were moments when it occurred to me that maybe we could have worked it out. Maybe I should have held up my end of the bargain, the one that says that being an actor is hard, but you stick it out, anyway. The one that says that despair is part of the agreement. Perhaps I could have worked on the relationship a little more; maybe I could have been more accepting and forgiving of the film industry's less charming attributes.

But for me, Acting was one of those men who purposely becomes so distant and intolerable that you are forced to leave them, so they don't have to break the ties and leave you some sad has-been who appears in *People* magazine's "Where Are They Now?" articles. Those articles always terrified me—the ones where a slightly dated photo of Famous You floats in an optimistic bubble over your current, un-famous self, while you try to justify to the world that you really haven't outlived your personal 'use-by' date. But being a student only allows so much time to sit and brood about why you are twenty-nine and just starting college. I had a foreign language requirement to fulfill.

It didn't take long for the word to get out around school about my old job. Walking down the hall created a buzz that made me feel as if there was a swarm of bees just behind me. Bees who watched a lot of movies. I stared at my shoes and tried to count the classroom numbers in my head so I didn't need to look up. I had dropped my glasses and scratched the lens, so I couldn't hide behind that social mask. I walked around brazenly in my contacts, putting my poster face out there for the world to see.

"Hey, *Doubtfire* Girl!" a guy yelled down the hallway.

I turned around. "Yeah?"

"Oh. Um…nothing. Sorry."

I sat in the stadium seating of Introduction to Something Important and reviewed my notes from last class. As I tucked my feet under so that a girl could pass by, she shoved her cell phone in my face and I heard the camera click. Out of instinct, I had even attempted to get my movie smile on my face in time for the shot but my acting skills were waning. The look was likely more reminiscent of a startled rabbit than anything. She walked away like nothing happened and I felt like part of a World's Fair exhibit.

It took me quite a while to make my first college friend. I tended to keep to myself and didn't live in a dorm or join any clubs or go to any events wherein social interaction would be necessary. For the first couple of semesters, my most notable communication consisted of asking the person next to me if I was in the right classroom or apologizing for dropping my pen under their desk.

Thankfully, two girls finally put me out of my loner misery and befriended me. My new friends were a six-foot tall blonde British bombshell and an Orthodox Muslim who wore a hijab with her jeans and flip-flops. When the three of us walked together, I faded into the background. It was an incredibly efficient way to hide. I didn't intentionally go out and find extraordinary-looking people, it just sort of happened that way. Perhaps it is just a case of people who are different being comfortable with people who are different.

My social anxieties lingered, so the classes where I could sit in the back and quietly take notes were my favorites. But these were rare, as the professors at UVA tend to be annoyingly engaged and interested in hearing from their students. I was convinced that whenever I was called on randomly and got the incorrect answer, tweets would immediately go out to the whole UVA community about how the *Doubtfire* Girl was stupid. I'd go home and find myself sprawled out on my neighbor's kitchen table, sobbing that I just wasn't cut out for college. Her three-year-old would watch me cry and then offer me a Cheerio. He was just trying to shut me up; he never really understood.

It took me an embarrassingly long time to realize that no one really cared about my answers; they were all much more worried about being cold-called themselves. It's challenging to clear your mind from that old Hollywood brainwashing, the one that insists that everyone must find you endlessly fascinating. It's quite freeing to think of yourself as just another frightened college student.

For many kids at school, once they got over the former actor thing, the fact that I was nine years older than them was far more intriguing. I was married and had a two-car garage and mortgage; these were fascinating and foreign concepts. I was different than rest of the students, but I had a role to play. They started calling me "Mama Jakub" because I always had Kleenex in my backpack, along with extra pens and some salient relationship advice. I told the boys to listen more and the girls to not get too serious, too fast. And then I told everyone that they needed to get more sleep and take vitamins.

Useless skills become useful

For some incomprehensible reason, there are still college professors that make their students perform skits. I hate skits. They transport me back to self-conscious acting classes in L.A., with all the pantomiming and melodrama. You can tell that both the performers and the audience are whole-heartedly humiliated by the experience.

My Italian class was divided into small groups and we were given a skit project. We would film the skit, so at least we got to skip the real-time humiliation of performing in front of our classmates. My group consisted of people who happened to sit near me. There were four of us: one guy I knew a little, who knew about my acting career, and two other girls he knew but I didn't. And whether they knew about me, well, I didn't know. The impending unease was obvious.

We decided to meet at the apartment of one of the girls and "write the script." This entailed figuring out how many Italian words we know between the four of us and then trying to stretch that into a story that fit the five-minute minimum. I arrived at the college apartment ten minutes late because apparently the first two years of college don't cover how to give coherent directions to your home. When I arrived, no one answered the door. I loitered in a hallway that smelled like weed and Hot Pockets, until a neighbor let me in to the apartment, which was not a huge accomplishment, as the door was unlocked anyway.

I waited, sitting quietly on the couch next to a guy who was passed out in his underwear. I looked around the apartment and tried not to touch anything, since the whole place seemed to be coated in something gluey. Let me just say that going to a college apartment when you are thirty-one-year-old married woman is a funny thing. Especially if it is your first college experience, and when you were nineteen you were usually living in hotels, and your most mutinous act was swiping an extra mini-shampoo from the maid's cart. It was kind of like going to a zoo to look at the animals. It's exotic and fascinating and there are many surprises, like the fact that there is half of a sandwich sitting on top of the toilet tank, or the eventual realization that no one knew who the sleeping-in-his-underwear guy actually was.

Finally, my skit partners arrived and we all sat on an unmade bed and wrote a ridiculous Italian tale of love and betrayal. I played the role of a server who watches all the drama unfold while attempting to offer the tormented lovers more food. This role was perfect for me as I was most confident in my restaurant Italian and *ravioli* counted as an Italian word. We did a couple of takes, with one of us inevitably forgetting that the double c in Italian is pronounced like a "k."

Near the end of the day, one of the girls contracted what we call in the film business a "giggle fit." This is a highly technical term, so let me explain; it's when you laugh uncontrollably as soon as the camera rolls. It's the stuff of great blooper reels and extra footage that plays under the final credits. My skit partner was doubled over with gasping laughter and just couldn't get it together. It was getting exhausting. By the tenth time we tried to film our stupid scene and she turned purple, I had to intervene.

"Just try jumping jacks."

"What?"

"Jumping jacks. Seriously. It'll work."

My skit partner did some dubious jumping jacks, which woke up the random sleeping guy on the couch. He looked around, rubbed his eyes, put on his pants and left. When we tried again, we got through the whole thing with no giggling and finally finished the damn skit.

"Wow." The girl looked at me. "That totally worked. Have you done a lot of skits before?"

Apparently I was wrong. Some of my acting skills did transfer over into my real life.

CHAPTER 20

I Am, Because We Are

College offered many experiences that I decided not to take advantage of. There was no keg stand at a frat party. There was no early morning Walk of Shame from some guy's dorm while still wearing a party dress and smeared mascara from the night before. I mostly avoided the greasy cafeteria and never got brave enough to "streak the lawn," running naked throughout the school grounds while my friends stole my clothes and threw them in the bushes. I was okay with skipping those things and loved watching my twenty-one-year-old classmates participate with unbridled enthusiasm. But there was one college experience that I couldn't pass up.

UVA offered study abroad opportunities. Students could take a class in a foreign locale and get college credit for it. It seemed like the perfect meeting of my two worlds. I could do my favorite part of a movie shoot—the traveling to a location for an extended period of time—but instead of being an actor, I could be a student.

Some people say that travel allows you to escape from your life. They say it's a form of avoidance that shelters you from intimacy and reality. I think travel brings life into exquisitely sharp focus. You realize that you can't escape yourself. All the good and all the not-so-good that makes up your soul is highlighted when you no longer have the safe confines of your routines. Travel leaves behind all the extraneous bits and pieces that never had any legitimate place in one's life to start with. There is simply no room for all that other garbage. Fear, anxiety, insecurity, self-doubt—they can't withstand the air that sweeps in off the Yucatán Peninsula or the sight of all those vibrant foods, piled up at the Boqueria in Barcelona. They can't climb to the top of the Siena bell tower or sit at the bar of the Raffles Hotel in Singapore. Those issues that you've been carrying just because you forgot to put them down get all brittle, dusty, and frail. When there is so much exotic energy swirling around, that junk simply gets carried off by the wind.

On a chilly spring morning, I attended a study abroad fair and wandered the booths full of colorful posters and eager students wearing berets or lederhosen while pitching the trips from which they had just returned. The options seemed endless; I could study engineering in Panama or learn Mandarin in Shanghai. My travel lust went into overdrive as I flipped through brochures depicting happy and self-assured students in racially diverse groups, holding pens thoughtfully while absorbing cultural experiences. All the options looked very nice but I knew which trip was mine the second that I saw it: Southern Africa.

I had always auditioned most enthusiastically for projects filming on the African continent and it had never worked in my favor. When the producers had passed on me for a part in *The Power of One* it had left me disappointed for weeks. My infatuation with the place began when I was about eight years old, fueled by my love for animals. I poured over musty stacks of National Geographics that confirmed that Sub-Saharan Africa was a magical wonderland, full of roaming troops of baboons and giraffes eating off the tops of acacia trees.

As I got older, I read about apartheid in South Africa and reconciliation after the black majority won their battle for independence from oppressive white rule. I fell for Nelson Mandela, who went from being a child in rural South Africa to lawyer to freedom fighter to prisoner to democratically elected president. South Africa seemed to be a place that steadfastly refused to be defined by its past.

I packed a small duffle bag and took my anti-malaria pills. Choking back tears, I hugged Jeremy and the dogs goodbye and got on a nine-teen hour flight. My student group traveled throughout South Africa and Mozambique for a month, studying the interaction between culture and environment for a class that was a co-listing with anthropology and environmental sciences. I trekked through wildlife parks, goat farms and villages. The first time I saw an elephant cross the path right in front of me, I lost my breath. I drank beer in sheebeens with members of the Black Consciousness Movement and talked to a traditional healer about how she cured her daughter's ovarian cancer. I yelled some very nasty things at a baboon who broke into my cabin, ate all my food, and ripped apart my bag, shitting on all my clothes.

That wall of fog that I always felt between me and everyone else seemed to disappear in South Africa. It slowly dissipated and allowed me to sit in a corrugated metal shack and enjoy a warm, sandy "Orange Drink" with the residents of a township and feel a blissful sense of com-fort in my own skin. I asked questions that I could never manage to utter at a Hollywood premiere. It turned out that people were very interest-ing. They were not just crazed fans that might kind of kidnap me. When I found enough voice to ask questions I got to hear personal stories that were much more varied and fascinating than mine. I learned how to talk to people without answering, "Yes, filming *Mrs. Doubtfire* was really fun." I laughed with perfect strangers and missed their company when we parted ways.

It was one of these strangers who told me about the philosophy of Ubuntu. It comes from the Bantu language and it means; *I am, because we are.* It's a worldview that focuses on community and the intercon-nectedness of us all. Ubuntu says that we cannot live in isolation, that generosity and compassion are what make us fundamentally human. When others thrive, you thrive. We're all in this together.

It was a far cry from the *every actor for themselves* mantra that I had adopted in Los Angeles. It was the opposite of the endless focus on individual achievement and personal success. In L.A., life had been so me-centered. Of course I had tried to be a good friend and a responsible member of the planet, but it was all about me and my stuff. My career, my unfortunate love life, my depression, my fear, my anxiety, my loneliness, my self-imposed isolation.

This sense of collectiveness suddenly felt tangible. Even when the details look notably different, we can all relate to the joy and suffering of the human experience. Our hearts all swell with happiness, and we all buckle with the pain of loss. The world opens up when you realize that you are not alone and not a freak—that everyone has to walk a different path, but that doesn't mean that any of us walk alone. We are all connected. Community can be created out of anything, and it is always available, if you are brave enough to put yourself out there. For the first time, I felt a deep desire to truly participate in my life and stop running away. I was never alone. I never would be. I just wasn't that special.

As I wandered through markets, freely chatting with the woman at the stall selling protein-packed Mopani worms and cheap Chinese flip-flops, that weight was completely gone. It was the weight of being burdened only with myself and my path in the world. I felt lighter when caring for others and when I felt that I could do something to contribute. This was not a White Man's Burden sort of thing; no one here needed me to save them. What I could do was ask someone how they were doing and really listen to the answer. I could help by having a meaningful conversation about the important things of life and sharing stories and laughing. I could connect.

At the end of each day, I scrolled through my photos, and saw shot after shot of me grinning. It became abundantly clear that I had forgotten how to smile pretty. I was showing more than the regulated bottom half of my top teeth. Good lord, I was smiling so big that my gums where showing. I would push up my already too-plump cheeks until crows-feet marched across my temples. I made that un-Hollywood smiley face that could hardly contain the joy of my life. I was no longer film-ready when I smiled, certainly not appropriate for the big (or even small HD) screen. But that smile was mine and it was overflowing with authenticity and happiness.

My best friend on the trip was named Abdel. He was a twenty-one-year-old college student from the politically ravaged country of Zimbabwe, who was studying to be an accountant. He had joined our group and was traveling around with us, seeing countries that were foreign to him, too. He was smart and knew it; he teased me with a kind of swagger that was equal parts endearing and infuriating. Abdel laughed at my addiction to sunscreen and said that judging by the way I spoke about my dogs, I had mistaken them for people. He quickly began to feel like a little brother to me.

Several weeks into our travels, while we sat in a restaurant in Mozambique, he asked me about being an older student. Why had I waited so long to go to college? I fumbled with my fork. Could I avoid the question? How was he going to react? I didn't want there to be another tectonic relationship shift. Not here. Not with him. I felt so much shame about the possibility of being rejected, of being thought of as profoundly different. My heart raced and the heat rushed to my face. I folded and unfolded my paper napkin while I found a way to explain myself.

"Well, um, I haven't mentioned this before because it's just sort of weird I guess, but I used to be an actor. Like, in movies."

Abdel touched my arm lightly, trying to calm my obvious nerves.

"I know. *Independence Day*. 'Welcome to Earth.' Boom!" He did a decent impression of Will Smith punching an alien in the face.

"Oh, I didn't know you knew about that. You saw that movie?"

"Everyone saw that movie." He rolled his eyes at me. "Even in Africa. We see movies, too, you know."

"Of course you do. I didn't mean…Sorry." I wasn't sure which was more offensive and culturally insensitive, assuming he had seen the movie, or assuming he hadn't.

He grinned at my attempt to be politically correct about an alien movie. "But movies are all done now, right?"

"Yes. All done."

"And you are happy to be done?"

"Yes. I am. I'm happy." I tried not to cry and look stupid.

I looked around this simple restaurant, not much more than a couple of plastic tables set out on a cement slab. I was overwhelmed by the beautiful food that had been provided to us. I was in awe of my new friend, who had offered me such kindness and understanding, despite the fact that our lives could not have seemed more different. I looked at my dirty jeans, which I'd worn every day for three weeks and still had some dust on the ankles, from where I had been sitting on the pressed cow dung floor of a healer's hut. My soul wanted to burst with the tremendous joy I felt. I was about to collapse under the weight of my gratitude.

"I'm very happy," I sputtered.

He took my hand. "Very good, my friend. Look forward. And be happy." I wiped away my tears that I just couldn't keep inside anymore. He laughed at me and I didn't mind.

What had I been waiting for? I had spent my entire life waiting. Waiting on the 405 freeway, waiting for auditions. Waiting for agents or managers or boyfriends to call. Waiting to see if I could become somebody. It never occurred to me that I already was somebody. I was me. "*Doubtfire* Girl" or not—it didn't matter. Happiness was a choice that was available. It was right there in front of me. I could live my life now and stop waiting for other people to give me permission to leave set to go to the bathroom or tell me to cry and think about dead puppies. It was time to focus my energy in better places. The dead puppy days were done.

That bliss was so clearly reflected back at me, standing at the place where the Indian Ocean meets the Atlantic. I stood at the Cape of Good Hope at the bottom of South Africa and looked out into the vastness. At the place where the two oceans meet, they create a small crest before flowing seamlessly into one another.

"Crazy, right? It's like this is the end of the world," someone behind me said.

I smiled and laughed because I knew there was no such thing.

This was just the beginning of a different part.

EPILOGUE

Namaste, Mrs. D.

t would never be so simple, really. It would never be just a flip of the switch. I always hated those stories where one revelation changes everything forever. Old habits die hard and I came home and started taking running water for granted and started doubting my capabilities in the real world. But that trip gave me something, and every day since, I've fought like hell to hang on to it. It's the knowledge that I am an integral part of something that is so much bigger and more important than myself. Since the days of playing craps with the teamsters, I had always been searching for my group, my community, and my connection. Ubuntu showed me that it had been there all along had I just opened my heart to it.

Shockingly, when I finally embraced my passion for words and found enough courage to write my story, it turned out that my life was relatable. The issues I had struggled with, that I always felt so alone with, were common. People are always considering changing jobs or going back to school or figuring out how to live authentically within the structure of their lives. People are always trying to wake up and find their way in the world. It's all the same stuff; taking a leap away from a social norm is always terrifying. It's just a little more unusual to live your dream by getting out of the film industry, rather than getting into it.

Every day I remind myself that I don't have to wait for someone else to give me permission to live. Sometimes you need to stop searching for happiness and just be happy. There is joy to be had, and it doesn't require a Hollywood career. It takes some courage, some compassion and some love, for yourself and others.

My revelation about all of this is nothing new. Religions are generally based on this idea of compassion and love. Jesus said it. Buddha said it. It's in the sacred texts of pretty much every faith in existence. Everyone is suffering, so stop thinking you are the only one who is special enough to be miserable and go make someone else's life a little better. Get over yourself, get over your past, get over your shit, and you will be better for it. (I'm paraphrasing.)

About a year after my graduation from UVA, as we were settling into our new house, I was curled up on the couch, looking for a chick flick to watch while Jeremy was traveling for work. *Mrs. Doubtfire* was on television. I hadn't seen it for seventeen years. I looked around suspiciously, feeling like I was about to watch something scandalous on Cinemax. I could just watch a little bit, couldn't I? Was that weird? I closed the curtains.

It was strangely familiar and yet there were so many things I had forgotten about. Then, there was me. I really was that girl. My mannerisms were the same, so was my voice. I now have curvier hips and some gray hair—but it was me. I still remembered all my lines.

It was just a movie. It was sweet and funny and silly. I'm grateful to that film for many things, it was a wonderful experience and it set me on the path to meet my husband and have the beautiful life I have now. It seems so futile that I spent seventeen years running and trying to not be labeled the *Doubtfire* Girl, because the movie was not some monster that was chasing me. A movie is just a movie, like Bobby Duvall had said when I was eleven. In that moment, I turned around and gave that movie a hug. I stopped trying to fight it. It touched people and gave me wonderful opportunities. That movie, and everything else that has ever happened, made me who I am. My life is not a secret to be kept.

I am that girl. But I'm a lot of other things, too.

APPENDIX

Almost Complete List of Acting Credits

2000   *Double Frame*

2000   *The Royal Diaries: Isabel—Jewel of Castilla*

1999   *Jack & Jill*

1999   *George Lucas in Love*

1999   *Mentors—"Raising the Siege"*

1999   *A Walk on the Moon*

1998   *Dream House*

1998   *Painted Angels*

1997   *Newton: A Tale of Two Isaacs*

1997   *On the Edge of Innocence*

1997   *The Beautician and the Beast*

1996   *Independence Day*

1996   *Reckoning*

1996   *Bermuda Triangle*

1995   *Picture Perfect*

1995   *Fight for Justice: The Nancy Conn Story*

1994   *Due South*

1994   *A Child's Cry for Help*

1994   *A Pig's Tale*

1993   *Vendetta II*

1993   *Mrs. Doubtfire*

1993   *Matinee*

1991   *The Story Lady*

1991   *The Rape of Doctor Willis*

1991   *Rambling Rose*

1990   *Night Court*

1990   *War of the Worlds*

1989   *The Phone Call*

1989   *Glory! Glory!*

1987-1989   *Friday The 13th The Series: Friday's Curse*

1989   *The Twilight Zone*

1988   *Once Upon a Giant*

1988   *Emergency Room*

1988   *Alfred Hitchcock Presents*

1986   *Christmas Eve*

1986   *Kay O'Brien*

1986   *Taking the Heat*

1986   *The Right of the People*

1985   *Eleni*

ACKNOWLEDGMENTS

One of the most important things I have ever learned is the power of practicing gratitude. Gratitude is so joyful and immense that it simply crowds out all the angst and suffering. I will attempt to express my appreciation here, and I'll undoubtedly fail to capture the whole of it. It's just that big.

Thank you to my trusted first readers, Lauren Macloed, Jen Higgins, Rachel Miller and Tracy Arbaugh—who gave loving feedback and laughed at the right places.

Thank you to Lizzie and my Yoga Soul Crew—for giving me a second home and a place to find myself.

Thank you to Bre and Eric Gregg, Karen and Graham Beatty, Serena Love, Sarah Cramer Shields, Loren Intolubbe-Chmil, Cecily Armstrong, Kirk Conard, Amy Kidd and Mara Wilson. You all know why.

Thank you to my parents—who have been with me since the beginning, teaching me humility, persistence and how to use a sledgehammer.

Thank you to my grandma, Arlene MacDonald—who transferred her love of words through the bloodline, even if her superior spelling skills didn't survive the journey.

Thank you to my agent, Gina Panettieri—for staying to meet the last writer in line at the Pitch Slam, and for the late night emails talking that same writer off the creative ledge.

Thank you to Megan Trank, Jocelyn Kelley, Felicia Minerva, Michael Short, Eric Kampmann and the entire team at Beaufort Books and Midpoint Trade Books—who believed there could be a worthwhile Hollywood story that didn't include rehab.

Thank you to my fellow writers, Scott Craven, Jacob Tomsky, Ben Lorr, Amanda Eyre Ward and Quinn Cumming—for offering advice and understanding the pleasure and pain of living a life devoted to the written word.

Thank you to all my blog readers—for their enthusiastic kindness, and for giving me a safe space to begin to share my work.

And thank you most of all to my husband—for having unwavering faith in me. Your support and encouragement made this all possible. You held my hand when I was terrified and you gave me the courage to be myself. Thank you for every moment at our kitchen table. Even the ones when I was crying. Maybe especially those.

And finally, thank you to Grace.